Reality is Spiritual

I0406852

Volume 2

The RTS Personality

Rational Theistic Self-analysis (RTS)
For Achieving Wholeness
Here and in the Afterlife
Based on the Spiritual Psychology
of Jung and Swedenborg

Leon James, Ph.D.

God, Immortality and Theistic Psychology Series

REGENERATION
MEDIA
PUBLICATIONS
KAILUA

http://www.theisticpsychology.org

Reality is Spiritual Series
By Leon James, Ph.D.

Volume 1
Dreams and the Spiritual World
Integrating the Psychology of
Jung and Swedenborg

Volume 2
The RTS Personality
Rational Theistic Self-analysis (RTS)
For Achieving Wholeness
Here and in the Afterlife
Based on the Spiritual Psychology
of Jung and Swedenborg

Volume 3
The RTS Interview
Rational Theistic Self-analysis (RTS)
Dialog On Consciousness, Immortality, Personality,
Marriage, God, and Afterlife Lifestyles
Based on the Spiritual Psychology
of Jung and Swedenborg

Volume 4
The RTS Exercises
Applying Rational Theistic Self-analysis (RTS)
For Regeneration of Personality

Reality is Spiritual. Volume 2. The RTS Personality

Based on the Spiritual Psychology
of Jung and Swedenborg

All quotes in this book from the work of Jung and Swedenborg were taken from public
domain versions made available on the Internet and downloaded freely.

This is the Second Edition published in November 2016

ISBN-10: 153914898X
ISBN-13: 978-1539148982
ASIN: B01LXD4UBJ

Dedication

This book is dedicated to

Dr. Christine Winskowski

Inventive Researcher, Author, Dedicated Teacher,
Loyal Friend, Follower of Christ
and a persistent student of spirituality and deep culture,
with a focus on Swedenborg's Writings on Conjugial Love

"We're all cultivating the gardens of the mind."
~Dr. Christine Winskowski

Topic Sections

**Click on numbers on the right to go to
the Section**

1. Definition of RTS

The title RTS contains three spiritual ideas: rational, theistic, and self-analysis.

Rational refers to the human ability to reason with ideas and truths.

Through education and culture we first develop our *natural*-rational abilities. This rational function consists exclusively of concepts that are time-bound, place-bound, measurement-bound, matter-bound, and energy-bound. This natural and materialistic form of the human rational ability constitutes our everyday natural consciousness from birth to adulthood.

Later in adult life, we have the opportunity to develop our *spiritual*-rational abilities. This consists of spiritual ideas only, which are not time-bound, not place-bound, and not measurement-bound. Spiritual ideas consist of mental activity and the spiritual world of the afterlife. It is little known that the mental world in which we all experience our daily life is the same as the spiritual world of the afterlife. They are one and the same known by two different words.

This means that we are born into the afterlife of eternity to begin with. Hence dying is not going anywhere but is to change our consciousness. You are already right now in the mental world of eternity. You were born into it through your spiritual body, but not through your physical avatar.

Thinking and reasoning with spiritual ideas constitute our spiritual-rational consciousness. The philosophy and practice that apply to RTS are based on spiritual-rational thinking and consciousness. Later we will discuss further the details of the human rational ability.

Theistic refers to God's omnipotence and how this power acts through cause-effect chains to produce and manage all events, both in the physical world and in the mental or spiritual world. The mental or spiritual world of eternity is the same as the afterlife of immortality.

The joint expression *"rational theistic"* indicates that in spiritual-rational consciousness we become aware that every event in our daily life and every perception and thought that enter our experiencing, is supervised and managed by the infinite power, unconditional love, and omniscient wisdom of God who is the original and infinite Human.

A distinction is made between "theistic" and "deistic". Those who hold a *deistic* view of the universe assert that God is the creator and originator of the universe and this includes the creation of natural laws that govern events. Hence it is these natural laws that determine what happens and not God directly. In contrast, the *theistic* view is that God directly and continuously intervenes and operates all events. God has specific purposes for creation and all its subsequent events.

Self-analysis refers to the daily lifelong activity of *witnessing our experiences* and of becoming aware of our moment-to-moment thoughts and emotions as we live our busy lives every day. The word "analysis" in regard to "self" implies that each of us is able to make objective and detailed observations of our personality, of our attitudes, intentions, and of our behaviors in interaction with others.

The full expression "rational theistic self-analysis" (RTS) refers to the systematic daily self-monitoring of our thoughts and feelings and their assessment in accordance with spiritual-rational ideas regarding God and the afterlife of eternity.

This book explains how people can raise their consciousness, their understanding, and their self-confidence by getting to know the philosophy and practice of *rational theistic self-analysis*.

These ideas about the mind and the afterlife are described in the work of Jung and Swedenborg, two of the past giants of psychology and spirituality. See Volume 1 of this book.

No one is born for hell; everyone is born for heaven. ~Swedenborg

Your perception will become clear only when you can look into your soul. -Carl Jung

What is conscious to us now becomes unconscious in the afterlife, and what is unconscious to us now becomes conscious after death.
~Leon James

Nothing happens TO me, everything happens FOR me. ~Abe Venter

---

2. Modern Civilization and Consciousness

The earliest generations of human beings on this earth were beautiful people, angelic in mind and intelligence. They were peaceful and lived in small family-communities in which they intermarried. They did not socially interact much with other family-communities. The reason given for this in the Swedenborg Reports is that the physical avatar they were given at birth differed across the family-communities and instinctively resisted mixing it up with other sub-cultures.

The precise appearance and abilities of the avatar they were given was determined by its correspondence with the typology of loves that formed their inborn personality. Each family-community had its own way of thinking, its own idea of God, its own pattern of preferences and sensitivities in their five senses, and its uniquely adapted traditions and daily habits of living. To intermarry and mix sub-cultures by intimate socializing was considered the death of who they are spiritually and eternally.

Being peaceful and celestial minds their avatars reflected this mental state by mild and respectful obedience to their inner personality. They were horrified at the idea that someone might want to take away or steal what belongs to another. They were ready to die for the sake of saving someone else. Despite their scarce social interactions with other communities they never threatened or invaded the other's normal territory.

I felt a sigh of relief when I read this in the Swedenborg Reports. I had been raised and educated in the idea that our most ancient ancestors were close to apes. So I pictured cave dwellers with hairy bodies and un-beautiful faces and bodies. Their "family-dwellings" were caves, trees, or crude huts.

They were warlike and competitive with other "tribes". Then I felt the secret pride that I was a modern person, far superior to them in "modern" civilization. And I felt much more beautiful and intelligent.

I did not realize that this view was pressing me down constantly. I did not know that this false notion was a spiritual plague that worked itself secretly to the core of my consciousness and kept it to remain natural and undeveloped of its inner spiritual potential as a human being.

But now I feel a sense of awe, admiration, and gratitude that God created human beings as celestial minds and bodies, like those earliest generations created by God. Celestial minds are in angelic consciousness from being in mutual love. Most of us are not conscious of our celestial thinking and feeling that is going on right now with everyone! We have three systems of functioning for consciousness: celestial, spiritual, and natural. The first human beings that God created on this earth were in celestial consciousness from birth onwards.

If this happened today to a person the medical prognosis would be schizophrenic or else motivationally underperforming and excessively shy, even anti-social. What a horrific diagnosis for a celestial human being or angel! Our thinking in our celestial consciousness is in itself unable to function at the natural consciousness level. In today's "modern" society the avatar of such a person would be categorized as "defective" and "irreparable", incapable of adapting, of learning, of surviving on its own.

But this is not a true picture. The earliest people born on earth had a natural consciousness learned through their avatar growing up under planetary conditions. But simultaneously they were also aware of the activity in their celestial consciousness. Today we are unable to do this. We are unconscious or not aware of our celestial consciousness, its perspective, its thinking, and its loving. The first generations were aware of their celestial functioning, thinking, and feeling. They were such that their natural consciousness did not oppose their celestial loves and thoughts of which they were aware internally. The natural consciousness that controlled the physical avatar body was perfectly aligned with the celestial order of thinking and feeling.

What an admirable mental state to be in! What an admirable community is formed when the people's avatars are under the obedience of celestial loves. Our life in society today must be endured surrounded by avatars that behave rudely, aggressively, selfishly, and form a physical danger to other avatars. Somewhere along the way in evolution and history, human beings closed up their celestial consciousness. At first they were in spiritual consciousness and had a natural consciousness that could be educated to learn obedience to spiritual reasoning and goals. Societies and cities in those days were also mostly peaceful and maintained polite diplomatic relations with each other.

But in the next evolutionary step of human experiencing on this planet darkness fell and blotted out the light. "Darkness" refers to inability to see that reality is spiritual. This is called materialism. The "light" that is blotted out is the light of spiritual consciousness, which gives us knowledge of God and the afterlife of eternity. I find it significant that the "rise of civilization" from primitive to modern, synchronizes with the "Fall of Humankind", which refers to being born with the inability to be conscious of the activity going on in the celestial and spiritual layers of our consciousness.

I thought much about this historical and evolutionary synchrony between "rise of civilization" and drop of consciousness. I came to the conclusion that this inverse relationship is created by God, who from love is in the constant effort of assisting people in their regeneration. I imagine that this can get pretty complicated! It involves managing all the main events and all the small events in a community in such a way that each person getting caught up in those events is benefitting from it.

Growing up in natural consciousness we learn to notice which acts of our avatar are contrary to the community's rules of order. So we acquire a way of thinking that is called "moral judgment", which is our "morality". If our thinking and feeling level now remains trapped in this natural consciousness system, then we are preventing ourselves from growing to the next necessary step, which is spiritual thinking and feeling. Practicing the perspective of RTS leads to the benefit of re-opening of this human possibility that gives us the experiencing of spiritual consciousness.

Now our rational consciousness completely changes! It is "reborn".

The result is that our natural consciousness is "purified" of mental contamination and corruption. This purification process is arduous and requires daily effort for years and decades. I call it "undergoing the regeneration process". RTS concerns itself centrally with that activity.

So it has come down to this. Our "modern advanced civilization" is strictly materialistic in method and explanation. This is what I call "being stuck in natural consciousness". God's incarnation opens up the anatomical function of rebirth and regeneration. By acquiring a natural physical avatar at its birth, God created specific anatomical or functional changes in this acquired avatar. These anatomical changes would make rebirth and regeneration possible for all avatars that were modeled on God's acquired avatar. This is another way of saying acquiring spiritual consciousness. Unless God had made these anatomical changes on the acquired Divine-Human avatar, no one would have the ability to be saved. Every individual would be born selfish with no possibility of reversing and becoming other centered. This is the same as saying that every individual would be born for hell. That is the end of all humanity.

Already at the creation of the world, God of course anticipated the need some day for the incarnation event in human history and evolution. God's love for humanity is so absolute and unconditional that God was willing to become humble and weak during that process of self-modification in an imperfect avatar. But how else could God change our anatomy so that we may have a heavenly life in eternity?

God incarnated into an ordinary imperfect avatar and through the avatar effected the anatomical changes in the natural consciousness that directed the avatar's behavior and appearance.

The actual imprinting of the personality changes from selfish to altruistic was achieved through success in resisting spiritual temptations. The natural consciousness that is embodied in the Divine-Human's acquired avatar was tempted spiritually for the purpose of giving the individual a voluntary free choice to reject every selfish love that came up in the temptations.

Without this voluntary rejection of a selfish thought or desire, there can be no permanent imprinting of the reborn personality.

This is the key to understanding regeneration and cooperating with God in its success. God would gladly imprint everyone with the love of good and truth. But such imprinting does not remain in consciousness. It has no roots and cannot grow. We remain selfish and return to it with greater love than before. So God cannot give mutual love to the individual who prefers selfish love. If God were to insist and force an individual to switch from being selfish to thinking and acting from mutual love, the individual would feel like some power possessed it and can no longer be oneself. This is a worse hell to be in than the one the individual was in before God's forced intervention.

Your destiny is the result of the collaboration between the conscious and the unconscious. ~Carl Jung, Letters Vol. I, p. 283

Christianity is the last word of mankind in the tremendous attempt to formulate the mysteries of the soul, and knowing nothing better we should acknowledge that we are still there; whether we like it or dislike it makes no difference at all, we are still there. ~Carl Jung, Visions Seminar, Page 135

If this [Religious] function is lacking, man as an individual lacks balance, because religious experience is an expression of the existence and function of the unconscious. ~Carl Jung, Letters Vol. II, p. 271

3. Definition of Spiritual

Anatomical knowledge does not tell us how we fill our own bodies but psychic experience does give us information on this point. We fill our bodies as if through inner streams. ~Carl Jung, ETH Lecture 26 Jan 1940

RTS defines two types of ideas, spiritual and natural, and more specifically, spiritual-rational ideas and natural-rational ideas. Some people make a dichotomy between rational and spiritual, and others between rational and symbolic. But the fact is that any natural idea can be spiritualized. For instance, the idea of a mountain is natural in itself because it belongs to the material or physical world. But we can make it into a spiritual idea by including the idea of creation by God. A mountain was created by God for the purpose of serving a useful function for humankind. In fact, everything that exists on our planet was created by God to provide a suitable environment in which human beings can be active and acquire knowledge and the ability to think rationally. The idea of mountain can thus be infused with the idea of God's intention of usefulness to humans. This spiritualized idea of "mountain" makes it into a spiritual idea.

The natural meaning of "mountain" is on the outside while the spiritualized meaning is then on the inside. In ancient times people considered mountains to be holy places and they worshipped on mountains, hills and groves. This is because they were thinking of what the mountain represents spiritually and it is this spiritualized meaning that they considered to be holy. Much later however there was a cultural decline as people became materialistic in their thinking and emotions. They then no longer knew what is spiritual. But they continued to worship on mountains and in groves thinking that these physical objects were in themselves holy. This type of thinking is of course empty and ineffective to regenerate the individual.

Consider the idea of "having an ambition". When you join that idea with the idea of motivational activity, you are beginning to spiritualize it. All human motivation involves the operation of psychic energy in the individual's mind. This mental power must have a source that is outside the personality or self. If you think of God as that source, then you are deepening the spiritual meaning of "having ambition".

The general principle is that any idea that we connect to God in some rational form becomes a spiritual idea.

There are therefore two types of rational thinking operations: ideas that we do not connect to God, which are then natural, and ideas that we connect to God, which are then spiritual. You might want to take a moment to think through some examples of your own.

Take as another instance the idea of "luck" or being lucky. In itself this is a natural idea similar to chance, randomness, and probability. We can spiritualize the idea of "being lucky" by connecting it to God through a rational explanation such as the following: There is an omnipotent God who has all the power. Hence if someone is being lucky, the source of it must be God since only God can order the distribution of probabilities and randomness. If there were such a thing as chance, then God would no longer be omnipotent, as things would happen that God did not make happen.

Now consider the idea of a catastrophe such as people dying in a car collision. Rather than calling it an unfortunate "accident", we can connect it to God by reasoning as follows: God's purpose in making that accident happen is to promote the spiritual welfare of all human beings, including the victims in the accident. More elaborate spiritual explanations of this event are obtained by connecting several spiritual ideas to it, such as the idea that death is a continuation of life and not an ending, and that no one can die except at the moment God brings it about, and that no one is born for self alone but for others.

As a further example consider what is wholeness and mental health. When we apply the idea of wholeness to the mind and personality we are reasoning in spiritual-rational consciousness, far above our everyday consciousness that we use to keep our physical body surviving and thriving. The physical body is temporary and subject at any time to illness and death. But our spiritual body remains intact, totally unaffected by anything that is physical, such as a virus or gun shot.

All human beings are therefore dual citizens, born with two bodies, one physical and temporary for the natural world, the other spiritual and immortal for the spiritual world of eternity in the afterlife. At death the physical body is separated and we continue life in the spiritual world with our spiritual body. It is the spiritual body that is the mind and nothing of the mind in terms of thoughts and feelings can exist in the physical body. Hence, when we awaken from the three-day dying-resuscitation process we are exactly the same person as before death.

The idea of wholeness is not applied to the physical body but only to the spiritual body or the mind. But as long as we are connected to our physical body on earth, growing towards our mental wholeness must take place through what we make our physical body do or not do, and what we think about it in our natural consciousness. *Mental development cannot take place in the abstract, but only in the experiencing.*

God manages our mental development with perfect wisdom and loving friendship. It feels good and contributes to our spiritual development, to acknowledge this spiritual truth of God's friendship. There then arises from within a feeling of total gratitude and appreciation for God's amazing goodness and humility to want to mange my thoughts and feelings from birth to endless immortality. What a true friendship! Who could think of something greater and better? No doubt this is what is meant by the saying, 'reality is greater than fiction'. How good and amazing God is to us. This is the spiritual reality. Nothing imagined or fictionalized can top that!

Once we acknowledge and learn to appreciate the spiritual truth that God is managing our thoughts, feelings, emotions, words, everything, then we can begin to consciously cooperate with God in that process of development. God is the manager, God has all the power, and further, *we have no intelligence or power from ourselves*. This may lead some people to conclude, "Well, it's useless to try anything. What's the point? God is doing everything." But this would be a tragic error.

Thinking in spiritual-rational consciousness we can clearly see that if we did not need to co-participate in our development, God would instantly make everyone healthy and whole forever. Why does God not do that? The spiritual-rational follow up answer is, "God cannot do that or else He would". So we conclude that every individual must cooperate with God and take an active role in healthy mental growth. The reason God cannot compel people to be happy and whole is that our very humanness is sourced in our freedom to choose for ourselves. If God takes this away from us we are no longer humans, but perhaps intelligent animals or artificial intelligence robots.

I developed the rationale for rational theistic self-analysis (RTS) in order to assist me and others in practicing a spiritual discipline in the course of the daily routines. We must understand what we are motivated to do or else we soon lose our motivation and involvement. But when we comprehend rationally, it actually makes sense. Blind faith in God doesn't get us as far as rational faith in God. God is the original *spiritual* being, which is rational. Reality is rational, which is spiritual. The higher the form of our rationality the closer we get to the awesomeness of God as our talking friend.

Swedenborg writes:
> *All of us are predestined to heaven and none of us is predestined to hell.*
> *We devote ourselves to hell by abusing our freedom in spiritual matters;*

then we embrace the types of things that emanate from hell. . . . We are all kept in the central area between heaven and hell, so that we are in an equilibrium between good and evil and therefore have free choice in spiritual matters. ~ Swedenborg, True Christianity, TCR 490

The purpose of rational theistic self-analysis is to gain the ability of cooperating with God in the lifelong process of regeneration.

This is an arduous task. We are born natural with the anatomical equipment of becoming spiritual. *The spiritual-rational mind is the beginning of the true human mind.* Below that, which is merely the natural mind, is not yet properly human. It is something we share with the higher animals, and although we can reach a more complex level of mental operation, nevertheless that increase in intelligence is continuous with that of the intelligent animals. The natural world is a lower degree of life than the spiritual world. What is physical is lower in universal function than what is mental.

God has provided a psychotherapeutic procedure for transforming our mind from merely natural to spiritual. This process is called "regeneration". A simple barometer as to when this happens is to examine your loves in daily interactions and thoughts. You will then see a change. In the natural phase of our thinking and emoting we are unable to believe that it is possible to love others as much as self and even more than self. Everything in natural consciousness comes down to self and ego. It is the basis and foundation of every love and every thought.

You will then see a change, a movement away from self-based ideas and feelings. You maintain a personal relationship with God and you study the spiritual truths that God gives in Sacred Scripture. This is the beginning of true reality in your mind, in your life, and in all your immortal future. It requires compelling yourself to think with respect of other people and of societal institutions, and to avoid disrespect and profanity because these are offensive to God and therefore injurious to your connection to God. This is the effort at self-compulsion, away from arrogance and disrespect, and toward conscience and compassion. This is the path, the way, the method that brings us to spiritual-rational consciousness and "salvation" from devolution to spiritual insanity and suffering.

The practice of RTS develops and strengthens our thinking about God and about eternal development and wholeness through a relationship with God. As Jung and Swedenborg demonstrate God is a biological idea. To be born human is to remain forever anatomically attached to God. This anatomy is not the temporary physical body or avatar we receive at birth along with the immortal spiritual body which is in the spiritual world and houses the mental organs such as the will, memory, personality, identity, loves and affections. All of these must be in the anatomy of the spiritual body. Hence it is that at death we awaken in our spiritual body and nothing is missing in our mental life.

Practicing rational theistic self-analysis consists of two activities. The first is to become familiar with theistic thinking in a rational mode. This is like reading and learning about a new marvelous planet that was discovered by space travellers. The second step, which goes on practically at the same time, is to start applying RTS thinking to one's daily life, especially to our reactions, our thoughts, our intentions, and our emotions.

Once we begin this spiritual process the going can get rough. We discover lo and behold that our thoughts are not pure but filthy and profane, and our emotions are not generous but jealous and cruel. At this point we must exercise RTS thinking to figure out why God manages in such a way as to immerse our thinking in filth and our willing in selfishness.

God comes through with an answer to guide us. Unless we were allowed to have those filthy thoughts and selfish loves we could not be saved from selfishness and the spiritual insanity to which it leads. Slowly we learn the lesson of love. Love is the good substance itself. It is the framework that holds the mind together as total unit. Love is the very essence of living substance, thus of all reality, mental and physical.

Love is anatomical and permanent. It cannot be excised without destroying the unity of the mind. Once we love something, whether it is one's beloved spouse or some strawberries, we are attached to that love forever. Love sticks permanently to the human personality. Now when we become adult and decide to practice rational theistic self-analysis, we come to God with a lot of mental baggage that sticks to us from our lifestyle habits and attitudes. Practically all our loves are selfish and self-serving, and all our thoughts and attitudes are spiritually false and irrational.

With this kind of distorted and deformed mental anatomy, removing what is contrary to good and truth is to destroy the whole mind and soul of the individual. This is why God cannot do it, not for His own sake, but for the sake of the individual, and God's love is such as to want the individual to be perfectly whole, happy, and intelligent.

Therefore regeneration of the old personality is necessary since it cannot be repaired despite God's omnipotence. And regeneration is a lifelong growth process, like growing a new tree that has been grafted on an old tree. The new tree must grow to maturity by growing and being nourished day and night for many years. And the more this process is going on the more God is able to isolate and neutralize the action of the loves in the old personality. Nothing is removed but only moved more and more to the far circumference of the personality in which the center matters and determines everything.

All the old selfish loves and all the old insane thoughts are disposed of in the process of regeneration. A new spiritually healthy personality gradually emerges by organic growth through our practice of new intentions, new attitudes, and new actions in our daily exchanges with others and society.

Upon the disconnection of our physical avatar at death we awaken with a personality that is well equipped to select and to enter a heavenly psychic society in eternity. But if we are not so equipped, we select to enter in a hell society. God honors the commitment of our loves and will assist us in making that selection.

The practice of rational theistic self-analysis is appropriate and effective regardless of religion, culture, or belief system. There is only one God and every nation or culture receives from God a religious Sacred Scripture that is suitable to the genius and life orientation of that community. When we read the Sacred Scripture of the world's major religions it is clear from the literal meanings and history that is presented that God is communicating with a particular culture and its people. God's commandments are worded in the thinking and the emotional capacity proper to that race or nation.

But when we use symbolism and correspondences we make out the spiritual meaning and message that is hidden within the literal verses. It is then that we enter spiritual-rational consciousness and perceive clearly that God communicates simultaneously to the entire vertical level of operation of the human mind. God's thinking and speech is the same in every individual's celestial-rational level of mental operation. It is also the same in the spiritual-rational level of consciousness. But it varies in the natural consciousness. Hence is given a variety of religions within cultures.

The spiritual practice in the RTS perspective helps the individual understand God in a higher and personal way, free of natural attachments that are in history, culture, and collective ritual. These are not in opposition but they are seen as distinct at different levels.

It is critical for regeneration, individuation, and self-realization that we understand rationally the biological connection that we have with Sacred Scripture.

Most people are educated and enculturated in the idea that Sacred Scripture is something that belongs to religion. It is correct to think that religion is based on Sacred Scripture and is a necessary part of it. All religions have their own *Sacred Scripture*. And this is the point to notice: every religion is a cultural practice. God provides a *Sacred Scripture* for every culture. There is only one God, and it is therefore the same God in every religion or culture.

When you compare the *Sacred Scripture* of different religions you will note some similarities and some differences. People who focus on the differences develop the idea that their own religion is the only religion that connects to the one God. The *Sacred Scripture* of other religions is then viewed as false, an attitude that has led to conflict and hostility between adherents of different religions. This has happened historically and is happening today.

Consider that religion can be practiced in natural consciousness and in spiritual consciousness. When *Sacred Scripture* is viewed in spiritual consciousness the differences in them disappear and it is plain that the content and ideas presented are the same for all *Sacred Scripture* that God has provided.

This makes rational sense. On the outside and on the literal surface meaning and topics of *Sacred Scripture* the cultural differences predominate in all topics. One sees differences and contradictions or disagreements, which then lead to conflict and hostility towards the "false" religions. This makes sense because God provides the text and content to suit the culture and genius of each nation or historically connected group of nations. If God did not do this, the religion would not be accepted.

People can accept only a religion that is suitable to their cultural thinking and adaptation.

The literal sense and content of *Sacred Scripture* must be sufficiently explicit to teach children and adults about God, about the afterlife or resurrection from death, about heaven and hell, and about what God tells us about how to live in order to avoid hell and to be happy forever in heaven. This makes it possible for everyone in natural consciousness to have a religion and to believe in God and God's commandments of living.

There are those who are willing to recognize that there is a spiritual consciousness that teaches a rational understanding of those things in the literal content. Without this rational understanding one cannot fully believe the things that are said in the literal historical sense and content. There is "blind faith" and "rational faith". In blind faith one cannot explain the many contradictions that are presented in the literal sense of *Sacred Scripture*. One cannot understand why an omnipotent God allows human suffering and evil to plague the human race. One cannot understand why it is said that God punishes those who sin and sends them to hell. This seems harsh and unjust to many people.

In consequence "blind faith" suffers and many begin to doubt and finally to reject God and *Sacred Scripture*. This is an awful regrettable consequence that cuts the individual off from salvation, regeneration, and mental health. Hence God constantly works in the background of the individual's mind to feel the need for regeneration and consciousness raising. This gradually turns the blind faith into the rational faith. Now the individual can perceive a new spiritual meaning to the content of *Sacred Scripture*.

Regardless of religion, culture, and the literal wording of their *Sacred Scripture*, people can now perceive the same meaning and content in all *Sacred Scripture*. The rational faith gives access to the universal truths that give understanding of God. The rational belief system becomes the biological science of God, which is called "theistic psychology". The *Sacred Scripture* of every religion contains the same theistic science. Rational faith or theistic psychology is therefore universal and biologically or anatomically unites the minds of all humanity.

In order for regeneration to proceed and grow towards the wholeness of individuation, it is necessary to acquire rational faith, which is faith in spiritual consciousness. One can then see more and more clearly every day how God runs the universe and the individual.

God is a God of pleasure and good feelings. The most appropriate time to thank God for the pleasure and enjoyment we experience is at the time we are gifted by God with these things. When you feel the pleasure and enjoyment of some feelings, sensations, perceptions, or ideas – that's the time to thank God by being affected with feelings of connection and closeness with God. Remind yourself that God is giving you these specific experiences and the consciousness of this experiencing. God is doing it because God loves you, created you, continues to create you towards your unique wholeness when you become connected spiritually to angelic society. This connection is eternal life and happiness.

The popular debate about whether or not God exists stems from a lack of sufficient knowledge about theistic psychology. The most basic spiritual facts are totally unknown. Here are some of the main spiritual facts that are little known or not known at all.

God has created two distinct worlds, one called the spiritual world and the other is called the physical world. Nothing physical can enter into the spiritual world, just as a physical chair cannot enter the mental world through imagination or dream. Instead, the physical and the spiritual are connected through symbolism, representatives, and correspondences. The chair in your imagination or dream must be made of something, some material or substance. The objects of your thinking and dreaming are real and are made of spiritual substance, which you can also call mental substance.

Most people believe that mental objects in our thinking or dreaming are not "real" and therefore are not made of some material. This is an error that may be attributable to the materialism of science that denies reality to anything that is not made of physical matter. We are raised and educated in this type of materialistic thinking, and hence we think that thoughts, feelings, and dreams are not real "but just something in your mind".

The spiritual truth is that all objects in the mind are objective constructions made of spiritual or mental substance or material. "Mental substance"? Yes. The physical world is constructed out of physical elements, energy, particles, and compounds thereof, such as rocks, fruits, air, or the physical body of animals and humans. The spiritual world is constructed out of spiritual substance originating and streaming out from the sun of that world called the "spiritual sun".

The physical world originates from the physical sun that rules the space around each star. Stars originate from the point of origin of the physical universe, which was a mass of tight packed matter that exploded and is known as the Big Bang. For the past few billion years the explosion, at the rate of the speed of light, has been expanding in all directions, thereby populating the endless physical universe with physical materials and energies that the stars and planets are made of.

While there are countless "suns" or stars in the physical universe, there is only on sun in the spiritual universe. This spiritual sun is the first presence of God in creation. It contains God's thoughts and intentions, which are infinite. God is substantial in an infinite mental presence. All of God's thoughts, feelings, and intentions are therefore substantial. The spiritual sun is also infinite and contains an infinity of human thoughts, feelings, sensations, affections, loves, imaginations, dreams, and so on.

We were created with a spiritual body that can receive this endless mental material streaming into the spiritual universe and outward to reach all human minds past, present, and future. Our spiritual body is anatomically equipped with organs that allow us to have consciousness, feelings, and sensations. The streaming mental objects going forth from the infinite spiritual sun spread out into the mental world where our mind exists, lives, and grows as a unique individual person.

You can see from all this that we are born with anatomical connections to God, to all other human beings past, present, and future. We are born into the spiritual world with a consciousness, personality, and identity that is immortal and lives on forever. Once a human, always a human. We are born to live temporarily attached and restricted by a physical body in the physical universe. Our spiritual body is born simultaneously with our physical body, the two being interconnected for as long as we live in this world.

The three-day dying-resuscitation process is a surgical procedure performed by God with loving attention by which our physical body is detached and becomes a lifeless corpse. Our spiritual body remains the same as before death. Now when we are resuscitated a few hours after death our spiritual body is no longer restricted as before. We now become conscious of our spiritual environment. This was not normally possible prior to death because our mental growth and personality development had to be established through the restrictive activity of the physical body to which we were connected by birth.

I think of my physical body as an "avatar" that gives me the ability to be conscious of the physical environment and to move and think natural thoughts that are mental representations of the physical objects and conditions by which my avatar is situationally affected. At death I no longer use the avatar and therefore lose all connections with the physical world. Now my conscious awareness is focused solely on the environment of the spiritual word.

When we awaken from the dying surgical procedure our thoughts, personality, identity, memory, habits of thinking and feeling emotions, are present with no change. This is because nothing whatsoever of our mental and feeling life could ever exist in the physical avatar, which is material and thus lifeless. No consciousness or sensation can ever exist in the physical brain. Right from birth our mental activity and personality were located in the spiritual body and were activities by the spiritual body. Hence after death nothing mental could have changed or been lost. This is the meaning of being immortal.

We now continue our immortal life in the spiritual world where we can encounter and interact with all other human beings that ever lived and passed into the spiritual world through the dying process. There is only one mental world, or one spiritual world and therefor all human life must be forever in that one mental world or spiritual world. This is wonderful news! It means we can meet and interact with anyone that has ever lived!

You know that there is only one physical universe where all matter is located regardless of how physically far they are from each other. You can see from this that there is only one mental world for the entire human race. Right now as you are reading this you can think about the anatomical fact that you are in one mental world that you share with all human beings. The only reason you cannot directly access other human beings mentally is that your mental activities are expressed in thoughts and ideas that are representatives to physical objects. Try to think of any idea right now that does not contain physical objects or conditions: matter, time, space, measurement, energy, motion, gravity, history, language.

These materialistic thoughts and definitions restrict your mind to what is called "natural consciousness". You are unable to connect and interact with others except through physical conditions. If they are too far, or have no communication devices, you cannot connect. But when you are in spiritual conscious all your ideas and thoughts have zero natural meanings or elements. Zero. Hence since there are no spatial limits or time limits in the mental world you can interact with anyone who is also in the spiritual world with their spiritual body.

You can be in spiritual consciousness anytime while you are still tied to your physical avatar. You can overcome the limitations of natural consciousness and rise to the level of spiritual consciousness simply by learning how to think with *only spiritual ideas*. The perspective of RTS is a method of learning this very thing.

Since birth everyone receives spiritual ideas from the spiritual environment of the spiritual body. These are necessarily spiritual ideas with no physical or natural elements in them. But by the time they enter into our natural everyday consciousness they take on physical elements and are no longer spiritual. The spiritual elements and meanings remain in our unconscious mind, which is the mind of humanity, the universal collective unconscious.

The collective unconscious is common to every human being. It is universal as there is only one spiritual or mental world. Our spiritual consciousness in this collective unconscious is not reachable with our natural materialistic ideas. We are conscious only of the corresponding representation that is expressed in a symbolic language. Without this "influx" or influence of our spiritual consciousness on the our natural consciousness we would not be rational human beings but merely a higher order animal more complex in functioning than the other animals on our planet.

But when we sleep and dream we are directly conscious in our spiritual consciousness. When dreaming we are being active in the collective unconscious. People believe that when they sleep they are unconscious. This is an error. We are fully consciously awake in our sleeping and dreaming, just as we are fully consciously aware when we have breakfast after waking up.

The proof that we are conscious while sleeping is that we can remember dreams. For if we were unconscious when sleeping we could not remember our dreams.

The memory of our dreams is incomplete not because we were not conscious but because we cannot express and be conscious of spiritual ideas when thinking in a natural language. I often have the experience of remembering a dream quite clearly and being totally unable to describe it in words of natural language. I've known 10 different languages before learning English as an adolescent. All natural languages have the same limitations. They are made out of ideas with physical properties. These cannot describe even a tiny aspect of a dream or other spiritual consciousness.

When people remember and describe dreams it is always in natural ideas, or physical objects like a crowd of people, a field of flowers, people on a beach, the taste of ice cream, the sensation of being physically touched, and so on. These are representations and correspondences of the mental activity and consciousness of the dream itself, which was performed through the spiritual body in spiritual consciousness.

> *Myth is not fiction: it consists of facts that are continually repeated and can be observed over and over again. It is something that happens to man, and men have mythical fates just as much as the Greek heroes do. ~Carl Jung, CW 11, Para 648*

Jung and Swedenborg made an intense study of these representations and correspondences in dreams, myths, and sacred literature. Freud's approach to dream analysis was not related to spiritual correspondences as they appear by representation in dreams and religious symbols. I describe their work in some detail in Volume 1 of this book. For example, when you dream about spiritual ideas and truths what you remember in natural ideas involve water in some form, like a lake, summer rain, winter rain, river, fountain, drinking cup, ice, steam, blood, and other liquids. Each of these forms of water in your memory of the dream corresponds to a different spiritual idea or feeling that you had in the dream.

Or, for instance, if you may remember your dream as you walking through a strange city and looking back and forth to find your way back to a house or place. This natural representation of the actual dream you had symbolizes your spiritual search for understanding a spiritual dilemma that takes place in your spiritual mind or consciousness.

You can grasp the idea of correspondences by looking at a person's facial expressions. This is especially clear with babies and infants. The facial expressions you see on someone's face are called "expressions" because each expresses a particular emotion or mood. The emotion and the mood are external or physical appearance or representation of an inner mental or spiritual activity. The physical expression on the face is a natural or physical representation of the spiritual emotion or mood that is happening within the mind. In a dream you may have a sad feeling that is remembered later as a physically "sad" facial expression.

When you remember a dream as seeing a high mountain you may have been experiencing during your dreaming as a spiritual connection with the Divine. Mountains and hills in natural consciousness correspond to a felt connection with God. Your spiritual experience in the dream as your love to God translates symbolically in your memory as seeing a mountain. Every animal species in your recall of a dream indicates some specific emotional activity that went on during your dreaming.

4. How To Spiritualize Everything

The word spiritual is much used and talked about today. For instance, a web search on that word shows over 300 million results, that is, web sites or documents that contain this word. Dictionaries offer these definitions or synonyms for spiritual: mystical, religious, divine, otherworldly, psychic, non-physical, transcendent, of the soul, and things of spirit. These are all good descriptions and every one appears accurate to me. However, our thinking needs to put these together into one idea. We can do this by expanding these dictionary descriptions.

People have used the word spiritual to refer to something mystical in the sense that it is not definable clearly or rationally. It is common to think that what is spiritual is difficult to comprehend. But this feeling may have come from the lack of clear and crisp definition of the word. The other descriptors are easier to comprehend: religious, divine, otherworldly, of the soul, and of the spirit. These concepts seem to coalesce into the idea of God and spirit or soul. So spiritual is whatever is related to God or the spirit or soul. In addition, spirit or soul is related to otherworldly and non-physical. This part of the description of spiritual establishes the idea of dualism or two independent worlds, one physical of this world, and the other spiritual or otherworldly, thus having to do with our afterlife and with immortality.

> God has never spoken to man except in and through the psyche, and the psyche understands it and we experience it as something psychic. ~Carl Jung, Letters Vol. I, p. 98

This is the surprise clincher for the word spiritual: psychic. What is psychic? We know this well from Jung and other literary traditions, namely, that psychic is related to consciousness and experience. In other words, spiritual means mental. This is a surprising and perhaps unsuspected conceptual relationship. When people talk about something "spiritual" what they are saying is therefore related to God, the afterlife, immortality, consciousness and the mental world of eternity.

What is the mental world of eternity?

Nothing can be more familiar to each of us since our life and experience is always a mental experience. We notice, we react, we feel an emotion, we think and analyze, we plan, we think of what to say, we think of what to do, we hear and sensate, we love and hate, we will. All these things are mental activities. Now since we are discussing this from the perspective of dualism, we can ask what is the mental world of eternity and how is it related to us in our own mental activity. And the astonishing answer is that they are the same. Our own individual mental activity overlaps and contains the mental activity of every other immortal human being. There is only one mental world and all human beings are born into it. Human beings are essentially mental beings. We an also say that they are spiritual beings since spiritual is the same as mental.

What an amazing realization this is! After thirty years of understanding this relationship through my reading of Swedenborg I am still excited with goose bumps every time I write about it. It is the most awesome scientific discovery and realization that we can make about our life, namely, that we are immortal because we are mental beings, and mental is in eternity.

Let's look at this again: mental is in eternity. We all realize this as soon as we think about it. The definition of the theistic dual universe is that God created the physical world with fixed time, place, and measurement parameters, but created the spiritual or mental world apart from fixed time, apart from physical location or size and quantity limits. We know this from our own experience in thinking, dreaming, and fantasizing. There are no fixed or physical limits in size, quantity, place, direction, or time when it comes to our mental world operations. We can produce whatever space, time, or construction materials we need to create the experience of a dream, story, or dramatic setting.

Now consider the word "spiritualize". What could that be referring to? From the word form itself we can tell that to spiritualize is doing something to something else that is related to spiritual. You can take anything around you and you can spiritualize it or say how it is related to spiritual. For instance, you see a dark cloud in the sky and you think about its spiritual or mental correspondence, which you expect to be something to do with not seeing something clearly or feeling despondent and fearful. To think of mental things when observing or thinking about physical things is to spiritualize.

Anything can be spiritualized because everything in the physical world corresponds to something of human mental activity in relation to God. This is the framework of scientific dualism. It connects the two worlds by the laws of correspondence that are built into everything created by God. God created everything from the substance of love and intelligence that are God's eternal mental activity. Hence the universe is created from mental substance called love and intelligence.

You can see from this that our immortality depends on our birth into eternity through a spiritual or mental body called the spirit and soul.

So now you need to reflect on this awesome new realization, which is that the mental world in which you live is the same mental word in which all human beings live, and further, that this mental world is called eternity because there is no fixed time, place, quantity, or measurement. We know this well from our dreams and fantasies.

One amazing conclusion from this new realization is that all human beings are connected anatomically past and present, while we are in this world and in afterlife world. But as Swedenborg has demonstrated through his living in both words simultaneously for 27 years, we are not conscious of others populating the mental world. It appears and feels to us as if we are alone in our mental world and that every individual is alone in his or her mental world. This is indeed the experience of the appearance.

But Jung and Swedenborg, and others, have shown that we can become conscious of the others while we are still in this world. But certainly after we are awakened from the three-day dying resuscitation process, each of us opens the eyes on the mental world of eternity and we can see present anyone we knew directly or through history of the past, plus innumerable others whom we did not know personally.

There is therefore an anatomical mechanism operating in our natural consciousness to prevent our awareness of others who are likewise in the mental world of eternity. Swedenborg was able to access and talk with many of his old friends who had passed on, many of the authors from antiquity whose books he had read, and an endless number of populations distributed from around the many inhabited planets of the universe. Such is the power and reach of our spiritual consciousness.

It makes sense that we are unable to detect the presence of others when we operate in our natural consciousness. Recall that in natural consciousness we are monists and materialists, believing the sensory appearances as being real. We are taught to minimize the mind and its thoughts as not really real, not as real as the body, money, or a stone. We say, "Oh, it's just thoughts. That's all. Nothing concrete."

But in spiritual consciousness we understand that the sensory appearances are real only on the natural plane of consciousness. God prevents people from interacting directly with spirits of the afterlife. This is necessary as a Divine precaution to protect people still on earth from being "possessed" and obsessed by those in the afterlife who have hostile intentions and purposes for trying to communicate directly with an individual.

———————

Jung writes:

> *I drew all my empirical material from my patients, but the solution of the problem I drew from the inside, from my observations of the unconscious processes. ~Carl Jung, 1925 Seminar, p. 35*

> *With our human knowledge we always move in the human sphere, but in the things of God we should keep quiet and not make any arrogant assertions about what is greater than ourselves. ~Carl Jung, Letters Vol. I, p. 125*

———————

Jung says that he went mentally mad for a few months when he was writing the famous *Red Book* ("Liber Novus") and became obsessed with the visions he had of the psychic world and the collective unconscious. He had multiple interactions with various psychic characters that came to him in his temporary madness, though at the time Jung feared that it might be permanent. He subsequently cautioned people to beware of the destructive and hateful devil coming out of the unconscious and attacking the sanity of the person.

> *You must be in the middle of life, surrounded by death on all sides.*
> *~Carl Jung, The Red Book, p. 370*

Since we can spiritualize anything we can benefit from this activity that will allow us to progressively raise our consciousness from natural to spiritual.

———————

Swedenborg writes:

It can never be said that heaven is outside anyone. It is within; because every angel accepts the heaven that is outside in keeping with the heaven that is within. We can see, then, how mistaken people are who think that getting into heaven is simply a matter of being taken up among the angels, regardless of the quality of their inner life, who believe that heaven is granted merely because of [the Lord's] mercy. On the contrary, unless heaven is within an individual, nothing of the heaven that is outside flows in and is accepted. ~Swedenborg, Heaven and Hell, HH 54

Conscience is a new will and a new understanding received from the Lord, and so is the Lord's presence with a person. ~Swedenborg, Heavenly Secrets, AC 4299

---

5. We Are Born Into Eternity And Immortality

It is important to know that the mind is a spiritual body with anatomical organs and functions like our physical body. When we are born our spiritual body is born in the afterlife of eternity and remains there forever. Our physical body is temporary and we lose all connection with it at death. While we are connected to our temporary avatar in this world our consciousness is completely restricted to the world of time, space, matter, measurement, and material explanations of their behavior. This is the materialist science that we learn in school and becomes part of our daily thinking.

But beneath this natural way of thinking is the unconscious activity of our spiritual thinking. At this unconscious level of mental activity we think and reason with spiritual ideas only. After the three-day dying-resuscitation procedure we awaken in our spiritual consciousness and its way of thinking. We now are fully aware of our spiritual thinking, just as we were aware of our natural consciousness prior to the dying procedure.

So the spiritual body grows up like the avatar from childhood ways of thinking to mature adult ways of thinking.

We awaken in our spiritual body and we are consciously aware of the sensory input from the afterlife world. We see other people who already live in the afterlife. This includes everybody who was ever born since the beginning of creation. If you have a special interest in someone you got to know from literature you can instantly be present face to face with that person. Swedenborg got to interview several people he knew from their books and who had lived on earth in ancient times.

While we are still functionally connected to our avatar here on earth, those who are already in the afterlife can see our spiritual body, though they cannot interact until after their avatar is removed. Our avatar on earth looks exactly like a material double of our spiritual body in the afterlife. Because of this similarity, people who knew each other through their avatar can recognize each other's spiritual body in the afterlife. The physical avatar is constructed from physical materials on earth. These are not living. They include minerals, water, oxygen, oils, chemical elements, atoms, energy, electricity, size, and location.

Hence the physical body cannot contain anything that is mental such as sensations, thoughts, feelings, awareness, consciousness. All these are in the spiritual body and its anatomical organs.

There is nothing mental that can exist in anything physical.

Hence it follows that the physical body is merely a temporary bio-technological model or avatar that is functionally connected to our mental organs. The avatar obeys all our mental orders. In this way, despite the fact that we are non-physical beings we can explore the physical world through our avatar. This exploration and experiencing allows us to grow and develop into adults that act and think in accordance with their natural-rational consciousness.

Once the natural-rational adult personality is achieved the individual is prepared to undergo regeneration of personality. This involves making a fundamental change in one's personality structure, from living with selfish loves and motives, to living with mutual love and altruistic motives. The more our regeneration progresses the more we enter into the level of our mental anatomy that functions in spiritual consciousness.

Regeneration proceeds by replacing the selfish loves with mutual love, one by one, area by area in the personality. The process of replacement always involves temptations or spiritual combats. These are situations, or opportunities, that God sets up for us in which we are tempted to give in and enjoy once more the delight and pleasure of consummating a selfish love. If we now resist the temptation and reject its delights, God immediately steps in and weakens the power of that negative love in our personality.

Through this gradual process of rejecting and weakening selfish loves there is a cleansing, cleaning, and healing of our personality from the action of these negative loves. *Our mind then becomes capable of altruistic intentions from mutual love.* This love now creates the conscious awareness of our celestial consciousness. This is called "entering heaven in eternity". All people who enter this high zone of the mental world of eternity meet each other and live in community as conjugial love couples.

All it takes to accomplish this amazing feat is to reject selfish love and to practice mutual love in our daily life. God does all the rest.

One of the saddest things for me to witness is to see people afraid of getting old and of dying. This thought spreads throughout one's natural consciousness and fills it with darkness and unreality.

It is spiritual insanity to think that death leads to our extinction.

Materialism, and the natural consciousness that it permeates, lead to the spiritual insanity of denying God, denying life after death, and denying that there is in the human mind both a heaven and a hell, and that this is eternity.

The return from spiritual insanity is in the attainment of spiritual consciousness, which is unperturbed and unaffected by materialism and its ideas of this world. Everyone must realize that life after death is entirely more important because it is immortal, going on forever, endlessly. *Your human personality right now is in that spiritual condition.*

The mind is spiritual, not material. The consciousness that is our mind is a non-material anatomical organ in the human form. The mind in its spiritual body is in the same form or appearance as the physical body or avatar.

This is because the bio-technological avatar is modeled or constructed as a material copy of the immaterial original, which is called the spiritual body or mental body. Your mental body, which contains the organs of your mind, is the original, and it counts as more important since it is immortal. The physical body may be called our material *avatar*, which is designed to give us control in the physical world.

Without the physical avatar our natural consciousness would be blind and deaf, thus unable to allow the personality to grow and develop into a mature human mind ready to be elevated into spiritual consciousness. This is the true human life. Below this in natural consciousness we are like "beasts", belonging to the animal kingdom. We have a distinctly human body and human intelligence but we think that our fate is like that of animals, namely dying of old age or being killed by various causes. Then nothing. Extinction. This fantasy removes our spiritual nature, and hence we lose our humanity and become like beasts.

God in *Sacred Scripture* calls this type of life "beastly". The earliest civilizations on this planet were spiritual, not natural. God's existence was known and was worshipped, along with prophecy and orally transmitted *Sacred Scripture* that served to develop their spiritual and celestial consciousness through becoming aware of spiritual truths and facts. It was known that there is a life after death, and a heaven and hell in eternity. God calls this type of life "human".

In other words, we are born natural and animal, with the normal growth potential of becoming spiritual and human. The human begins in the spiritual while the natural that is below it is not yet human.

At birth we acquire two bodies. One is the mental body or the spiritual body. It is our spiritual consciousness or the spiritual mind. It is immortal and is in eternity. The second body is a temporary avatar built out of the materials of the physical world and equipped to sense, move around, and displace objects in obedience to what we want in our mental body or mind.

The temporary physical avatar has the same appearance as the permanent mental body since it is a copy of it. The lower organic portion of the mental body is immersed in the ideas and feelings specifically adapted to the world of the physical avatar. We sense and perceive the physical world through the receptor organs of the avatar that are functionally attached to the mental or spiritual body.

The purpose of being born connected to a physical avatar is in order that our mental body or mind may be able to develop our natural consciousness. In this mode of thinking everything we think is by means of ideas that represent material models and adapted to a natural rationality. This is marked by love of survival and love of being the greatest, the richest, and mightiest. When our natural consciousness reaches adult maturity, God gives us the reasoning power and the motivation to acquire spiritual ideas that can build up our spiritual consciousness. Without first acquiring a mature natural consciousness we would be physiologically incapable of acquiring spiritual consciousness. The consequence of that is the inability to live in an eternal heaven, or state of peace and fulfillment. Much is at stake here!

Hence God gives us a physical body to allow us to complete our growth in natural consciousness. Then God leads us into spiritual consciousness and into a life of loving others more than self, which is the true human being as an image and likeness of God, who is the original Human, and the infinite Human. I very often think how amazing it is and how fortunate for us that God is human, omnipotent, and our intimate best friend and loving father who has a passion and love for making every human being like Himself, loving others more than self, and deriving the greatest pleasure and satisfaction when we are able to make another person happy through our effort. Knowing this about God is the most precious knowledge that we can possess. It elevates our consciousness to ever-greater wisdom and happiness, endlessly, to eternity!

You can now better realize that everything spiritual is made of mental things like love, emotion, affection, worship, spirituality, happiness, goodness, virtues, and their opposites, anger, hate, stupidity, irrationality, cruelty, suffering, hell etc. *These words are spiritual ideas and they refer to mental activities of human beings. There is nothing spiritual that is not mental.* Hence what is known in the literature as "the spiritual world of the afterlife of heaven and hell" is nothing but the mental world that is so familiar to each of us. What is heaven and hell, or happiness and suffering, but mental activity of the mind?

The afterlife of eternity is nothing else than your own mental world that you already know! *You were born into the afterlife of eternity.*

This is surely the most amazing spiritual fact that I have ever discovered and experienced.

It solves all sorts of "heavy" problems that people have on their mind and have had in the past centuries, as we know from the world literature and history. Searching for immortality is futile and blind. Desiring immortality is useless.

We are born into eternity and immortality.

Our consciousness is not in physical space and time, but is in the non-material mental world where space and time are instantly manufactured by what we desire and love, and what we know and believe. Everyone is familiar with this capacity from the nature of our dreams and imagination.

Our consciousness makes us human by giving us *spiritual rationality*, the basis of which is that God is present in our mind's growth and that God guides us to our eternal happiness to the extent that we freely cooperate. This consists of willingly rejecting the natural consciousness philosophy of "self first", which is from self-love, and willingly accepting and practicing the life of "God and others first", which is from mutual love. This modified perspective and daily practice is known by various names, as for example, "regeneration", "individuation, "self-realization", "wholeness", "mental health", etc.

The three-day dying-resuscitation procedure disconnects us from our physical body and physical world. Now at last we are consciously in eternity. This allows us to receive sensory input directly from the mental or spiritual world and no longer filtered and restricted through natural consciousness. When our physical avatar becomes a corpse through death, we lose forever all input from the physical world.

And now a wonderful discovery: our environment in the mental world of eternity is filled with similar things as in the physical word, namely, other people, animals, buildings, trees, food, space, time, objects, gold, diamonds, etc. But none of these things are made of physical matter so their nature and properties are entirely different from the physical world. We have plenty of familiarity with living in this type of non-material world through our dreams and imagination. Have you ever wondered what those people, or trees, or automobiles, or fruits and vegetables are made of in your dreams or thoughts? In natural consciousness one would answer that "They are made of nothing. They are just dreams, thoughts." But in spiritual consciousness one would answer that "They are made of non-material elements called spiritual substance."

Everything in the spiritual or mental world of eternity is made of mental substance, the chief ones being love-substance and truth-substance.

Mental substance is needed when you sense, feel, think, dream, or imagine anything. These mental things cannot exist from nothing, as this is illogical and irrational. Something cannot be made of nothing. In fact all mental objects such as thoughts, meanings, jokes, stories, music, and memories, must be made of mental substance, the basis of which is love-substance and truth-substance. These two types of mental substance are eternal and infinite. For endless millennia human beings can extract new meanings and experiences from love-substance and its truth-substance.

This living human immortal organic mental substance issues from the Spiritual Sun that is at the center of the mental world of eternity. This is where infinite God can be seen to enter the finite created universe. Love-substance with its truth-substance around itself, streams out of the Spiritual Sun and extends itself and fills the entire mental world of eternity. Anyone anywhere receives this substance and ingests it through the mental organs that are called the will and the understanding. In technical language these are called the affective and cognitive systems.

This mental "food" is necessary for the experiencing of consciousness. Love-substance with its truth-substance is this mental food that feeds the stream of our thoughts. Without this mental food constantly flowing in our mind would be like a plant whose source of water was cut off, so that it shrivels, dies, and turns into dust. The entire human race past and present would plunge into darkness and a mental coma if this food were to be cut off by God.

The will is the affective system of the mind and is an anatomical organ that can absorb love-substance from the mental environment in eternity. From this constant absorption of love-substance, the human will is able to have motivations, loves, interests, pleasures, and intentions. Truth-substance is absorbed through the organ of the understanding, which is also called the cognitive system of the mind. This continuous absorption of love and truth substance creates and supports our immortal consciousness and spiritual rationality. God's infinite love is a Divine, living, and eternal substance. It streams into the mental world of humanity, creating in us consciousness, loves, and intelligence.

When you evolve your spiritual understanding you will perceive that love with its truth is a living and eternal mental substance that exist in God's Human mind in infinite variety. Then you will realize that it is through this living mental or spiritual substance by which God is omnipresent in the mind and in the universe. Whatever exists is constructed of God's love-substance and truth-substance as its infrastructure and inmost form. And since love with truth are God's feelings and thoughts, and are infinite, God cannot give these away to human beings. When love with truth-substance is functioning and active in human beings it is still God's love and intelligence. They remain God's own consciousness. *This gives God omniscience, omnipresence, and omnipotence.*

How amazing it is that this God is Human and loves each of us like a Father.

We acknowledge this deep spiritual truth by talking to God! That is the beginning of wisdom or spiritual rationality.

Talking to God every day and throughout the day is the sane acknowledgment of spiritual reality.

When you do this, God opens up your spiritual consciousness by allowing you to perceive spiritual ideas, such as the idea that you must switch your character orientation from loving self more than others to loving others more than self. No one is born for himself or herself. Everyone is born for others. To reject this spiritual fact is to deny reality, and hence to become spiritually insane. This spiritually dysfunctional mental state prevents wholeness and leads after death to suffering, misery, insanity, and sub-human lifestyle.

> *The Lord is present with you the moment you start to love the neighbor. ~Swedenborg, Heavenly Secrets, AC 904*

God creates everyone for improving the lives of others in a special and unique way. We each receive a different packet of potentials in order that every individual may provide his or her own special abilities to others. In this way the happiness and intelligence of all humanity continues to progress into the endless future. This growth process is interrupted and interfered with when an individual clings to self-love and persistently refuses to accept mutual love as an alternative personality structure.

Rejecting God is selfish because it is a rejection of mutual love, which is to love God and others more than self. To reject mutual love is to reinforce self-love. All selfish loves hang together in a collection or community within the personality structure of every human being. To cling to one selfish love is to cling to all.

It is a spiritual fact that you either love God or you love self.

Making use of the RTS perspective helps us to train ourselves to think with spiritual ideas and to practice them in daily life. The first step is to stop harming others, in our mind or in our interactions. The second step is to wish well to others and to assist them in their needs for comfort, security, and respect. And finally, to acknowledge that none of this modification is done by self but by God when the self talks to God and strives to please God by obeying God's wishes and rules. This heals the mind from its spiritual insanity and prepares it for eternal conjugial happiness in heaven. In this mental state a oneminded married pair together make up and appear as just one angel.

6. Selfish Loves
Are Self-Destructive

> *One must never look to the things that ought to change. The main question is how we change ourselves.* ~Carl Jung, Letters Vol. I, p. 314

Everyone can benefit from learning how we can change ourselves. This activity is the adaptation process of living. By definition, living requires constant growth. Plants continue their physiological and biochemical activities every second for as long as they remain alive. This is the universal organic process. Our mind is a mental reception organ capable of capturing or being affected by the mental substances and forms that are present everywhere in the mental world of eternity.

These substantive mental structures are external appearances or extensions of God's mental substance, which is infinite in variety and fills every human being's mental states. God's mental substance is our mental food, the "spiritual bread" that feeds our mind moment by moment, allowing us to experience emotions, thoughts, and intentions.

The mental body, or spiritual body, is therefore continuously engaged in its growth and development from birth to immortal eternity. However, the process of our mental growth is at risk when it is under the attack of self-centered loves and intentions. Carrying out these self-motivated intentions provides us with the experience of delights and satisfactions. Self-love or selfishness is a genetically inherited mental virus that causes the personality structure of the individual to grow in a spiritually deformed manner and direction.

Individual life requires a collective existence that includes a collective consciousness. This condition requires mutual love, or loving others more than self. This other-centered personality structure is healthy and achieves a happy immortality in eternity.

We are born naturally self-centered and compulsively inclined to self-love, which is to love self exclusively or to love self before all and more than anything. Partly this is due to inheritance and partly it is due to the natural consciousness that is maintained in culture by materialist ideas and thinking. As human beings reach the state of adulthood, God awakens in each person the deeply experienced desire for seeking spiritual truth with the intention of becoming more spiritual. This is our starting point for undergoing regeneration and becoming a fully spiritual person, which is the beginning of being a true human.

We need therefore to know how to change ourselves. This becomes the most important spiritual task ahead. Rational theistic self-analysis (RTS) provides the opportunity to learn and understand rationally the basic facts of reality, God, and life. This spiritual knowledge is presented, discussed, and explained throughout this book.

Making use of the RTS perspective is the process of practicing the spiritual skills of changing our personality structure in a fundamental way. It is a difficult task to perform to stop thinking about "self first, and others and everything else as second". In actuality when we try to do this in our daily life we repeatedly learn the shocking experience of complete failure. Most of us feel powerless to abandon our self for the sake of others and for God. We can only pretend to do so by covering up and hiding the underlying bottom floor where the self lies, watches, commands, and dictates. The self is a ruler of our loves in life.

This is when God moves us from within to appeal to Him to help us, to save us. *If we give in to this inner directionality we succeed.* God leads us through the forest of evil intentions and organically like a surgeon detaches them one by one from their grip of spiritual destruction. God calls us "dead" or "not living" when our spiritual is destroyed. We are then existing forever in the depths of hell in our mind. It is very important to understand that this is by no means a punishment. God can never punish because He is pure and infinite love and support.

7. God Never Punishes

God desires to save everyone regardless of how they have lived and what personality structure they have. There are no past sins, as many people believe. There are only *current* sins that create their own punishment or inability to continue growing in a healthy form. It is the self-centered personality structure that rejects the healing that God desires and longs for every person to have. Sadly, it is the spiritual insanity of self-love that keeps the person in mind's hell. The dysfunctional consciousness of the person desires this life of hell and finds in it aspects to love and lust after. When the person no longer desires in any way whatsoever to "reform". This is why God calls this lowered living "dead" or spiritually insane.

Even so, God continues to exert control over the individuals in that sub-human mental state, continually holding them back from precipitating themselves into lower and more debased mental states. As a result of God's presence in their mind they retain a semblance of rationality and understanding of truths, but they hate them and do not allow them to enter the   mind.

It is spiritually hurtful to refuse to give up the idea that God punishes. This irrational idea stands as a barrier to theistic rationality. Many people fall into irrational traps, as for instance, the idea that God is the source of both good and evil. But when you give up false and irrational ideas about God you are gaining spiritual sanity and rationality.

_____

Swedenborg writes:
> But the fact is that the approach to the numinous is the real therapy and in as much as you attain to the numinous experiences you are released from the curse of pathology. ~Carl Jung, Letters Vol. I, p. 377

> I am not, however, addressing myself to the happy possessors of faith, but to those many people for whom the light has gone out, the mystery has faded, and God is dead. ~Carl Jung, CW 11, Para 148

> The reason the recently dead [following the three-day dying resuscitation procedure] find this likeness in everything [they see around them] is that their minds remain exactly as they were in the world [before death]; and because the mind is not confined to the head but pervades the whole body, it has a similar body, for the body is an organ of the mind and runs without a break from the head.

> The mind is therefore the man himself, but he is then not a material but a spiritual man; and because after death he is the same man, he is presented in accordance with the concepts in his mind with things similar to those he possessed at home in the world. But this lasts only a few days. That the mind pervades the whole body, and is the man himself who lives after death, is perfectly plain from the synchronisation of the speech of the mouth and the actions of the body with the mind's wish and thought. For the mouth instantly utters what the mind thinks, and the body instantly executes what the mind wishes.

> The error of believing that man after death lives as a soul or mind, and that this does not have human shape, but is a kind of vapour as of the breath or a bubble full of air, is due to ignorance that the mind constitutes

the interior form of the whole body. ~Swedenborg, Memorable Relations, 5 Mem n. 5

---

8. Human Beings Are Anatomically Connected

A fundament principle in RTS thinking is that every individual is mentally connected to other individuals, especially those who have undergone the three-day dying resuscitation process. They are then conscious in their mental body and mental environment in eternity. People already living in the mental world of eternity may be called "spirits" in general, and more specifically, "angels" for good spirits and "devils" for evil spirits. Angels who are mentally connected to you desire to support you, to help you, and to give you strength against the enemy of self-love and its vast cohorts in the spheres of hell. Devils are evil spirits who desire to harm others, this being their strongest lust of life.

When you experience a healthy and constructive life you are actually experiencing the life of the good spirits that are mentally connected to you. You are now experiencing their personality structure, though it feels like it is our experiencing alone. The presence of the spirits is not perceived and most often it is denied and disbelieved when instructed about it.

The presence of evil spirits is experienced as mental illness and personality dysfunctions. For instance, we may feel neurotic compulsions that are harmful to our spirit. We may feel joy when seeing our enemies defeated and delight in their suffering, even to the extent of desiring to torture them. We may be disaffected, unhappy, scared, worried, stressed, and we may lead an unhealthy lifestyle. We may feel impatient with learning truths and fall prey to sub-cultures that teach irrational and harmful ideas or encourage the practice of self-love and denial of God and the afterlife.

Note carefully that these ordinary daily negative mental activities do not originate in the individual, and thus do not belong to the individual. The mental hell belongs to the evil spirits to whom we are mentally connected.

We often fall for the false appearances and do not want to know that what we are experiencing is not ours but theirs. But if we can get through that resistance we can come to understand rationally how we can change ourselves.

The only way possible to change ourselves is to agree to the regeneration process. God is managing the details of our mental activities. God connects us and reconnects us mentally to various spirits, angels and devils. This creates a specific daily schedule of experiencing spiritual temptations. If we need to feel adulated and praised by others, God will arrange for those emotions by connecting us to particular spirit personalities. If we need to experience a personal tragedy, God will let it happen. God does this for the sake of our regeneration, of making progress in abandoning a life of self-love and acquiring a life of mutual love with others.

As we come to become aware of this spiritual reality we begin to feel some freedom from our negative neuroses and compulsions. They are not at all "ours". None of them. All our bad feelings, our lusts, our stupidities are theirs. Hence we can actually break the mental connection we have with them. The moment we do this, the symptoms begin to release their grip and we feel more and more free to choose mutual love over the self-love.

This is the spiritual process of regeneration, of individuation and self-realization, the process of becoming truly human more and more to eternity.

It is wonderful to keep remembering that God who created and manages the universe is God-Man, the original and only Human. God is the infinite Divine Human. Everything that is created and exists must be finite as two infinites are impossible and a logical contradiction. Since God is infinite everything must exist within that infinite. This is how we can understand that God is omnipresent. God is present everywhere because everywhere and everything is within God. More specifically, everything is within God's Mind. All things are made of that mental substance that exists in God in infinite variety. And that mental substance cannot be detached from God as it is infinite and the infinite cannot be given away to created finite things.

Since all things and all events are constructed of God's own mental goods and truths, we can see how it is that God is omnipresent through His mental substance.

Eastern religions and philosophies are known to teach that the universe exists in God's mind. When we Westerners hear of that idea we are puzzled. We do not fully believe that it is so. That's because we think with material ideas and in that natural consciousness what is mental is less real or not real at all. People say, Oh it's just a thought. Just a dream, Just my imagination." Why "just"? This implies that thoughts are not actually real like rocks, or trees, or gold and diamonds. Thoughts come and go, and are gone. Where is their reality?

But when we begin to think in spiritual consciousness we understand that God's thoughts and feelings are the only thing that is real. Everything else is derived from God's mental substance, which therefore is the only reality that gives realness to everything else. We then confirm the Eastern wisdom that declares all creation to be in God's mind.

People think about the infinite and omnipotent God, who is said to be pure love and who loves every created human being like a Father. Why is there suffering and ugliness in the world? Why does God allow bad and horrific things to happen to people? The inability to explain this rationally sometimes leads people to begin to doubt that God is really omnipotent or even to doubt that God is only goodness and love.

But later in spiritual consciousness we begin to understand in what way we can say that this world is perfect. First, we know that God manages every detail of the universe and of all events. This is what "omnipotent" means. We know that God manages the good and the bad, the good times and the tragic. Hence we adopt the point of view that God is perfect and all things God does is perfect. We then try to resolve the issue of evil and suffering by remaining consistent with the premise that God is perfect and all things are perfect. *We then come to the realization that God manages the bad for the sake of the good.* This is the sense in which we can think that this world is perfect. The bad things that happen do not mean that God is not fully in control or that the bad things reduce the perfection of the world.

One helpful spiritual idea is to know that God uses some negative things to help manage and heal other negative things. Remember that we are born in natural consciousness, as this is restricted to the sensory input of our physical avatar or body. In natural consciousness we tend to love self above all things. This leads to a state of devolution and mental illness, from which comes bad thoughts, bad intentions, bad behaviors. Others are impacted negatively. Community life becomes risky and hostile. We are fearful, unwise, shortsighted, unhappy, unable to use our human potential.

God must intervene in order to save us from this negative existence. God's interventions are executed within the freedom of the individual, so it is not a straightforward or simple thing to accomplish. God never forces the person to "be good" because this would be useless for the person's salvation, that is, of becoming spiritual by loving others more than self. When we are forced to be good we do not love it, and what we don't love cannot enter our core personality. When we are forced to be good, we always eventually reject it and return to our self-love.

Hence God uses intermediary states of progression by which we can learn how to love to be good. God uses bad things and bad people to allow us to follow in our love on a gradual basis. For instance, God allows tragedies or misfortune to befall us, which function as a wake-up call to reform or to reduce our unwise pursuits and lusts. Undisciplined excesses lead to negative consequences such as sickness or accidents. We learn from these contingencies.

God manages everyone's death. A person can die only if God allows it on the basis that it is better for the person spiritually to start a new life in the mental world of eternity. An accident or tragedy that kills people is nothing but that sort of care that God brings about on a controlled basis. When an innocent infant or child dies it is a sad thing but not a useless thing. That particular child is better off growing up in the afterlife. We cannot know all the contingencies of people's lives but God does.

Infants and children are born with much evil tendencies that must be healed for the child to grow up spiritual and to enter eternal happiness in heaven. Some children need this while others do not, but need other things and experiences that are in this world. All children who pass on into eternity are taken care of by loving mothers and caretakers under full provision and protection of God. They grow up educated in spiritual things and become angels who love others more than themselves.

It is in this sense that we can rest rationally assured that this is a perfect world because all things in it serve the eternal welfare of every human being. Whatever negativity that does not serve that positive and humane purpose cannot come into being, cannot occur or exist.

In all chaos there is a cosmos, in all disorder a secret order.
~Carl Jung

9. Moving From Natural To Spiritual Consciousness

Swedenborg writes:

The seat of faith...is not consciousness but spontaneous religious experience, which brings the individual's faith into immediate relation with God. ~Carl Jung, The Undiscovered Self

The medicine-man is also the priest; he is the saviour of the soul as well as of the body, and religions are systems of healing for psychic illness. ~Carl Jung, Psychotherapists or the Clergy

There is no conflict between religion and science in the East, because no science is there based upon the passion for facts, and no religion upon mere faith; there is religious cognition and cognitive religion. ~Carl Jung, CW 11, Para 768

It is of course essential for the psychotherapist to have a fair knowledge of himself, for anyone who does not understand himself cannot understand others and can never be psychotherapeutically effective unless he has first treated himself with the same medicine. ~Carl Jung, Letters Vol. 1, p. 455

The truths and falsities of the natural man [when we are in natural consciousness] *are called cognitions and knowledges; but when the truths themselves have acquired life, which is effected by a life of faith, which is charity, they belong to his spiritual man* [when we are in spiritual consciousness].

These with their affections and pleasantnesses do not appear to man's manifest sense and sight [self-knowledge or awareness], *as the cognitions and knowledges of the natural man do, for the reason that so long as a man [human being] lives in the world he thinks naturally and speaks naturally [this being in natural consciousness], and this a man sensibly feels and perceives by a kind of sight that belongs to his understanding.*

But his spiritual thought, which is conjoined to the affection of truth or of falsity, is not apparent until man has put off the natural body and put on the spiritual body, which takes place after his death, or his departure from this world and his entrance into the spiritual world; then he thinks spiritually and speaks spiritually, and not naturally as before.
~Swedenborg, Apocalypse Explained, AE 654

There are two states or phases of human consciousness: natural consciousness and spiritual consciousness. This book discusses how we can move from natural to spiritual consciousness.

There are great psychological benefits that we can enjoy when moving up in consciousness. Everyday negative emotions, neuroses, despondency, worry, and dysfunctions of all types are mental experiences that exist and thrive In natural consciousness. All our fears, depressions, resentments, jealousies, felt limitations, and emotional weaknesses are mental activities that are entirely immersed in natural consciousness. *They cease to exist when we raise our thinking to spiritual consciousness.*

Our natural consciousness works only with material ideas and conclusions.

The perspective of rational theistic self-analysis (RTS) gives us practice in thinking with spiritual consciousness.

Making use of RTS as a perspective on oneself offers a spiritual discipline for raising consciousness above the natural emotional weaknesses of our habitual way of thinking in daily activities.

Where does this habitual way of thinking come from?

The fact that people ordinarily think in natural consciousness implies that it is a biological and a cultural inheritance.

Few people realize that we inherit our way of thinking. The two sources of inheritance are biological genes and cultural genes. You can observe the way people differ in appearance and in habits as you travel across the continents. These cross-cultural differences are sourced in people's biology and in their traditional social attitudes or psychology.

Consider that your way of thinking is shared by many others who grew up in the same geographic locality, and promoting the same social and cultural attitudes and rules of life. You can also observe multiple sub-varieties of attitudes in one general culture and biology. For instance, it is common for public issues to have some people be supportive of it and other people who oppose it. And yet both sides of the issue agree in how to think about it conceptually despite their occupying opposites positions on a scale of attitude or support. In fact, you can be on one side of a public issue one day, and then changing your mind and ending up on the opposite side. This shows that there is a conceptual or cultural framework that gives rise to the controversial issue and makes it meaningful to all sides.

This shared culturally inherited way of thinking and reasoning is time-bound and place-bound. In other words, all such concepts and ideas are framed within the limits and conditions that apply to the natural world or physical world. These natural ideas and principles of thinking are suitable for living on this earth. This way of life includes competing against others and hoarding what we can in wealth, reputation, influence, and recognition. This is the earth-way of thinking and living. It is called "worldly" thinking. And you can witness and experience the horribly negative consequences of such worldly natural existence. Such thinking and living may be called sub-human or pre-human. A famous saying by Hobbes is rendered "*Homo homine lupus est*", which is Latin for "Man to man is a wolf".

And yet every individual can rise above this natural and world-dependent level of thinking, reasoning, emoting and loving. The beginning of becoming a whole human being is to think and reason in spiritual consciousness. This is the great dividing line that initiates the "new birth" or "rebirth". We are born animal or worldly, thus as pre-human, with the capacity of becoming spiritual and whole human. *We are not human in the genuine sense as long as we are still thinking, reasoning, and emoting in the natural consciousness that we have inherited by biology and culture.*

The perspective of rational theistic self-analysis (RTS) provides a way out of the inheritance trap and mental enclosure. The idea of RTS involves a new type of knowledge that may appear to many as "difficult" or complicated, when it is not. There is an appearance of difficulty and complexity when learning to think in spiritual meanings and to reason with spiritual ideas. But this perception and experience of difficulty comes from the interference of natural consciousness in your mind that wants to jump in and continue to control the boundaries of your thinking. If you are motivated to seek spiritual truth and spiritual reality then this illusion of difficulty dissolves in the beauty and simplicity of spiritual knowledge and thinking.

This book provides you with that knowledge and leads you into its daily use.

To be more precise, we are going to use the expression "natural-rational consciousness" instead of just "natural consciousness". Similarly with spiritual-rational consciousness. This usage will help you to keep in mind that human consciousness is always rational and that there are two types of rational reasoning operations in our mind, one that is based on natural ideas and the other on spiritual ideas.

Natural-rational consciousness may be called *"the register of captivity"*. It is the experiencing of life as hostile, brutal, and short. But spiritual-rational consciousness is the experiencing of immortal human life, human love and compassion for one another. Everyone is born with a mind that is operating in natural-rational consciousness, but with the capacity or potential to operate in spiritual-rational consciousness.

Every human being is immortal and born for heaven, which is the mental state of eternal happiness, marital joy, and the continuous development of our endless potential as individual and unique human beings.

10. Some Major Spiritual Truths

To elevate our consciousness from natural thinking to spiritual thinking we need to counteract the aversion and even hatred that natural-rational consciousness experiences for spiritual ideas and truths. Swedenborg observed that in the afterlife, those who hate spiritual truths feel sick in the stomach as soon as they are exposed to any spiritual ideas such as God, correspondence, incarnation, regeneration, love of self, marriage, innocence, infants, justice, good and truth, etc.

This indicates that we need to train our rationality to think with spiritual truths. This self-training is accomplished through regeneration when the individual acts and thinks in accordance with mutual love and holds in aversion the thought of hurting others for selfish gain. Becoming a "spiritual" person means to learn spiritual truths and to use them in our thinking and reasoning about our daily activities.

The principal spiritual truths are these:

1. There is one God who is the original human. God is the infinite Human. God is uncreate as a Human, and all parts of the Human are uncreate and infinite. Uncreate means that it has always existed and is infinite. God is omnipotent, omniscient, and omnipresent. Hence God is infinite in power, love, and wisdom.

2. God is pure love and mercy and creates human beings that they may become spiritual and be happy forever in eternity, after death. Pure love and mercy cannot punish or be angry. Hence God never punishes anyone. But all deeds and thoughts have built-in unavoidable eternal consequences. These inevitably bring about punishing experiences.

3. God is present in the mind of every individual, organizing and maintaining all unconscious and conscious operations. God does this for the sake that every individual may develop mentally and become spiritual. This new becoming is accomplished by regeneration. It is also called "being reborn" because pour core

personality structure is modified from selfish loves to mutual love. This is the love that creates community and society. All selfish loves are opposed to mutual love.

4. God supervises every step of the rebirth and regeneration of every individual. To be possible and successful, this regeneration process requires the cooperation of the individual in total freedom so that it is motivated by the desire to become a heavenly person.

5. The key element in the success of regeneration is love. We start with inherited natural love, which is the love we have for ourselves, or for those who are connected to us, and those who are our supporters or admirers. To undergo regeneration we must switch over from this self-centered love to love of God and of others. We must love others as much as our self, or more than our self. We must love God above all. If we strive to live this way in our daily activities we gradually acquire a heavenly personality. Upon dying, we resuscitate and enter the heavenly state forever in partnership with the person we love.

6. We must realize that if we do not regenerate we remain natural. After we resuscitate from death we live in the spiritual world of eternity with a natural consciousness. As a result, we sink into the negative and murky depths of spiritual insanity and moral depravity. This is called life in hell.

   No one keeps people there by force. But their natural thinking and self-centered love make it impossible for them to raise their thinking into spiritual consciousness. Heavenly mental states in eternity require a spiritual-rational consciousness. Hellish mental states in eternity function in a natural-rational consciousness.

In order to make these spiritual ideas real in our life we must understand them. They are useless for our regeneration if we do not understand them *rationally.* This means using our rational common sense thinking to figure it out until it makes sense. You can feel a distinct internal relief when you finally can see it clearly. We can sense it through our avatar when it experiences a deep breath of relief from prior constraint.

To become aware of our spiritual-rational consciousness we need to make the effort of reflecting on the topic of some spiritual truth, and trying to figure it out until we feel that "it makes sense!"

The RTS perspective involves the practice that allows you to develop spiritual-rational thinking in everyday life. The spiritual is not something separate from the natural. The two worlds are always connected and operating synchronously by the laws of correspondences, which will be discussed. This is also true for consciousness. Every meaning or principle in natural-rational consciousness can be "spiritualized", which consists of connecting the natural to the spiritual by means of spiritual ideas or truths. It is equivalent to supplying a spiritual context to a natural idea or act.

Every one of our daily activities and thoughts can be infused with spiritual ideas and their justifications.

Common activities such as eating, walking, working, watching a video, buying clothes, conversing, having fun, driving a car, etc., can be infused with spiritual significance. *By doing this we become more and more spiritual-rational until we have regenerated our natural-rational character from selfish and self-centered to altruistic and God-centered.*

In natural consciousness it is impossible to stop being selfish and self-centered. We share this evolutionary trait of survival with many intelligent animals. This is why it is said that we must be "reborn" and "regenerated", which refers to changing the loves in our character. This self-modification process is not instantaneous but must progress steadily over a lifetime. When we awaken from the three-day dying resuscitation procedure we experience our new eternal life in accordance with our regeneration.

Swedenborg writes:
> The first kind of faith any of us ever have is faith handed down from the past. It becomes a saving faith later on when we become spiritual as a

result of the way we live. . . . [A traditional faith] does not save us until we live a life of faith, which is a life of goodwill. That is the point at which we will and do what we believe. Willing and doing are matters of love, and love binds us to the One whom faith causes to be present. ~Swedenborg, Apocalypse Explained, AE 815

Without undergoing regeneration our character remains with self-centered loves and their natural-rational justifications. In the afterlife, this old inherited consciousness seeks out others with like attitudes and justifications. But those who undergo regeneration prior to death, awaken from the dying process able to function in spiritual-rational consciousness. They seek out others who are like-minded. Hence are formed the spiritual communities and societies of eternity.

Those who rise in consciousness through the love of others and the love of God experience together a social life of friendship and mutual compassion and good will. They live in heavenly cities and paradises that are outward reflections of their inward character.

But those who remain natural retain their self-centered character and lead a social life with others who are similar in character. Hence people who are hypocritical and practice deception live with others who also are deceptive and crafty. People who are violent and cruel live with those who are violent and cruel. Such is the spiritual law of eternity.

You can now see from this information why regeneration is called "salvation", given that the old inherited self leads directly to a life of hell in eternity, while regeneration saves us from that horrible fate by changing our love for self only to a love for others and for God.

Many people believe that the good they do outweighs the bad they do. They also think that no one is all bad and that everyone has some good in them. This thinking is natural and self-centered. It is false and ignorant. *The spiritual fact is that no one can do good or be good from themselves but only from God.* Hence if you say that people can do both good and bad, or that no one is all bad, then you are ignoring that the so-called "good" they do is not actually good but only appears to be good in natural perspective.

Hence it is a false idea to think that people can do both good and bad. When people do something bad or selfishly motivated they are unable to do something good or unselfishly motivated. The two cannot exist in the same personality. Spiritual understanding shows that we must first stop doing bad before we can do good. In other words, we must first give up selfish thinking before we can think altruistically. This then is the process of regeneration. First, we acquire spiritual knowledge and truths that show us the way. Second, we repress and resist any form of selfish thinking, intending, or delighting. This can only be done successfully by acknowledging and invoking the help of God. Third, we receive and accept from God the regenerated love for others and for God. Now at last we can do good that is good. And with this new capacity we can live in heaven or eternal human happiness.

Jung writes:

> As a doctor it is my task to help the patient to cope with life. ~Carl Jung, CW 12, Para 32

> The labours of the doctor as well as the quest of the patient are directed towards that hidden and as yet unmanifest "whole" man, who is at once the greater and the future man. ~Carl Jung, CW 12, Para 6

> But no matter how much the parents and grandparents may have sinned against the child, the man who is really adult will accept these sins as his own condition which has to be reckoned with. ~Carl Jung, CW 12, Para 152

> To find out what is truly individual in ourselves, profound reflection is needed; and suddenly we realize how uncommonly difficult the discovery of individuality is. ~Carl Jung, CW 7, Para 242

> The patient must learn to go his own way. ~Carl Jung, CW 16, Para 26

> My soul is my supreme meaning, my image of God, neither God himself nor the supreme meaning. God becomes apparent in the supreme meaning of the human community. ~Carl Jung, Liber Novus, Footnote 92, Page 240

He who can risk himself wholly to it finds himself directly in the hands of God, and is there confronted with a situation which makes "simple faith" a vital necessity; in other words, the situation becomes so full of risk or overtly dangerous that the deepest instincts are aroused. ~Carl Jung, CW 18, Para 1539

Religion is the fruit and culmination of the completeness of life, that is, of a life which contains both sides. ~Carl Jung, CW 11, Para 71

One needs death to be able to harvest the fruit. Without death, life would be meaningless, since the long-lasting rises again and denies its own meaning. To be, and to enjoy your being, you need death, and limitation enables you to fulfill your being. ~Carl Jung, The Red Book, Page 275

Like plants, so men also grow, some in the light, others in the shadows. There are many who need the shadows and not the light. The image of God throws a shadow that is just as great as itself. ~Carl Jung, Liber Novus, Page 230

Our natural model is Christ. We have stood under his law since antiquity; first outwardly, and then inwardly. At first we knew this, and then knew it no longer. We fought against Christ, we deposed him, and we seemed to be conquerors. But he remained in us and mastered us. ~Carl Jung, Liber Novus, Page 293

Acquiring the perspective of RTS is to do the work of regeneration in daily life.

11. Can Rich People Enter Heaven?

Swedenborg writes:

It is not contrary to order to look out for one's self and one's dependents. Those have "care for the morrow" who are not content with their lot, who do not trust in the Divine but themselves, and who regard toward a happy state to eternity. ~Swedenborg, Heavenly Secrets, AC 8478

Moreover the goods [skills and enjoyments] *of the external man* [natural consciousness], *which so long as the man* [individual] *lives in the* [physical] *world are the delights of life, are good only insofar as they partake inwardly of this* [genuine] *good* [from God through heaven].

For example, the good of riches. Insofar as [physical] *riches have spiritual good* [received from heaven] *within them, that is, insofar as they have as their end* [intended goal] *the good of the neighbor, the good of our country or the public good, and the good of the church, so far they are* [genuinely] *good.*

But they who conclude that the spiritual good [mutual love] *of which we are speaking is not possible in a condition of worldly opulence, and who therefore persuade themselves that to make room for heaven they must divest themselves of such things, are much mistaken. For if they renounce their wealth, or deprive themselves of it, they can then do good to no one, nor can themselves live in the world except in misery and thus can no longer have as their end the good of the neighbor, and the good of their country, nor even the good of the church, but themselves only, that they may be saved, and become greater than others in the heavens.*

Moreover, when they divest themselves of worldly goods, they expose themselves to contempt, because they make themselves of low estimation in the sight of others, and consequently useless for performing services and discharging duties. But when they have the good of others as their end, they then have also as an end, or as means, a state of being in the capability of effecting this end.

The case herein is precisely as it is with the nutrition of a man, which has as its end that he may have a sound mind in a sound body. If a man deprives his body of its nourishment, he deprives himself also of the condition needed for his end; and therefore he who is a spiritual man does not despise nourishment, nor even its pleasures; and yet he does not hold them as his end, but only as a means that is of service to his end. From this as an example we can judge of all other things. ~Swedenborg, Heavenly Secrets, AC 3951

In other words, it is necessary that we make a distinction between genuine good and non-genuine. *Genuine good* is what we receive from our unconscious celestial consciousness that is "coming down" or inflowing into our still unconscious spiritual consciousness, and finally into our natural consciousness where we become conscious of it and interpret it in accordance with our love and understanding. Even though our love is still selfish, we learned to cover it up by putting on the appearance of mutual love. We act considerate and generous in our daily interactions with others for the unspoken goal that regards self only, rather than from a desire to benefit others. Hence we appear good when we are not.

One symptom of this "selfish good" is that we become incensed and vengeful against those whom we are benefiting, as soon as they do not acknowledge us, or no longer favor us, and do not reciprocate the favorable treatment we give them. But it's different when we benefit others *altruistically*, that is, from a feeling of wanting to benefit others for their sake, or for the sake of what is genuinely good, which is only from heaven from God. When we benefit others for a selfish gain or only for our reputation, we corrupt or distort this inflowing genuine good by turning it to ourselves and away from others.

People are often confused about what is "charity" and "loving the neighbor" that are commanded by religion and morality. They may feel guilty about not contributing their full "ten percent" to charities and to helping institutions or to fund-raising campaigns. By the same token they feel good about themselves when they do contribute, and especially when they contribute more than expected. But when we continue to make progress in our regeneration and as we elevate our thinking to spiritual-rational consciousness, we can perceive that this kind of charity is not genuinely good, but is thoroughly steeped in selfishness, serving the self only. To feel sinful for not contributing enough and to feel merit in contributing more, is not a spiritual act but natural.

Genuine good is associated with spiritual truth, and this gives us the spiritual-rational perception that we deserve zero merit for doing good to others since we did not do it from ourselves and with our own power. Hence there is no credit whatsoever that can be assigned to the person doing good to others. The spiritual commandment to love our neighbor as much as we love ourselves does not mean to love the person or individual, but rather the good and truth that are in the person from God. We must love God above everything, hence when we love the neighbor we are not loving the neighbor per se, but the good and truth in the neighbor, and therefore we love God by loving the neighbor. God has the only merit because all the truth and good we have is from God.

People are confused about who is the neighbor who ought to be loved. Everyone? But this is psychologically impossible, and hence it cannot be a Divine commandment since God would not command us to do something that we cannot do. All commandments are things we can do, if we want to. So we cannot love everyone the same way, or with the same love. This gets resolved in our understanding when we begin thinking in spiritual-rational consciousness. The neighbor we are commanded to love is the good and truth in the neighbor that is from God, since all genuine good and truth are from God alone.

Hence it is that our love of the neighbor must be adjusted in each individual case according to the genuine-good and truth that we can perceive in an individual. We do not love a violent criminal, a child molester, or a terrorist who targets innocent people. We simply look for any good and truth in such persons, and not finding any, or finding the opposite, we therefore withhold our love. The only consideration that we retain is to respect the humanity of such persons, and thus to refrain from violating their human rights as prisoners. It is clear from this that the commandment to love the neighbor must be applied, not to the person, but to the genuine-good and truth that remain in the individual.

Here is how Swedenborg presents this issue:

> It is known in the churches that by the goods which man does he can merit nothing, for they are not his, but the Lord's; and that meriting or merit looks to man, and thus conjoins itself with the love of self, and with the thought of pre-eminence over others, and consequently with contempt for others. For this reason works done for the sake of reward are not good in themselves, because they do not spring from the genuine fountain; that is, from charity toward the neighbor.

Charity toward the neighbor has within it the desire that it should be as well with him as with ourselves; and with the angels, that it should be better with him than with themselves. Such also is the affection of charity; and therefore it is averse to all self-merit, and consequently to all the doing of good that looks to reward.

To those who are in charity, the reward consists in being able to show kindness, and in being allowed to do so, and in the kindness being accepted. This is the delight, nay, bliss itself that is enjoyed by those who are in the affection of charity. From this it is evident what that "reward" is that is mentioned in the Word, namely, the delight and bliss of the affection of charity; or what is the same, the delight and bliss of mutual love; for the affection of charity, and mutual love, are the same thing. From all this it is evident that by "reward" in the external sense is here signified mutual love. ~Swedenborg, Heavenly Secrets, AC 3956

12. Swedenborg: Some Ways People Can Find Out About Life After Death

---

Swedenborg writes:

When someone's body can no longer perform its functions in the natural world in response to the thoughts and affections of its spirit (which it derives from the spiritual world), then we say that the individual has died. This happens when the lungs' breathing and the heart's systolic motion have ceased. The person, though, has not died at all. We are only separated from the physical nature that was useful to us in the world. The essential person is actually still alive. I say that the essential person is still alive because we are not people because of our bodies but because of our spirits. After all, it is the spirit within us that thinks, and thought and affection together make us the people we are. We can see, then, that when we die we simply move from one world into another. ~Swedenborg, Heaven and Hell, HH 445

I have been permitted to speak on this subject with very many in the other life [afterlife] who were from the Christian world, and with the more learned also [philosophers and theologians]; *but wonderful to say, scarcely anyone of those with whom I have been permitted to speak knew anything about it, when yet they might of themselves have known much about such things if they had only been willing to use their reason. But as they had not been solicitous about the life after death, but only about life in the world, such things had no interest for them.*

The things which they might have known of themselves had they chosen to use their reason, are the following:

First, that when man [on earth] *is divested of his* [physical] *body, he comes into the full exercise of a much more enlightened understanding than when living in the* [physical] *body, for the reason that while he is in the* [physical] *body, corporeal and worldly things occupy his thoughts* [natural consciousness], *which induce obscurity* [to spiritual ideas]; *but when he is divested of the* [physical] *body* [at death], *such things do not interfere, and it is with him as with those who are in interior thought* [spiritual-rational consciousness] *by abstraction of the mind from the things of the outward* [physical] *senses.*

From this they might know that the state after death is much more clear-sighted and enlightened than the state before death; and that when a man dies, he passes comparatively from shade into light, because he passes from the things of the [physical] *world to those of* [spiritual] *heaven, and from the things of the*[physical] *body to those of the spirit* [body]. *But wonderful to say, although they are able to understand all this, they nevertheless think the contrary, namely, that the state of life in the* [physical] *body is relatively clear, and that the state of life after being divested of the* [physical] *body is relatively obscure.*

The Second thing that they may know if they will use their reason, is that the life which man has procured for himself in the world follows him; that is, he is in such a life after death. For they may know that without dying altogether no one can put off the life which he has acquired from infancy; and that this life cannot be changed into another in a moment, still less into an opposite one.

For example: he who has acquired a life of deceit, and has found in this the delight of his life, cannot put off the life of deceit, but is still in that life after death. He who is in the love of self, and thereby in hatred and revenge against those who do not serve him, and those who are in other such evils, remains in them after the life of the body; for these are the things which they love, and which constitute the delights of their life, and consequently their veriest life; and therefore such things cannot be taken away from them without at the same time extinguishing all their life. And so in other cases.

––––––––––––––––––

Swedenborg's discussions with those who are in the afterlife, especially the recent "arrivals", led him to discover that although they had known about life after death from their religion, they did not actually believe it. In their interior thinking, which is perhaps not fully conscious when it is ignored, they rejected the idea of life after death. Such rejection was correlated with a lack of interest or curiosity about life after death, which to me is still astounding. How could they not be interested? Swedenborg points out that everything spiritual is disliked when we are in natural consciousness because the spiritual things are contrary to the natural things and threaten them. As for instance selfishness, which is a proper part of natural consciousness, hence also the logic of competition and superiority over everyone else.

When we base our daily interactions on selfishness we feel threatened by spiritual ideas such as the life after death where selfishness becomes insanity and hell. Not wanting to hear this message is the reason why they are not curious about finding out what happens in the afterlife, which is a spiritual life, not natural. This is true even when people are being "religious", although in that case they imagine a life after death that is on this earth, and one that is similar to what they now have, but more grandiose.

Another example is the spiritual idea I discussed just above that tells them that they cannot receive merit for the good things they did to other people to benefit them. They also hate the idea that it is God who acts for them because they then feel manipulated by God and no longer a free agent.

The Third thing which a man may know of himself, is that when he passes into the other life he leaves many things behind which have no place there, such as cares for food, for clothing, for a place of abode, and also for gaining money and wealth, as well as for being exalted to dignities, all of which are so much thought of by man in the life of the body; but in the other life are succeeded by others that are not of this earthly kingdom.

Therefore the Fourth thing a man can know is that he who in the world has thought solely of such worldly things, so that he has been wholly possessed by them, and has acquired delight of life in them alone, is not fitted to be among those whose delight is to think about heavenly things, that is, about the things of heaven.

From this follows also a Fifth thing; namely, that when the externals of the body and the world are taken away, the man is then such as he has been inwardly; that is, he so thinks and so wills. If his thoughts have inwardly been deceits, machinations, aspiration for dignities, for gains, and for fame thereby; if they have been hatreds and revenges and the like, it can be seen that he will still think such things, thus the things that belong to hell, however much he might for the sake of the before-mentioned ends have concealed his thoughts from men, and thus appeared outwardly to be worthy, while leading others to believe that he had not such things at heart.

That all such externals, or simulations of worth, are also taken away in the other life, may likewise be known from the fact that outward things are put off together with the body, and are no longer of any use. From this everyone may conclude for himself what kind of a man he will then appear to the angels.

The Sixth thing that may be known is that heaven, or the Lord through heaven, is continually working and inflowing with good and truth; and that if there is not then in men--in their interior man which lives after the death of the body--some recipient of good and truth, as a ground or plane, the good and truth that flow in cannot be received; and for this reason man while living in the body ought to be solicitous to procure such a plane within himself; but this cannot be procured except by thinking what is good toward the neighbor, and by willing what is good to him, and therefore doing what is good to him, and thus by acquiring the delight of life in such things.

This plane is acquired by means of charity toward the neighbor, that is, by means of mutual love; and is what is called conscience. Into this plane the good and truth from the Lord can inflow, and be received therein; but not where there is no charity, and consequently no conscience; for there the inflowing good and truth pass through, and are turned into evil and falsity.

In other words, it is necessary for people to realize by spiritual-rational thinking that an individual's personality habits and loves become a permanent part of the immortal self. After death this permanent portion functions as a necessary basis for future development of the personality in eternity. This former basis cannot be replaced any more than the foundations of a house without pulling it down and destroying it.

This is why it is necessary to undergo regeneration prior to death, which is the only process provided by God to modify our personality habits in a fundamental way, from loving self exclusively to loving others more than self. This requires a lifelong effort of repressing and inhibiting older habits that are based on selfishness. God is very involved and active in this process, providing the sequence of experiences that bring the individual to temptations. Through spiritual temptations the individual receives a second chance to react differently from before.

If we acquired habits of unfair competition and deceit in our daily interactions, temptations now give us the opportunity to just say No to selfish habits of lying, cheating, stealing, and taking revenge. When we persist in these reversals and apply them to everything in our daily lives, God can modify our basic personality by putting our former loves and ideas to the side, to the circumference of our personality where they are neutralized and rendered inactive. To the extent that this occurs, to that extent the individual can be "reborn" mentally or spiritually, and acquire a personality composed of altruistic loves and innocent pleasures and enjoyments of life.

Swedenborg writes:
> The Seventh thing that a man can know of himself, is that love to God and love toward the neighbor are what make man to be man, distinct from brute animals; and that they constitute heavenly life, or heaven; while their opposites constitute infernal life, or hell. But the reason why a man does not know these things is that he does not desire to know them, because he lives the opposite life, and also because he does not believe in the life after death; and likewise because he has taken up with principles of faith, but none of charity; and consequently believes in accordance with the doctrinal teachings of many, that if there is a life after death, he can be saved by faith,

no matter how he has lived, even if his faith is received in his dying hour. ~Swedenborg, Heavenly Secrets, AC 3957

That there are three heavens, is known, namely, an inmost heaven, a middle, and an ultimate; or what is the same, a third, a second, and a first. The inmost or third heaven is celestial; for the angels [people in heaven] there are called celestial because they are in love to the Lord, and are therefore most fully conjoined with the Lord, and are consequently in wisdom above all the rest, are innocent, and hence are called innocences and wisdoms.

These angels are distinguished into the internal and the external, the internal being more celestial than the external. The middle or second heaven is spiritual; for the angels there are called spiritual because they are in charity toward the neighbor, that is, in mutual love, which is such that the one loves the other more than himself; and because they are such they are in intelligence, and are hence called intelligences.

These angels are also distinguished into the internal and the external, the internal being more spiritual than the external. The ultimate or first heaven is likewise celestial and spiritual, but not in the same degree as the prior ones; for what is natural adheres to these angels, and they are therefore called the celestial natural and the spiritual natural. These also are in mutual love, yet do not love others more than themselves, but as themselves. They are in the affection of good and knowledge of truth, and are likewise distinguished into the internal and the external. ~Swedenborg, Heavenly Secrets, AC 4286

In other words, there are three levels or planes of existence in the human mind, and therefore also in the afterlife. Which plane we live in is determined by what our chief love is. The higher the level, the more one enjoys intelligence and wisdom, and the happier one can be. The universal key to eternal life is the love that affects us, whether we love ourselves only, which is infernal or hell, or whether we love others as much as self, which gives us spiritual-rational consciousness, or whether we love others more than self, which gives us celestial-rational consciousness. The higher our consciousness is, the closer we are to God, and the more God can benefit us in everything that is good and true.

Jung writes:
> The unconscious is not just evil by nature, it is also the source of the highest good: not only dark but also light, not only bestial, semihuman, and demonic but superhuman, spiritual, and, in the classical sense of the word, "divine." ~Carl Jung, The Practice of Psychotherapy, 1953

> Out of honest contrition for sin comes divine grace. That is not only a religious but also a psychological truth. ~Carl Jung, C.G. Jung Speaking: Interviews and Encounters, p. 154

Swedenborg writes:
> Faith in its essence is truth, and that everyone is able to acquire truths from the Word, and that so far as anyone does acquire them for himself, and loves them, he implants in himself the beginnings of faith. ~Swedenborg, The True Christian Religion, TCR 356

> As far as one is in the stream of Providence, so far one is in a state of peace. Such alone know and believe that the Divine Providence of the Lord is in each and all things, yea, in the least of all things. ~Swedenborg, Heavenly Secrets, AC 8478

---

13. Consciousness In the Afterlife

What most people overlook or seem unable to understand is the fact that I regard the psyche as real. Carl Jung, CW 11, Para 751

Swedenborg lived in dual consciousness for 27 years before he left this world through the portals of dying. Thus for nearly three decades he was able to meet with the people who were in the afterlife, interview them, and write eyewitness ethnographic reports of the conditions of life and society in the world of mental eternity. His best-known report is the book titled

Heaven and Hell in which we can read the details of their daily lives, both in "heaven" and in "hell".

Every human being is born with an immortal spirit body that houses the organic mental structures of the mind. We are unable to see the spirit body with the eyes of our physical body. Our natural consciousness is under the illusion of the appearance that it is the physical body that sees and hears and senses touch. The three-day dying-resuscitation procedure separates the spirit body from the physical body, and upon awaking in the afterlife we continue our activities with the spirit body to eternity. *Our immortality is due to our spirit body that is born into eternity.* We receive sensory input from the physical body and world as sensations that are felt in the spirit body.

The physical body is not alive and is constructed of dead matter. But it is so constructed that the spirit body (or mind) can sensate and become aware of the physical things in the natural world that enter the senses of the physical body. I think of the physical body as my avatar through which I can see into the natural world and act in it. This dual existence allows us to develop our natural mind that will serve us as a "plane" or basis for developing the spiritual mind and the celestial mind. This is why no one is born directly into the afterlife of eternity for in that case we would not have a natural mind as a plane for the spiritual mind to develop and evolve in eternity.

As a unique exception Swedenborg on the other hand was conscious in both the natural body and the spirit body at the same time for 27 years from age 57 to 83, when he passed on. This was unlike the normal case, which would be to be conscious through the physical avatar only of the things of the natural world, and after death to be conscious with our spirit body of the things of the spiritual world of the afterlife. Swedenborg was therefore able to report through his physical body in a natural language what he saw and experienced through his spirit body and how he interacted with the people there in a universal and inborn spiritual language.

In the afterlife what is conscious now becomes unconscious and what is unconscious now becomes conscious.

This is truly amazing! It was fully confirmed by Swedenborg in his spiritual ethnography of the afterlife. As we awaken from the three-day dying-resuscitation surgical procedure we still have our memory from our life on earth. But very quickly this memory sinks into the sub-conscious and is no longer available except when God allows access for the benefit of the individual in the afterlife. At the same time, the individual is connected telepathically to people still on earth. Those in the afterlife now begin a new life that consist in living from the memory with those on earth to whom they are connected by God for specific purposes.

God continually connects and disconnects the mind of an individual on earth to bring about telepathic contact with specific others in the afterlife of eternity. Without some telepathic contact from many others no one can think or live. The entire human race is so connected by God in infinitely complex patterns that only God's infinite wisdom can manage and make grow. In general individuals are connected more extensively to the extent that they share particular loves and affections.

For instance, if your personality is marked by habits of anger and lack of compassion you are being connected to individuals and societies in the afterlife who share that habit of anger with lack of compassion, thus a desire to punish and take revenge. *The afterlife crowd that is connected to you through the shared love has access to your memory.* They each now think themselves to be you! As long as they are connected to your mind through your shared loves, they will continue to live from your memory on earth. They then think of themselves to be living again on earth. Isn't this amazing!

Here is a selection from Swedenborg on this subject. He uses the word "spirit" for those who are in the afterlife of eternity. Each of us will be "spirits" following the three-day resuscitation procedure. When we are still on earth we are referred to as "man", which refers to the people still on earth, or still attached to a physical body. As spirits we have our immortal spirit-body or spiritual body with which we were born and which contains the operation of our memory and personality.

Swedenborg writes:

Concerning Memory. In the other life it is not allowed that one should use his own memory for the reason, that everyone who draws the past from his own memory, is not only anxious concerning the future, and vexes himself from the fact that the present is unlike the past, but he indulges grief in whatever state he is; and then also, as was perceived, he wishes to live only from himself, for to live from one's own memory is to live, as it were, from himself which for many reasons, is not allowed to a spirit, but to a man more than to a spirit. As a spirit, thinking from the memory of a man, thinks himself to be a man, if he were to use his own memory he would think he was not the man, but himself; wherefore for reasons of use, in order that he may be subservient to man, it is not allowed to exercise his own memory. - 1748, November 13. ~Swedenborg, Spiritual Experiences, SE 3962

In other words, in the afterlife, God does not allow us to have access to our earth-life memories in order to protect us from thinking that we live for ourselves and from ourselves. This psychologically harmful belief would prevent us from undergoing regeneration, without which we cannot live in happiness to eternity, but in misery instead. A lot is at stake here! Moreover, the spiritual reality is that no one is born for self, but everyone is born for others. To believe that one is living from self leads to the belief that one is born for oneself and not for others. This harmful belief again prevents regeneration, thus the experience of eternal happiness.

As well, by being connected to people on earth, the people in the afterlife (spirits) serve a useful social and psychological helping function in the personality development of people still on earth. Spirits are therefore essential in our regeneration.

You can see from this that spirits are active participants in our dreaming. *We are not alone in our dreams.* Many spirits are present and fulfill useful functions to bring us the images and events that are so realistically represented and duplicated in our dreams.

Swedenborg writes about what life is like to the people in the afterlife (spirits). He spent nearly three decades in dual consciousness so that he was simultaneously aware of his physical body and daily activities and of his spirit body and the people in the afterlife with whom he interacted on a daily basis for 27 years. This is a unique situation in the history of science as there has never been a scientist who could write a spiritual ethnography of the afterlife by direct observation over several years.

Swedenborg Writes:

The dwellings of the blessed [those living in heaven] *in the other life are of many kinds, and are constructed with such art as to be as it were embodiments of the very art of architecture, or to come straight from the art itself. These dwellings appear not only to the sight, but also to the touch, for all things there are adapted to the sensations of spirits and angels, and hence are such as do not come to bodily sense like that of man* [physical body], *but to that possessed by those who are there* [spirit body].

I know that this is incredible to many, but this is because nothing is believed which cannot be seen by the [physical] *bodily eyes and felt with the hands of* [physical] *flesh. For this reason the man of this day, whose interiors* [spiritual mind] *are closed, knows nothing of the things which exist in the spiritual world or in heaven. He does indeed say from the Word* [Sacred Scripture] *and from doctrine* [religion] *that there is a heaven, and that the angels who are there are in joy and in glory, but he knows no more about the matter.*

How the case is there he would indeed like to know, but when told he still believes nothing, because at heart he denies the existence of such things, and his desire to know about them is prompted solely by his curiosity from doctrine [blind acceptance], *and not by any delight grounded in faith* [rational understanding]. *They who are not in* [rational or spiritual] *faith also deny at heart; but they who believe* [dualism] *get ideas from various sources about heaven and its joy and glory, each person from such things as are of his own knowledge and intelligence, and the simple from the things of bodily sensation. ~Swedenborg, Heavenly Secrets, AC 4622*

Science today is materialistic and opposes dualism and theistic explanations. Even those who are in a religion are taught that when we die we are unconscious until the Day of Resurrection when God's angels will cause the skeletons of the dead to reassemble by miracle and the person could then be awakened from the sleep of death. People who believe in an afterlife believe that the "raising of the dead" will take place in this physical world. Their thinking about religion remains materialistic, not believing that there is a separate spiritual world of eternity.

While we function in natural-rational consciousness we do not and cannot believe in a separate spiritual world. Our thinking is composed of only materialistic concepts, ideas, meanings, and reasoning patterns. Spiritual ideas or truths cannot exist in such a mental atmosphere. When hearing or reading about spiritual ideas the natural mind will always interpret it materialistically.

The thinking and feeling operations of our mind completely change when we cross from natural to spiritual consciousness. Now we can perceive the rationality of explanations that are drawn from spiritual truths and realities. Now we can see below us or behind us the limitations of our thinking when we are immersed in materialistic consciousness. Now it is obvious to us by rational perception that God creates and manages a physical universe and a mental or spiritual universe, and that the two are locked into each other and operate as cause and effect.

We can also perceive as obvious the fact that our connection to God makes us immortal. Further, we can also see that the purpose of life on earth is to allow us to form a natural-rational mind and personality that can then be made human by entering eternal life in spiritual and celestial consciousness.

We can also see the clarity of Swedenborg's distinction between "blind faith" and "rational faith". To believe the mysteries of religion and doctrinal teachings without understanding them is called blind faith. Swedenborg shows that blind faith ceases in the afterlife and is tucked away in the background of awareness, leaving the individual without any faith, that is, knowledge of God and heaven. But rational faith remains in the afterlife and then serves as a basis from which to evolve endlessly in deeper understanding and rationality of spiritual and celestial truths, and the endless varieties of love that are within these truths.

Carl G. and Emma Rauschenbach Jung
at their home at Küsnacht, near Zurich, before 1955

Carl Jung's Vision of his wife after her death.

We shy away from the word "eternal," but I can describe the experience only as the ecstasy of a non-temporal state in which present, past, and future are one. Everything that happens in time had been brought together into a concrete whole. Nothing was distributed over time, nothing could be measured by temporal concepts.

The experience might best be defined as a state of feeling, but one which cannot be produced by imagination. How can I imagine that I exist simultaneously the day before yesterday, today, and the day after tomorrow? There would be things which would not yet have begun, other things which would be indubitably present, and others again which would already be finished and yet all this would be one.

The only thing that feeling could grasp would be a sum, an iridescent whole, containing all at once expectation of a beginning, surprise at what is now happening, and satisfaction or disappointment with the result of what has happened. One is interwoven into an indescribable whole and yet observes it with complete objectivity.

I experienced this objectivity once again later on. That was after the death of my wife. I saw her in a dream which was like a vision. She stood at some distance from me, looking at me squarely. She was in her prime, perhaps about thirty, and wearing the dress which had been made for her many years before by my cousin the medium. It was perhaps the most beautiful thing she had ever worn.

Her expression was neither joyful nor sad, but, rather, objectively wise and understanding, without the slightest emotional reaction, as though she were beyond the mist of affects. I knew that it was not she, but a portrait she had made or commissioned for me. It contained the beginning of our relationship, the events of fifty-three years of marriage, and the end of her life also. Face to face with such wholeness one remains speechless, for it can scarcely be comprehended.

The objectivity which I experienced in this dream and in the visions is part of a completed individuation. It signifies detachment from valuations and from what we call emotional ties. In general, emotional ties are very important to human beings. But they still contain projections, and it is essential to withdraw these projections in order to attain to oneself and to objectivity.

Emotional relationships are relationships of desire, tainted by coercion and constraint; something is expected from the other person, and that makes him and ourselves unfree. Objective cognition lies hidden behind the attraction of the emotional relationship; it seems to be the central secret. Only through objective cognition is the real coniunctio possible. ~Carl Jung, Memories Dreams and Reflections.

Swedenborg points out that anyone can know things about the afterlife and heaven from various sources and personal experiences, but many people do not care to investigate the matter and therefore do not see them and do not believe them, despite their declarations from pure belief that is required by membership in a religious community.

Swedenborg reports that our sensations are purer when we no longer have the physical avatar to captivate our immediate attention and awareness. This is something I look forward to!

_____

Swedenborg Writes:

Nevertheless most people do not apprehend that spirits and angels enjoy sensations much more exquisite than those of men in this world, namely, sight, hearing, smell, something analogous to taste, and touch; and especially the delights of the affections [pleasures and loves]. *If men* [on earth in natural consciousness] *would only believe that their interior essence is the spirit, and that the* [physical] *body and its sensations and members are adapted to uses in this* [physical] *world merely, and that the spirit and its sensations and organs are adapted to uses in the other life, then from themselves and almost of their own accord they would come into ideas about the state of their spirit after death; for they would reflect that the spirit must be the man himself* [ego-personality] *who thinks, and who desires, longs for things, and is affected with them; and further that all the power of sensation which appears in the* [physical] *body belongs properly to the spirit* [body or mind], *and to the* [physical] *body merely by influx* [from the spirit body or mind]; *and they would afterwards confirm themselves in this idea by many considerations, and in this way would at last take more delight in the things of their spirit* [mind] *than in those of their* [physical] *body.*

It is also a real fact that it is not man's [physical] *body which sees, hears, smells, and feels, but his spirit* [body or mind]; *and therefore when the spirit* [mind] *is divested of the* [physical] *body, it is in its own sensations, the same as when it was in the* [physical] *body, only now far more exquisite; for the things of the* [physical] *body, being comparatively gross, had rendered the sensations obtuse, and this the more because the man had immersed them in earthly* [physical] *and worldly* [natural] *things.*

This I can aver--that a spirit has much more exquisite sight than a man in the [physical] *body, and also much more exquisite hearing, and, astonishing to say, the sense of smell, and especially the sense of touch; for spirits* [those in the afterlife] *see one another, hear one another, and touch one another.*

_____

This is amazingly good news! When we "pass on" and become fully conscious in the spirit world we are in company of countless other people who have already passed on before us and with whom we can now have a relationship. Countless others and endless opportunities, as you can imagine! By death we are not passing into an impoverished world but a much richer one, with more exquisite social experiences, pleasures, enjoyments, and delights.

Swedenborg Writes:

Moreover, anyone who believes in the life after death might infer that this is the case from the fact that no life is possible without sensation, and that the quality of the life is according to the quality of the sensation, nay, that the intellectual faculty is nothing but an exquisite sense of interior things, and the higher intellectual of spiritual things; and it is from this that the things of the intellectual and its perceptions are called internal senses.

As regards man's power of sensation immediately after death the case is this: As soon as a man dies and all things of his [physical] *body grow cold* [corpse], *he is raised up into life, and at the same time into a state of all sensations; insomuch that at first he scarcely knows but that he is still in the* [physical] *body, for the sensations he then enjoys lead him so to believe.*

But when he observes that he has more exquisite sensations, and especially when he begins to speak with other spirits [inborn universal spiritual language or thought-language]*, it dawns upon him that he is in the other life, and that the death of his* [physical] *body has been the continuation of the life of his spirit* [ego-personality]*.*

I have spoken with two of my acquaintances on the day of their burial, and with one who through my eyes saw his coffin and his bier; and as this man enjoyed all the sensation he had in this world, he spoke to me about the burial rites while I was following in his funeral procession, and also about his [physical] *body, saying that they should throw that away because he himself was alive.*

What an amazing drama! Swedenborg was speaking with his neighbor who had just passed on and whose funeral Swedenborg was attending. The man thought his family and friends ought not to be sad and pretend that he was dead! Elsewhere Swedenborg mentions that the man asked him to tell the people at the funeral that he was not dead. But Swedenborg refused because he said that they would not believe him and would think him to be mad.

Swedenborg Writes:

Be it known, however, that they who are in the other life can see nothing whatever in this world through the eyes of any man [still on earth]; *but that their being able to do so through mine was because I am in the spirit with them and at the same time in the body with those who are in the* [physical] *world. And be it further known that I did not see with my* [physical] *bodily eyes those with whom I have spoken in the other life, but with the eyes of my spirit* [body]; *and yet I saw them as clearly, and sometimes more clearly, than with the eyes of the* [physical] *body; for of the Lord's Divine mercy the senses of my spirit have been opened* [dual consciousness].

But I am aware that what I have so far said will not be believed by those who are immersed in bodily, earthly, and worldly things (that is, by those of them who have such things as their end), for such people apprehend no other things than those which are dissipated by death. I am also well aware that those will not believe who have thought much and investigated much about the soul, and who have not at the same time comprehended that the soul of man is his spirit, and that his spirit is the man himself who is living in the body; for such persons could have no other notion about the soul than as of a thinking principle, whether of flame or of ether, that acts solely into the organic forms of the body, and not into those purer forms which are of the spirit in the body; thus that the soul is such a thing as must be dissipated together with the body. And this is especially the case with those who have confirmed themselves in such things by views that are inflated with a persuasion of their own preeminent wisdom. ~Swedenborg, Heavenly Secrets, AC 4623.

But be it known that the life of sense with spirits is twofold, namely, real and not real. The one is distinguished from the other by the fact that everything is real which appears to those who are in heaven, whereas everything is unreal which appears to those who are in hell.

For whatever comes from the Divine (that is, from the Lord) is real, because it comes from the very being of things, and from life in itself, but whatever comes from a spirit's own is not real, because it does not come from the being of things, nor from life in itself. They who are in the affection of good and truth are in the Lord's life, thus in real life, for the Lord is present in good and truth through the affection; but they who are in evil and falsity through the affection, are in the life of what is their own, thus in a life not real, for the Lord is not present in evil and falsity. The real is distinguished from the not real in this--that the real is actually such as it appears, and that the not real is actually not such as it appears.

They who are in hell have sensations equally with others, and are not aware but that everything is really or actually just as it appears to their senses; and yet when they are looked at by the angels, the same things appear as phantasms, and disappear, and they themselves do not appear as men, but as monsters. It has also been given me to speak with them on this subject, and some of them said that they believe things to be real because they see and touch them, adding that sense cannot deceive. But it was given me to reply that no matter how real these things may appear to them, they nevertheless are not real, and this because they themselves are in things contrary or opposite to the Divine, namely, in evils and falsities, and moreover are themselves nothing but phantasies insofar as their thoughts are concerned, to the extent that they are in cupidities of evil and persuasions of falsity; and to see anything from phantasies is to see things that are real as not real, and things that are not real as real; and that unless it were given them of the Lord's Divine mercy to have their senses affected in this manner, they would have no sensitive life, consequently no life at all, because that which is sensitive constitutes the whole of life. To adduce all my experience on these subjects would be to fill many pages.

Therefore when you enter the other life beware of being deceived, for evil spirits know how to conjure up illusions of many kinds before those who come fresh from the world, and if they cannot deceive them, they nevertheless thereby endeavor to persuade them that nothing is real, but that all things are ideal, even those which are in heaven. ~Swedenborg, Heavenly Secrets, AC 4622

Few people realize that life after death is an exciting new adventure for every human being. It helps to remember or to realize that human beings are created for the afterlife of eternity, and that our temporary life on earth is but a brief transition phase towards our real home and life. This life is a stage of preparation for something much grander and exciting. Our fear of death or dying is not based on reality but on superstition and ignorance. The natural mind is afraid of death because it does not comprehend or believe that we are immortal.

The purpose of my writing this book is to share the happy knowledge of the afterlife. I present a system of thinking that allows people to apprehend our dual nature, natural and spiritual. Above all, this new knowledge brings us closer to God, to the purpose of creation, and to greater awareness of the rational method of management that God uses to run the universe and to bring every individual to eternal happiness.

The purpose of rational theistic self-analysis is to help us to see this knowledge more clearly and to apply it to our regeneration. This is the process of individuation that brings us to full development in wisdom and higher consciousness. The more clearly we understand this process the better we are able to cooperate with God in undertaking this awesome journey.

> *Doing good when the possibility exists and doing it with all ones heart, is loving [the neighbor]. ~Swedenborg, Heavenly Secrets, AC 6073*

14. Overview of
Rational Theistic Self-analysis (RTS)

Acquiring the RTS perspective is an approach to self-healing, individuation, and regeneration that is at once rational, theistic, and has a self-directed focus whose goal is to assist in the growth of the individual into full maturity and potential.

It is essential for positive human growth and good mental health that we acknowledge our immortality and dependence on God in everything that is in our mind, emotions, loves, and thinking. This acknowledgment to oneself is needed to allow the individual to restore inner freedom that is not merely part of our customs. Inner freedom is the essential condition for releasing and experiencing every individual's unique inborn human potential. That essential inner freedom to think and to love has been derailed and set aside by our education that inculcated into us the perspective of materialistic science and its reductionism of reality into monism.

We are taught as young and inexperienced minds that a material world in time and space is the only one that must be acknowledged as real. We are trained to reject the idea that there is another world that is not physical and is not in time, what "some people" call a "spiritual world". And therefore the idea of an afterlife in eternity is to be considered imagination, not reality.

But reality is spiritual. Materialism and "monism" deny that there exist two independent worlds that God created and is managing. Hence to live with materialistic thinking is to live in un-reality. And this is harmful to every individual's happiness, potential, and eternal future.

The reality is more usefully and accurately described in scientific "dualism", which is the past and the future of science. The twentieth century has allowed the solidification of a materialistic science that has broken with the past and the future of humankind. Consider the enormous and tragic consequences of the majority of our society living in materialistic lifestyles. On a societal and community level there is criminality, conflict, terrorism, war, and hostile competition. On a personal level there is unhappiness, dysfunctional relationships, unhealthy lifestyles, unfulfilled lives, unfulfilled creative potential, lack of enthusiasm, much stress, depression, selfishness, hatred, and numerous neuroses and psychopathologies. This is living in un-reality.

The fact is that everyone at any time can put a stop to it!

You don't need to change others or society in order to get back to the personal work of restoring balance and growth of human potential. By acquiring a spiritual-rational way of thinking you will be able to see and understand what is obscure and unknown in materialistic thinking that uses a natural-rational base instead of a spiritual-rational base. You will then be able to see that you can be happy, fulfilled, and growing in potential by discovering how your mind works and how you can manage it. This is inner work, private, and free. Society is purely external to you, including all its science and dangers. Unhappiness, stress, and lack of enthusiasm are mental states that the individual can control by spiritual thinking and discipline of life.

The perspective of the rational theistic self-analysis (RTS) is free for the having and requires no special skills or knowledge. RTS is the self getting to know the self and managing it towards positive growth and health.

Many people are suspicious of something involving "theistic" or God. This is understandable given the widespread confusion that equates God and religion. People are put off by those who try to "push" their religious beliefs on others who don't want them. This is also why we have a tradition and legal structure for prohibiting public schools and institutions from promoting or teaching religion. This is the attitude in natural-rational thinking. It is useful in preventing religious conflicts and discrimination as was practiced in the past. Religious intolerance is still being practiced in many parts of the world.

But spiritual-rational thinking allows us to rise to a higher and more universal way of understanding. We can clearly see that there is an actual distinction to be made between religion and God. Religion belongs to advocacy and possible intolerance. God belongs to science in the dualism mode. Religion is part of culture, history, and politics. These belong to the natural world here on earth. God is part of universal reality and belongs to both our temporary natural existence and our immortal spiritual life of eternity.

Religious people may claim God for their religion or for all religion. Materialistic science may deny God and all religion. This is natural-rational thinking. But in spiritual-rational thinking we can see that God does not belong to religion alone, nor to science alone. Most importantly and relevant to each person, is that God belongs to the individual human being. God is not merely the creator of the universe. God is omnipotent and omniscient, and this means that *God cannot give away any power whatsoever* to nature, to scientific laws, to religious leaders, or to the individual. If God did that He would no longer be omnipotent and managing everything. And this is impossible.

Hence the first and most basic fact that we adopt in spiritual-rational thinking is that *God is present in our mind, managing every detail of its growth and its potential.*

Much needs to be filled in and explained to make this spiritual truth completely understandable in a rational way. All that is presented in this book. It is not complicated or difficult. No special skills are needed to fully comprehend the set of facts of spiritual reality. And we must fully and clearly comprehend it, or else we cannot believe it and we cannot practice it. It is useless. And we go wanting. Hence in this book I present and explain these spiritual facts in more than one context and with sufficient repetition to allow you to consider, reflect, and expand.

Once we understand rationally that God is present in our mind and how He manages all its details and growth, we experience an immense relief from the enormous burden and stress imposed by the materialistic idea that we are alone and in charge of our mind.

If we are alone and in charge of our mind then we are also to be blamed for our failures, unhappiness, fears, and shortcomings. This is a crushing burden to carry, and it is a false burden, useless and unnecessary. God constantly works in our mind to bring us out of this delusion of life. But we also need to understand that God will not compel us to accept the truths that can liberate us. Why not? Why does God not use this omnipotence to make us happy and intelligent in spiritual truths and a life in accordance with them?

God will not compel anyone to change because such forced change is useless and actually harmful, making the individual sicker and unhappier. God's love for every individual prevents His omnipotence from spiritual compulsion. Only voluntary and free self-management can last and enter the inner framework of our personality, the portion we need in the afterlife to lead an eternal happy existence.

Rational theistic self-analysis is an approach we can practice to fix our thinking from natural to spiritual, and to fix our feelings from selfish to altruistic. To be happy here and in eternity we need to labor to regenerate our inherited and inborn love of self. Everything we do and think in natural-rational consciousness is for the sake of self. We approve of those who favor us and may act well towards them, but we hate those who disapprove of us or are different from us, and we act by intolerance and condemnation of them. This is selfishness. It loves only the self and wants to dominate everyone and everything for the sake of self. This is also the life of hell in the human mind.

Only love has spiritual power and is eternal. Love determines our personality and ego consciousness. Selfish inborn love is natural, while mutual love or spiritual love is eternal. Loving others or respecting them for our own benefit and for our sake is a selfish love that leads to devolution and hell in the human mind. Loving others for the sake of others, or for the sake of God, or for the sake of good, is mutual love. Loving others is, firstly, not to do them any harm, overt or mental, and secondly, to strive to do them all good through what we know and have.

This is the spiritual reality that God created and is maintaining. Loving self for the sake of self leads to a mental hell here and in eternity, while loving others for the sake of others or God leads to a mental heaven in eternity. Understanding this reality in a rational way, with all the supporting spiritual facts, will heal you and expand your consciousness and reality to whatever you desire. That will be the incalculable and happy benefit of practicing rational theistic self-analysis.

Religion is not involved in RTS. But many people do have religion and are loyal to it. You will discover that there is nothing in RTS that is opposed to religion or contrary to it. In fact RTS is based in the wisdom of God's Word as presented in *Sacred Scripture*, especially when *Sacred Scripture* is read with spiritual meaning and not merely historically. This too will be fully explained here.

Some readers may wonder at this point that if God is omnipotent and manages every detail of our mind then why is it that we are responsible to fix our selfishness and materialistic thinking. This too will be fully accounted for, as otherwise the RTS view cannot be agreed with and practiced. But for now I can summarize the general facts of the matter by pointing once again to the spiritual reality that love is the only thing that lives permanently in our personality and makes us immortal humans.

Everything we think, choose, or do is done from some love. Our ego-personality or unique self as an individual is made of out of our love and of nothing else. At the very core of our soul or will, we have a ruling love that commands all other loves and arranges them into a desired order beneath itself. God cannot compel the individual to change this inborn and reinforced love-structure. The result cannot stand because it is not constructed from the love of the individual, and especially the particular ruling love.

The only biological solution that God has made available through creation is called "regeneration", as well as other expressions. Since our mind is a spiritual organ and grows similarly to a plant or tree, it is clear that the only way to heal the unhealthy personality is to grow a new one by means of new loves. This organic growth process is called regeneration, which is to grow a new organ.

It is a simple situation that we teach our children and they can understand it. There are good loves and bad ones. The bad ones are all managed by a ruling love or "tyrant" called *"loving self only"*. The good loves are managed by a "king" called *"loving others as much a self"*. Loving self only leads to dysfunction, pathologies, unhappiness, foolishness, and finally, hell. Loving others as much as self leads to mental balance and growth, and to intelligence and wisdom, and finally to heaven.

Why is this so? As you think more and more in the spiritual-rational mode, it becomes clear that there is no other way that God can fulfill His goal and desire in creating human beings and a universe for their service and habitation. This goal is to bring every created individual into a collective consciousness called heaven in eternity. In this highest human organic mental state and ability people live together as angel couples forming endless communities of love, each type of love attracting others who are in that same love.

Heaven is therefore a community of mutual love. It is in this mental state that God can make everyone more and more perfect, more and more happy and intelligent, every day to eternity. Further, people from all over the inhabitable universe pass into the other life on a constant basis, where each individual adds his or her unique love and personality to the collective consciousness. Everything in heavenly communities reverberates through its members so that the unique love perception, and emotion of each is communicated and enriches every other member.

But there is an additional rational fact that must be consulted when we decide to strive to love others as much as self. Of course this is a gradual process as we learn to discern what it is in others that we must love as much as self. Spiritual-rational thinking informs us that it is wrong and impractical to love others as persons. What if it is a bad person? How can we love a bad and predatory individual who loves only himself or herself and despises others, community, the law, and God. We must not love such a person nor can we.

So what we must love in others as much as self is the good and truth that we can perceive to be in others. Since there may also be falsity and evil in the person we surely must not love that. So the spiritual law that we must love others as much as self, actually means that we must only love what is good and true in anyone.

This coincides with loving God because all good and true can only come from God and is God in the human mind. From this you can see that we love God when we love what is from God in self and others. And only heavenly love and truth are in God, and therefore God in others. What is false and not good or evil is never from God. It is only from the individual's selfishness that turns the good and the true flowing in from God into their opposite. We must not love that.

Swedenborg Writes:
> *Everyone is created to live forever.... The reason not everyone gets to heaven, though, is that people immerse themselves in pleasures of hell that are contrary to the blessedness of heaven. People who do not enjoy heaven's bliss cannot enter heaven because they cannot stand the place. ~Swedenborg, Divine Providence, DP 324*

This is the perfect universe that God has created and is maintaining forever. Part of this perfection is to put individual freedom above all other principles of God's omnipotent management system. This is because human life is nothing else by the individual's love. Remove that love and the individual has no life, thus no longer exists. This is why God will not compel people to be good and thus to go to heaven. People who choose in total freedom to deny God and to make self god, cannot be turned away from that choice without killing them spiritually, thus in eternity. To provide for these people as well, God created the mental state of hell where many choose to enter immediately after death when they become spiritual beings.

––––––––––––––––

Swedenborg Writes:
> *Our entire sense of self resides in our will. The first time we are born, the self is evil. The second time we are born, the self becomes good. The first time, we are born of our parents; the second time, we are born of the Lord. ~Swedenborg, True Christianity, TCR 658*

––––––––––––––––

Rational theistic self-analysis is nothing else than a daily discipline to assist God in the person's process of regeneration. God has all the power doing the organic regeneration by which our personality is re-grown or regenerated. The only power we have is to cling by free choice to loving others as much as self. *We do this not by declarations but by deeds.*

For instance, consider your daily normal annoyances. They mostly have to do with disapproving of others and their lack of considerateness. It may be being noisy, or having too many parties, or forgetting about their obligations and promises, or being clueless when it comes to pleasing others or taking care of their needs. And besides other things such as cheating, deceiving, lying, stealing, gossiping, threatening, damaging, etc.

Now having thought of the selfishness of others and how they affect you negatively, think of how you affect others negatively. Quite likely your two lists are similar. We act like the other people who act inconsiderate, selfish, and dishonest. Regeneration involves a new way of thinking and acting hour-by-hour and minute-by-minute. You can see why the process is slow and takes years or decades of build up.

You can see from this why RTS is called self. We have to be aware and conscious of what we are thinking all day long. There is no special technique for assisting God in the process of our regeneration. It is normal for human beings to be aware of what they are thinking and emoting, and to be able to recall and report much of it for further consideration and analysis.

At the same time I don't believe that just any kind of self is effective. It is a common experience to make a resolution or promise and then see ourselves irresistibly breaking it. I review the issue in Volume 1 especially as explained in the work of Jung and Swedenborg. More on this will be presented as you read further along. In spiritual-rational thinking about God's omnipotence we can see that we have zero power in acting against an established love in our personality structure. A tree will not be able to fly regardless of its development or longevity. The human ego-personality cannot act against its love because it is nothing but that love and love cannot act against itself.

This is why God's intervention is required or there is no change in our inborn loves and our immortal personality is pre-destined to a miserable life in eternal hell. God's love requires that He intervenes and save the individual from such inhuman and cruel fate. This is why God in sacred Scripture calls Himself "Savior", the only one there is, the only one who can regenerate our personality from hell to heaven.

But this God can do only to the extent that the individual is willing to cooperate freely, not out of fear of person or hell, but out of love of others as much as self. Can you make yourself be affected by this love and emotion? Are you willing to learn to be so affected? If yes, then rational theistic self-analysis can assist you in this process by showing you how the process works and how you can cooperate with it.

Swedenborg Writes:
> The Word is the Divine Truth which is in the Lord and from the Lord Divine Truth has power in itself, and such power that, by means of it, heaven was created and the world with all things therein. ~Swedenborg, Heaven and Hell 137

---

15. Jung's Explanation of
The Role God Takes In Our Regeneration

Jung writes:

All religions are therapies for the sorrows and disorders of the soul. ~Carl Jung, Commentary, The Golden Flower

The word becomes your God, since it protects you from the countless possibilities of interpretation. The word is protective magic against the daimons of the unending, which tear at your soul and want to scatter you to the winds. ~Carl Jung, Liber Novus, p. 270

It may be useful to first read Volume 1 to become familiar with the thinking of Jung and Swedenborg on what is "rational", what is "theistic", and what is "self" (see: Reality is Spiritual. Volume 1. Dreams and the Spiritual World: Integrating the Psychology of Jung and Swedenborg (2016).

Jung's analytical psychology gives God a central role in the process of regeneration, which he called "individuation". To Jung, human development and wholeness involved the process of bringing God from its dark unconsciousness into the light of individual consciousness. This is what God desired and achieved by incarnating and suffering the psychic war of individuation.

By letting the Divine unconscious come into our individual conscious awareness we form a union with God, seeing God as Human and who can be our friend, guide, and protector. But Jung warns that this path or activity is fraught with psychological danger. We must be careful to distinguish our shadow from the devil:

When a patient in our days is about to emerge from an unconscious condition, he is instantly confronted with his shadow and he has to decide for the good, otherwise he goes down the drain. (quoted below).

The process of individuation starts with this dangerous war in our psychic constitution. If we lose we are lost in hell and live a terrifying existence immersed in darkness, unable to judge what is real, what fantasy.

In dealing with darkness, you have got to cling to the Good, otherwise the devil devours you. You need every bit of your goodness in dealing with Evil and just there. (quoted below).

The unconscious contains not only God but also the devil!

_____

Jung writes:
This meeting with oneself is, at first, the meeting with one's own shadow. The shadow is a tight passage, a narrow door, whose painful constriction no one is spared who goes down to the deep well. But one must learn to know oneself in order to know who one is.

For what comes after the door is, surprisingly enough, a boundless expanse full of unprecedented uncertainty, with apparently no inside and no outside, no above and no below, no here and no there, no mine and no thine, no good and no bad.

It is the world of water.....where I am indivisibly this and that; where I experience the other in myself and the other-than-myself experiences me.
The Archetypes and the Collective Unconscious, p. 21

_____

Because our conscious mind has an organic anatomical connection to the collective unconscious it is clear that we possess in our personality both heavenly and hellish. The hellish exists in the background or the depth of our personality. Therefore it is not clearly seen without special effort. The hellish loves beckon to our conscious personality or ego, and try to seduce the conscious ego into liking it more than the heavenly traits that we also possess. *The heavenly fights back with truth in our rational understanding.* Truth brings rational light that is more powerful than any fantasy or spell in which we are immersed from birth and heredity.

Heavenly and hellish loves or traits needs to be defined anatomically, not psychologically. The mind and the individual consciousness is part of the overall anatomy of the mental world of eternity, which is better known as the afterlife or the spiritual world. So heaven and hell are part of our mental anatomy. Each is a mental state that is available to enter by anyone anytime. Navigation to heavenly zones in the mind and navigation to the hellish zones in the mind, is effected by our loves, and especially, our ruling or chief love that governs and arranges under itself all other loves in the personality.

We all start our adulthood in a selfish mental state. Most of us do for sure. This is inherited and few people work hard against their inherited tendencies. Only spiritual knowledge can motivate the person's free will to start resisting their enjoyable and well-liked hellish loves. Yet without this there is not salvation from natural consciousness.

One of its sad characteristics is that natural consciousness gradually devolves into lower and lower levels of activity of human consciousness. At that level of functioning the human being has turned into a human-beast, spiritually insane, incapable of reasoning, rationally, and horrifically cruel to others whom they can capture under their influence and turn into cowering slaves.

The anatomical definition of heaven and hell is this: When the ruling love of the individual is mutual love and the love of God's good and truth. This altruistic love is the anatomical connection to the heavenly states of consciousness in the human mind. Similarly with the anatomical definition of hell: When the ruling love of the individual is mutual love and the love of God's good and truth.

Jung writes:

> What is important and meaningful to my life is that I shall live as fully as possible to fulfill the divine will within me. This task gives me so much to do that I have no time or any other. Let me point out that if we were all to live in that way we would need no armies, no police, no diplomacy, no politics, no banks. We would have a meaningful life and not what we have now—madness.

Here is what Jung wrote concerning the necessity of theistic self-analysis:

_____

The analyst must help life as long as he can. There is a prejudice that analysis is the art of letting out the unconscious, like opening the cages in a zoo. That is part of analysis, but it must not be done in an irresponsible and foolish way. This is only the preparatory part. The main analysis is what to do with the things that have emerged from the unconscious. One must see what the underlying trend is—what the will of God is. ~Carl Jung, 1958, Talk With Students

From the psychological standpoint the experience of God the creator is the perception of an overpowering impulse issuing from the sphere of the unconscious. ~Carl Jung, 1953, Letters Vol. II, p. 133

Though Christ was God, as Man he was detached from God and he watched the devil falling out of heaven, removed from God as he (Christ) was separated from God inasmuch as he was human. In his utter helplessness on the cross, he even confessed that God had forsaken him. ...
But becoming Man, he becomes at the same time a definite being, which is this and not that. Thus the very first thing Christ must do is to sever himself from his shadow and call it the devil.

When a patient in our days is about to emerge from an unconscious condition, he is instantly confronted with his shadow and he has to decide for the good, otherwise he goes down the drain.

The first step on the way to individuation consists in the discrimination between himself and the shadow. In this stage the Good is the goal of individuation, and consequently Christ represents the self.

The next step is the problem of the shadow: in dealing with darkness, you have got to cling to the Good, otherwise the devil devours you. You need every bit of your goodness in dealing with Evil and just there. ...

As a matter of fact, our society has not even begun to face its shadow or to develop those Christian virtues so badly needed in dealing with the powers of darkness.

Our society cannot afford the luxury of cutting itself loose from the imitatio Christi, even if it should know that the conflict with the shadow, i.e., Christ versus Satan, is only the first step on the way to the far-away goal of the unity of the self in God.

It is true however that the imitatio Christi leads you into your own very real and Christ-like conflict with darkness, and the more you are engaged in this war and in these attempts at peacemaking helped by the anima, the more you begin to look forward beyond the Christian aeon to the Oneness of the Holy Spirit. He is the pneumatic state the creator attains to through the phase of incarnation.

He is the experience of every individual that has undergone the complete abolition of his ego through the absolute opposition expressed by the symbol Christ versus Satan. The state of the Holy Spirit means a restitution of the original oneness of the unconscious on the level of consciousness. ... ~Carl Jung, Letters Vol. II, p. 133-138

I suspect them [the great Eastern philosophers] of being symbolical psychologists, to whom no greater wrong could be done than to take them literally. If it were really metaphysics that they mean, it would be useless to try to understand them. But if it is psychology, we can not only understand them, but we can greatly profit greatly by them, for then the so-called 'metaphysical' comes within the range of experience. If I accept the fact that a god is absolute and beyond all human experiences, he leaves me cold. I do not affect him, nor does he affect me. But if I know that a god is a powerful impulse in my soul, at once I must concern myself with him, for then he can become important... like everything belonging to the sphere of reality. ~Carl Jung, Psyche and Symbol, 1958

The seat of faith...is not consciousness but spontaneous religious experience, which brings the individual's faith into immediate relation with God. ~Carl Jung, The Undiscovered Self

What is important and meaningful to my life is that I shall live as fully as possible to fulfill the divine will within me. This task gives me so much to do that I have no time or any other. Let me point out that if we were all to live in that way we would need no armies, no police, no diplomacy, no politics, no banks. We would have a meaningful life and not what we have now—madness.

God seeks consciousness in man. This is the truth of the birth and the resurrection of Christ within. As more and more thinking men come to it, this is the spiritual rebirth of the world. Christ, the Logos—that is to say, the mind, the understanding, shining into the darkness. Christ was a new truth about man. Be what God means you to be. ~Carl Jung, Jung Speaks, p. 75

In these selections Jung is discussing individuation and God's role in it. There are various levels of greater individuation and perfection as we fight progressively against the devil or the evil that is in us from inheritance, biology, and a selfish lifestyle. We fight and win through the good and truth that is also within us and to the extent that we honor these through daily lifestyle choices, thoughts, and actions.

Regarding this progression of individuation, Swedenborg discusses three levels of consciousness that we can discover in the perspective of RTS and of regeneration. When we are immersed in the lowest level of consciousness, we are called spiritually a "dead man". But in next level higher we are called a "spiritual man", and in the highest level we are called a "celestial man". These are three phases of the self that we get to know through the RTS perspective. Here is Swedenborg writing in his work *Heavenly Secrets.*

Swedenborg Writes:
This chapter treats of the celestial man, as the preceding one did of the spiritual, who was formed out of a dead man. But as it is unknown at this day what the celestial man is, and scarcely what the spiritual man is, or a dead man, it is permitted me briefly to state the nature of each, that the difference may be known.

First, then, a dead man acknowledges nothing to be true and good but what belongs to the body and the world, and this he adores. A spiritual man acknowledges spiritual and celestial truth and good; but he does so from a principle of faith, which is likewise the ground of his actions, and not so much from love. A celestial man believes and perceives spiritual and celestial truth and good, acknowledging no other faith than that which is from love, from which also he acts.

Secondly: The ends which influence a dead man regard only corporeal and worldly life, nor does he know what eternal life is, or what the Lord is; or should he know, he does not believe. The ends which influence a spiritual man regard eternal life, and thereby the Lord. The ends which influence a celestial man regard the Lord, and thereby His kingdom and eternal life.

Thirdly: A dead man, when in combat [of temptations] almost always yields, and when not in combat, evils and falsities have dominion over him, and he is a slave. His bonds are external, such as the fear of the law, of the loss of life, of wealth, of gain, and of the reputation which he values for their sake. The spiritual man is in combat, but is always victorious; the bonds by which he is restrained are internal, and are called the bonds of conscience. The celestial man is not in combat, and when assaulted by evils and falsities, he despises them, and is therefore called a conqueror. He is apparently restrained by no bonds, but is free. His bonds, which are not apparent, are perceptions of good and truth. ~Swedenborg, Arcana Coelestia, AC 81

Prior to initiating the process of regeneration we are spiritually dead. This means that we live and think in false beliefs, not knowing what is fantasy or unreality, and what is truth and reality. What maintains the fantasy life as if real is the love of self only, which is evil, and is called the devil in our psyche. This is the cause of our destruction as a human being and therefore we are then dead despite our immortality. If the individual does not change this state there is no other place to exist after death then trapped forever in the hells of our mind. This tragic lot must be avoided.

Regeneration or individuation begins with the acknowledgement that God is present in our mind and is always active, constantly trying to reduce our involvement with evil intentions and false justifications. And as this proceeds with our willing cooperation we awaken from being a dead man to becoming a spiritual individual. Such a "new man" or individual receives the power to grow from clinging to the spiritual truths that are like a sword wounding and chasing away the distorted truths of false beliefs that justify remaining in self-love, thus in evil and in cahoots with the devil. The truths we cling to invite the good that chases and defeats evil.

And there is a still higher level of human operation called the celestial individual or mind. This is initiated and maintained by clinging first to heavenly love, which is to love others even more than self. Our consideration and respect for the welfare of others is even more intense than our desire to take care of our own comfort and benefit. Our highest pleasure and delight comes when we are able to benefit others and to see their delight from it.

Jung writes:
If you are a gifted person, it doesn't mean that you gained something. It means you have something to give back. ~Carl Jung

Individuation can only occur if we engage our usefulness to others. Individuation is not an intensification of consciousness, it is very much more. For you must have the consciousness of something before it can be intensified, and that means experience, life lived. You can only bo really conscious of things which you have experienced, so individuation must be understood as life.

Only life integrates, only life and what we do in life makes the individual appear. You cannot individuate, for instance, by locking yourself up in a cell, you can only individuate in your concrete life, you appear in your deed; there you can individuate and nowhere else.

Real consciousness can only be based upon life; upon things experienced, but talking about these things is just air. It is a sort of conscious understanding, but it is not individuation.

Individuation is the accomplishment through life. For instance, say a cell begins to divide itself and to differentiate and develop into a certain plant or a certain animal; that is the process of individuation.

It is that one becomes what one is, that one accomplishes one's destiny, all the determinations that are given in the form of the germ; it is the unfolding of the germ and becoming the primitive pattern that one was born with.
~Carl Jung, Visions Seminar, p. 758

Your visions will become clear only when you can look into your own heart. Who looks outside, dreams; who looks inside, awakes. ~Carl Jung

---

16. The Idea of God:
Natural, Spiritual, Celestial

All consciousness is rational. This is because God is the only consciousness and we have our consciousness only from what flows into our mind from God. God's consciousness is pure truth, pure rationality, pure intelligence, and pure wisdom. Hence it is that the consciousness that we receive as human beings is also intelligent and rational. Our rationality from God is not pure like that of God because our mental reception organs are not perfect and infinite as it is for God. Hence we have an imperfect and less pure rationality than God. The purity of our reception is proportional to the kind of love that dominates our life. This is explained below. Each level of rationality operates or exists at its own anatomical level.

There are four levels of rationality in purity and perfection:

1.   Divine rationality, which is perfect, infinite, and omniscient. It is not only the source of all rationality in human beings it is in the rationality of human beings so that their rationality is not from themselves, but from God's rationality. Rationality is substance and is the outer part of love that forms the inward part. God created the universe and human minds using this substance. God is omnipresent in His substance, and from there He is omniscient. Divine rationality is essentially human. We are human only because God's Human rationality forms our consciousness and reasoning. As rationality-substance fills the sphere of creation, it is everywhere and

can be received by the mind of any individual. The anatomy of the human mind was so contracted by God as to be able to receive into itself the Divine rationality-substance. This reception varies uniquely with each individual's unique mental anatomy or mind.

2.   Celestial rationality, which is the highest for human beings and closest to God. It is received by those who love God and love others more than they love themselves. They are called angels, live married in the highest heaven with other couples like them. They instantly know everything there is to know about something as soon as they think about it. They are in conjugial love that makes them indescribably happy, wise, and beautiful, and in the full vitality of young adulthood. They live in spiritual palaces and gardens and their dwellings are indescribably artistic and meaningful. They are not ever in want or need of anything because God is with them close and furnishes everything, including the magnificent clothing in their closets that appear different and new every morning, and the tasty bites and delicious fruit unknown on this planet that appear on a table when desired. Swedenborg has witnessed and observed these facts that I am relating here.

3.   Spiritual rationality, which is the reception we experience when we love God more than self and love others as much as self. Spiritual-rational consciousness gives us the ability to rise above the natural world intelligence of materialistic science. We are able to understand spiritual ideas that seem mystical and obscure in natural-rational consciousness. We are able to study God's meanings in Sacred Scripture viewed in its spiritual sense that is apart from the historical and literal meanings. This allows us to cooperate effectively with God in our regeneration. Our new consequent personality is wise, peaceful, capable, and whole. We are fully equipped to live with others like us in a spiritual heavenly community in eternity. We live as conjugial couples and enjoy having an occupation suitable and useful for the heavenly citizens. We are studious and enjoy learning new knowledge and applying them to spiritual life.

4.   Natural rationality, which is the reception we experience when we love ourselves more than God and more than others. This is what is familiar to most of us, especially when we have not yet begun our life's spiritual journey called regeneration. Our thinking and reasoning in natural-rational consciousness is partly from education and its materialistic science

courses, and partly from our hereditary biological pre-disposition. Our mind is constructed by God to undergo a growth process from birth to regeneration. In our childhood and adolescence growth stages we think with concrete ideas and abstracted ideas that are based on the concrete ones. Hence everything we think is limited in conception to what has time, space, quantity, and measurement. The result is that we deny spiritual reality, deny God's existence, deny life after death, deny heaven and hell. Even if we do not deny and practice a religion our idea of God and the afterlife is still materialized and limited, hence not genuine but pure fantasy.

In natural-rational consciousness our idea of God is that He created natural forces and laws and these are governing every phenomenon. Science tries to discover what are these fixed laws. In this perspective God is far away somewhere in the sky or universe.

Jung writes:

What is the nature of an advancement toward interior things is not apparent to anyone in this world; but in the other life it is plainly apparent, for there it is an advancement from a kind of mist into light, because they who are in exterior things alone are relatively in a mist, and by the angels are seen to be in one; whereas they who are in interior things are in light, and consequently are in wisdom, for the light there is wisdom; and wonderful to say, they who are in a mist cannot see those who are in light as in light, but they who are in light can see those who are in a mist as in a mist. ~Swedenborg, Heavenly Secrets, AC 4598

But above all protect me from the serpent of judgment, which only appears to be a healing serpent, yet in your depths is infernal poison and agonizing death. ~Carl Jung, Liber Novus, Page 238.

My soul is my supreme meaning, my image of God, neither God himself nor the supreme meaning. God becomes apparent in the supreme meaning of the human community. ~Carl Jung, Liber Novus, p. 240

The three days descent into Hell during death describes the sinking of the vanished value into the unconscious, where, by conquering the power of darkness, it establishes a new order, and then rises up to heaven again, that is, attains supreme clarity of consciousness. ~Carl Jung, Liber Novus, p. 243

Death is the hardest thing from the outside and as long as we are outside of it. But once inside you taste of such completeness and peace and fulfillment that you don't want to return. When you can give up the crazy will to live and when you seemingly fall into a bottomless mist, then the truly real life begins with everything which you were meant to be and never reached ~Carl Jung, Letters Vol. I, p. 357-8

The collective unconscious does not understand the language of the conscious. The unconscious can be reached and expressed only by symbols. The symbol is the primitive expression of the unconscious, but at the same time it is also an idea corresponding to the highest intuition produced by consciousness. ~Carl Jung, Commentary, Secret of the Golden Flower

---

17. Collective Consciousness

One of the most startling discoveries I made through my study of the Swedenborg Reports is about collective consciousness.

The three-day dying-resuscitation process removes the function of individual consciousness and removes the physical avatar and its sensory input to our individual natural consciousness.

We then are conscious in the spiritual body. This consciousness is collective. *In the spiritual afterlife of eternity only collective consciousness is available to experience.*

Those who appear near to each other in a tight group are now mentally conjoined as well. The reason is that mental conjunction produces the group. The visual group is an embodiment of the mental conjunction, which means that they are now immersed in collective consciousness. This is our consciousness in conjugial pairs and in heaven that are composed of such pairs.

We experience affections spontaneously. The others who are "near us" and "with us" are also affected spontaneously and in a similar way. An instance is when suddenly each individual breaks out in spontaneous voicing. The sweet song and music that the others can hear is the embodiment of the affection being consummated. And all the voices sing the same song with a sweet and pleasant harmony. *This spontaneous and shared group expression and experience may be called the collective conscious.*

What else would you call it? This collectivity of spontaneity is in contrast to our life here in natural consciousness, which is individualistic. Consider people standing or sitting in a tight group in some room. What creates this natural group is the outward coordination of their avatars. Each person makes their avatar cooperate for their own reason that is not shared with the group. If it were, the group would break up. This individual consciousness is not collective.

But in heaven and all other spiritual societies in the afterlife there is no independent individual consciousness.

18. How Consciousness Varies With Our Love

Only in quietness do we posses our own minds and discover the resources of the Inner Life. ~Helen Keller in "The Beauty of Silence," The Home Magazine, May 1935

In spiritual-rational consciousness we can see that it is impossible for God to be away somewhere while things are running themselves. God is omnipotent and omnipresent and therefore everything that exists or is going on must be governed by God, although we cannot see this directly.

In celestial-rational consciousness we can perceive that God is omnipresent through the substance of good and truth that permeates the sphere of the physical and mental worlds. In other words, God creates everything out of the substance of good and rationality that is in Himself in infinite variety. But God cannot give away a portion of Himself, or a portion of the good and rationality-substance that exists in His mind, otherwise He would no longer be omnipresent. The infinite cannot be split or else it would no longer be infinite. The universe and the human mind are created from good and rationality -substance that is God's mind. Whatever exists is constructed out of God's good and rationality-substance that is the very anatomy of His mind. This is the meaning of the oft-repeated assertion in Sacred Scripture that God is in us and we are in God, or that we have our being in God. It is an anatomical reference.

God is in us because His mental substance of good and rationality composes the anatomy and organs of our mind, and as they continually flow in from the universal sphere, our mind is filled with that substance, as a result of which we can enjoy consciousness, rationality, intelligence, love, emotion, happiness, and immortality. This makes it clear what is the continual inflow and constant presence of God in our mind. This view is very different from the natural-rational view of God or from the spiritual-rational, although closer to the latter than to the former.

We can also understand in celestial-rational consciousness that God cannot be divided into pieces, for then He would not be infinite, and therefore the good and rationality-substance that is from God and is God, inflows into every individual equally and fully (not partially). But since every individual mind is unique and no duplicate is possible to eternity, the reception of the good and rationality-substance also varies uniquely. No two people can ever receive God's substance in the same way. And we know and can observe that we can distort and misuse and invert whatever good and truth that flow in, turning it into selfish evil with its falsified truths that agree with those evils and even justify them as being good.

What is good and rationality-substance? Note that this is the same as, What is love and truth-substance, since good is the same as love in the will or affective system, while truth is the same as rationality and intelligence in our cognitive system. Our mental anatomy is constructed to have affective and cognitive systems of reception, one for love-substance, and the other for rationality-substance.

It took me several years to really understand the meaning of substance. It is a spiritual idea and therefore difficult to express in natural language, which is constructed to handle concrete and abstract concepts, but not spiritual or celestial. We first think of abstract concepts as spiritual, but this is an error that we acquired through being taught materialistic science throughout our public school years. The closest that monistic science can get to any spiritual idea is to see it as abstract, thus not concrete. There is much that has been written in the history of philosophy concerning what is substance, and along with it, what is form and quality. Needless to say there is no agreement about what substance is or what it means. You can do a survey of these views in online encyclopedias freely available on the Web.

But readers of this book are likely to have gathered sufficient spiritual-rational knowledge that is able to understand the reality of substance.

To begin with consider the spiritual idea that God is the only reality and the only substance. This is the departing platform, the base underpinning of everything spiritual. Every spiritual idea contains the idea of God at its center or inmost semantic portion. This is because God's omnipotence applies to every molecule, ant, tree, or planet. Similarly, to every thought, idea, feeling, emotion, or word.

We know from knowledge and experience that our mechanical devices stop running without electricity, battery charge, or other source of power. Nothing runs without God's power continuously being applied to each thing that runs or functions. If God withdraws his power, nothing runs, everything stops dead. No thoughts running around in our mind, no sensations, no feelings, no plans, no relationships, nothing. Everything is powered by God's omniscience and omnipresence.

God's power is substance. Recall that substance is God or God's mind. Substance is the power. Power is the substance. Power cannot be nothing. It must be substance. This substance is called – are you ready? – love.

You can see now why the most fundamental reality is substance, which is God's mind. Nothing exists except substance, and therefore, everything that exists is constructed out of God's mind, which is the only substance.

Love is that substance.

Everything therefore is made of love, whether an atom or planet, or memory or personality. This is astonishing to those of us who have read about eastern philosophy and religious scriptures where Westerners first encounter the idea that the world is made of consciousness, that only consciousness exists all else being an appearance or illusion, that everything that is exists in God's mind, that consciousness is everywhere, that a stone is unreal while an idea is real, and others like these. But now in our rational and theistic science approach we can see that all these facts are true and yet not so complicated to understand as it seems at first.

What makes the difference is that we start rationally from the spiritual idea of substance that is defined as the only stuff that exists. Substance is not created. It has always existed as God's mind. When God created the universe there was nothing but the substance of love and intelligence in God's mind. What then can the universe be created from? It is clear that it had to be created out of substance in God's mind.

Creation is therefore the exteriorization and delimitation of God's eternal and infinite substance of love and intelligence. This substance exits or flows out from God as a living sphere of Himself into the whole universe in which everything is. All this existence and world is therefore nothing but Himself, that is, His love and intelligence, and therefore His consciousness, His omnipresent and omniscience. Hence we can understand rationally how we are in God and God in us, or how everything in the universe is in God, or that only God's mind-substance is real and permanent, while all else is less real and perfect, or that love and consciousness are real while a stone is not.

This idea cannot be comprehended and therefore accepted in natural-rational consciousness. That level of reasoning is being weighted down and limited by time-space-quantity conceptions. Spiritual substance refers to a spiritual-rational idea and cannot be made meaningful in a natural-rational idea, though it can be copied or abstracted from it. It may then sound alike in natural consciousness but grates as opposites in spiritual consciousness. There is not physical time, space, or quantity of matter in spiritual reality. There is no natural time since it is in eternity, and there is no physical space since spiritual reality is mental or spiritual having to do with the mind and its mental operations. Our mind can create any amount of space or quantity of something. We do this from love or desire. It is spontaneous.

Love is known to be experienced as a feeling and as a certain attitude of attraction and care. This shows that love is mental substance. God's love is that substance and power that runs everything. Everything in the two worlds is therefore constructed out of God's love-substance. And the character of love is to desire to make others happy, to will to benefit them in every possible way, and to derive the deepest enjoyment and delight from doing this and seeing the other's happiness from it. This is God's love and therefore all genuine love that human beings experience.

Think about the people you love dearly and whether this description rightly describes your experience.

Swedenborg Writes:

Is there anyone who does not know—or who cannot know—that what is evil comes from hell and what is good comes from heaven? Can anyone, then, fail to see that we abstain from hell and turn away from it to the extent that we abstain and turn away from evil? On this basis, can anyone fail to see that we intend and love what is good to the extent that we abstain and turn away from evil, and that in fact the Lord releases us from hell to that same extent and leads us to heaven?

All rational people can see this provided they know that hell and heaven exist and know where evil and good come from. If, then, we reflect on the evils in ourselves, which is the same as self-examination, and abstain from them, then we extricate ourselves from hell, turn our backs on it, and make our way into heaven where we see the Lord face to face. We may say that we are doing this, but we are doing it in apparent autonomy, and therefore from the Lord. ~Swedenborg, Divine Providence DP 321

---

19. How Love-Substance
Is Our Spiritual Nourishment

This rational theistic approach gives us a rational understanding of how God is omnipresent. God's love-substance is the same as good-substance that is associated with truth-substance or intelligence-substance. Since everything is constructed out of love-substance and its associated truth-substance, God is present in everything and everywhere, inside and outside of physical things and mental thoughts or emotions. Recall that God's substance is living and is God's mind, His love and His truth or wisdom. God creates and runs every object's molecules and every thought or feeling by means of love and truth-substance.

God cannot give away any good and truth-substance because it is infinite and created things are finite. The infinite cannot be divided which is why God is present in every individual fully as Himself. This presence is closest and purest in celestial-rational consciousness, then it descends into spiritual-rational consciousness, and finally exits into natural-rational consciousness where we become aware of it if we pay attention to it or wish to see it.

When the natural-rational personality has been regenerated it is called being in spiritual-rational consciousness. This higher consciousness to be effective must have the natural-consciousness rearranged by regeneration from the love of self only to the love of others as much as the love of self. This is achieved by the individual's daily struggles to practice loving other as much as self. That is possible to the extent that the individual is willing to compel their self to give up and repress all things of their personality and loves that were built up from the love of self only. This self-compulsion is called spiritual combat and it is closely managed by God so as to present appropriate situations and temptations by which the person can practice giving up selfishness that is at the expense of others.

The conclusion is now clear: God is the inside, outside, and around everything because it is made of Him, His mind, his will, his love, his wisdom, his infinite inventiveness, His mutual love, and so on. This is how God is omnipresent, since there is no "place" or thing that is not where God is. Everything is within God since there is nowhere else to be.

Now the second major point to recall is this. God created the universe for the sake of human minds.

Since God cannot be nothing, God is something. That something is substance. This substance is eternal, infinite, living, intelligent, and omniscient. The substance in the inner layer of God's mind is called good or love, and in the outer layer is called truth, rationality, intelligence, or wisdom. Good and truth-substance, or love and wisdom-substance, are distinct but united as one. Good-substance is also called love-substance, while truth-substance is also called intelligence-substance.

God forms the human mind as an image of His Divine Human mind, so that our inner organic layer is called the affective-circulatory system in the spiritual body, which is the will in the mind and is the seat of loves and feelings. This is what makes our life. Hence love or good-substance is anatomically layered in the inmost regions of the spiritual body or mind. Love-substance in God's mind or spiritual body corresponds to the blood and its nourishment in our spiritual body or mind.

The nourishment in the blood of the physical body is material, mineral, and chemical arranged in little organic factories that can break down the complex chemicals and nutrients into particular components that is appropriate for each type of cell function. In our spiritual body the affective system corresponds to the circulatory. The nourishment is mental and composed of spiritual substance arranged in various forms of reception such as experiencing a motive or emotion, intending a plan of action, feeling attracted or repelled to various things, enjoying a delight or pleasure in something, and so on. So the nourishment and blood of the mind is this constant circulation and processing of emotions, motives, enjoyments, thoughts, fantasies, dreams, and so on.

Besides the primary and inmost layer of the affective system, our middle organic layer is called the cognitive-respiratory system in the spiritual body. The cognitive system receives the inflow of intelligence-substance while the affective system receives love-substance. The inflow into these two layers makes them operate synchronously or by simultaneous correspondence so that they act as one.

The result of this joint operation between a feeling and a thought is the operation of our sensorimotor-skeletal system that is relatively on the outside of our mind. This is the anatomical layer that is closest to the environment and is suited for it. Sometimes this is referred to as corporeal-consciousness that is not capable of rational thinking, and hence is discretely below our daily natural-rational consciousness. Without the rational we become corporeal, not unlike any of the animals with which we share some intelligence and emotional disposition. As well, being stuck in corporeal-consciousness turns people into a pack of wolves and predators on each other. Humanity could not survive without the rational.

20. God's Intimacy With Human Beings

Our ability to will and intend from love and desire comes from the inflow of love-substance into our affective system. Our ability to think and reason with rationality and intelligence comes from the inflow of truth-substance into our cognitive system. Our ability to move, sense, and perceive in the external environment comes as a result of the joint action of our will (affective system) and our thinking (cognitive system). In this way you can understand rationally and scientifically how God creates the universe and how God operates on our thinking and willing from birth to everlasting eternity.

You can also see how God must be omnipresent in our mental activity and that we cannot have a single idea or a single sensation without God giving this to us as a gift through the good and truth-substance that flows in every moment of life. All life and existence would instantly stop and disappear if God withdrew or withheld the inflow of His substance into every object, mind, idea, or feeling. This is the celestial nourishment we must have to live. Because this nourishment is spiritual and celestial, it is eternal, and hence our personality or mind is immortal from birth. Further remember that this food we consume is not material but substance. Hence we consume or digest God's substance, which is God. God's consciousness cannot be withdrawn from Himself when we are nourished by His mental substance. Therefore God is inside the formation of every thought or feeling. God is conscious of Himself being in us as love and Intelligence-substance. You can clearly see from this that there are no secrets we can keep from God or hidden emotions of which God is unaware.

Can anything be closer and more intimate to us than God?

I read about a movement among some women to want to make God into a female figure. They apparently resented the despotism of the men over women in religion and public life. Furthermore, they felt that God as Woman would be able to understand women and could be trusted, while a God-Man could not in the same intimate way. However when we begin to think in celestial-rational consciousness we realize that God is present and participating in every woman's thought, feeling, and sensation, as described just above. God is present in our mind not as Man nor as Woman but as living and conscious love-substance and truth-substance out of which our thoughts and feelings are constructed and activated. A woman's thoughts, emotions, and sensations are constructed out of the same substance of God's mind as a man's thoughts, feelings, and sensations. There is no sensation, thought, or emotion without God being at the center of it and at the periphery of it.

There are some men who state that they have experienced a mystical union with God and that it cannot be described in words since it is above language, rationality, and human thinking. But in celestial-rational consciousness we can see that God is rationality itself, truth itself, and intelligence itself. There is no mystical meaning or experience that can be above God's truth and rationality. It is through good-substance and rationality-substance that we come closest to God, and in fact we are one with God through truth-substance and love-substance that flows into our mind and life or will. We are in union with God the more we receive love-substance and truth-substance without the distortion of self-love and its arrogance.

It is called arrogant because it 'arrogates" or appropriates to self what belongs to God. To think that we live from ourselves destroys spiritual reality in the individual's natural mind and thinking. As a result there is no guidance from truth-substance that flows in from our spiritual-rational consciousness as to what is good and what is evil. When we are arrogant we lose the ability to make the distinction, calling good what we love, and evil what we don't want. This mental state is spiritually insane. It prevents all regeneration of character. The individual simply continues on insane psychological pathways, joined by other minds who are also in that mental state. Sadly, the end of the pathway at death is one's eternal immortality that must now be spent in insane animal-like states of mind and emotion.

Union with God is the good and truth-substance that we receive in us genuinely and without resistance, thus with humility and obedience. We receive the inflowing love and truth-substance first in our celestial-rational consciousness. This is an unconscious operation of God on our mind. However, in the afterlife those who have loved others more than self and have acquired such a personality structure, exist consciously in the celestial-rational plane of human consciousness.

While we are still in this life, the reception of love and truth-substance in our celestial-rational system has determinative effects on the lower level spiritual-rational operation and consciousness, although we are not conscious of this. The two levels of our mental anatomy, celestial and spiritual, correspond to each other and act synchronously. The higher celestial level induces or produces a corresponding activity in the spiritual level.

The reception of good and truth-substance now spreads down into the middle level of mental operation. This activity too is unconscious until our afterlife if we lived this life by loving others as much as self, and thereby have developed our personality structure to allow our consciousness to function permanently at the spiritual-rational level. Without this regeneration process in this life, the personality in the afterlife cannot live or survive in heavenly communities in eternity. God therefore provides an alternative to heaven, which is a mental level of operation at the natural-corporeal level. Here everyone who loves themselves more than others can find existence with each other.

Finally as it descends in the anatomy structure, the spiritual-rational operation induces or produces a corresponding operation at the natural-rational level of consciousness and operation. This now we are fully conscious of, if we wish to pay attention to it. Prior to regeneration we totally oppose and repel the attempt of the spiritual-rational to re-arrange the thoughts and intentions so as to correspond with the spiritual-rational. Hence we cannot be guided or led by anything spiritual.

Everything that we are motivated to do and learn is due to natural rewards and punishments. Such a personality cannot begin regeneration. Only by compelling ourselves to rearrange our priorities and philosophies can we begin regeneration. This new order in our mind must correspond to the spiritual-rational order, Then we can go ahead and equip our personality with the altruistic traits that we must have in order to exist in eternity at the spiritual and celestial levels of consciousness.

As a result of this three-step corresponding incorporation of love and truth-substance in our mind, we are able to have thoughts, to reason, to be aware of our thoughts and reasoning, to have emotional reactions, and affections or loves. In other words all of our life is produced by God through good and truth-substance that constantly flows into our spiritual body or mind, giving it all its abilities, thoughts, dreams, fantasies, intelligence, and endless potential for developing to eternity. It is a beautiful, orderly, and perfect anatomical system that ties God's mind to ours in an unbroken and intimate co-participation with every unique individual and immortal life. It is also how the human race is tied together anatomically and grows and functions together. Every human being is tied anatomically to every other human being past and present, and to God.

Jung writes:

Jungian analysis is not simply a mechanical application of technique. It is a unique encounter with the depths of your own being, helping you to become the person you were meant to be. ~ Jason E. Smith, Jungian Psychoanalyst

The Jung Foundation for Analytical Psychology is dedicated to helping people grow in conscious awareness of the psychological realities in themselves & society. New York, NY • cgjungny.org

But if you want to go your individual way, it is the way you make for yourself, which is never prescribed, which you do not know in advance, and which simply comes into being of itself when you put one foot in front of the other. ~Carl Jung, Letters Vol. I, Pages 132-133

---

21. Three Stages of Individuation and Regeneration

Jung writes:

Healing may be called a religious problem. ~Carl Jung, CW 11, Para 523

The soul possesses by nature a religious function. ~Carl Jung, CW 12, Para 14

Be what God means you to be. ~Carl Jung, Jung Speaks, p. 75

"The Resurrection of the Christ within" is perhaps one of the most important and fundamental, and crucial of Jung's assertions; I know it as I experience it likewise. ~Gail Green, 2016

Swedenborg Writes:

Actually, we are bad trees right from our seed, but we are granted a scion or graft from shoots taken from the tree of life, through which the sap rising from our old roots is changed into a sap that brings forth good fruit. I offer this comparison to show that if the process of divine providence is so unfailing in the growth and reproduction of trees, it must by all means be unfailing in our own reformation and regeneration. We are far more important than trees. ~Swedenborg, Divine Providence, DP 332

Keep in mind that the goal of rational theistic self-analysis is to train yourself to think about yourself in a new spiritual way. *To the extent that you adopt this new spiritual thinking in daily life, to that extent you will feel empowered to manage all your psychological issues that are associated with human growth.*

Ordinary daily character weaknesses are responsible factors in bringing people's lives down to a purely natural or animal level of functioning that prevents individuation and humanization, and promotes a downward slide to de-individuation and de-humanization. These negative mental states are maintained by a false representation in one's mind of life, of God, and of our immortality. *Rational theistic self-analysis (RTS) brings a new way of thinking and a deeply needed relief from the tyranny of materialism and selfism that dominate our personality in natural consciousness.*

Jung writes:

But the soul suffers great need, since outer freedom is of no use to it. . ~Carl Jung, Liber Novus, p. 311

Salvation is a long road that leads through many gates. These gates are symbols. ~Carl Jung, Liber Novus, Page 311

If one accepts the symbol, it is as if a door opens leading into a new room whose existence one previously did not know. But if one does not accept the symbol, it is as if one carelessly went past this door; and since this was the only door leading to the inner chambers, one must pass outside into the streets again, exposed to everything external.
~Carl Jung, Liber Novus, p. 311

The symbols used by the unconscious to this end are the same as those which mankind has always used to express wholeness, completeness, and perfection: symbols, as a rule, of the quaternity and the circle. For these reasons I have termed this the individuation process. This natural process of individuation served me both as a model and guiding principle for my method of treatment. ~Carl Jung, CW 7, Para. 187

Individuation means becoming an "individual," and, in so far as "individuality" embraces our innermost, last, and incomparable uniqueness, it also implies becoming one's own self. We could therefore translate individuation as "coming to selfhood" or "self-realization." ~Carl Jung, CW 7, Para 266

The aim of individuation is nothing less than to divest the self of the false wrappings of the persona on the one hand, and of the suggestive power of primordial images on the other. ~Carl Jung, CW 7, Para. 269

Swedenborg Writes:

For a person is born natural, but becomes spiritual through regeneration; and if he does not become spiritual he is in hell. The knowledge which the natural man, that is, a person who has not been regenerated, possesses dwells in the light of the world, whereas the intelligence which the spiritual man, that is, a person who has been regenerated, possesses dwells in the light of heaven. And as long as a person sees things solely in the light of the world he is in hell; but when he sees them at the same time in the light of heaven he is in heaven.
~Swedenborg, Heavenly Secrets, AC 10156

The individual needs to progress through three main stages of individuation as shown in this Table:

STAGES OF INDIVIDUATION	TYPE OF CONSCIOUSNESS	MENTAL ACTIVITY
1	Natural	Loving self more than others
2	Spiritual	Loving others as much as self
3	Celestial	Loving others more than self

People develop, mature, and become adults, all in stage 1 of the individuation process. At some point in adult life they must move on to stage 2 individuation or else they are stuck in stage 1. This means suffering a downward course to the road of de-individuation. Natural consciousness is well suited for our daily activities in this life, allowing us to develop our personality and reasoning, and to acquire social skills and personal management skills. *But after that it leads to a dead end!* Natural consciousness is actually only a stage of development and a new stage must succeed for mental health and further development.

> *Individuation is an expression of that biological process—simple or complicated as the case may be —by which every living thing becomes what it was destined to become from the beginning. ~Carl Jung, CW 11, Para 460*

Now we need to realize that individuation is always to be defined in the context of *collectivity.*

The individual is a member of the collectivity called a community or society, and all members together make up the collectivity. Such as are the members, such is the collectivity. *There is no individual apart from collectivity.*

Individuation is the process of becoming more and more an individual within the collectivity.

A collectivity becomes more and more perfect as its members become more and more individuated.

De-individuation is the opposite psychological process whereby the individual becomes less and less an individual, and more and more a role of uniformity.

Individuality requires distinctiveness in all its parts and throughout its various levels of activity or functioning. Inhibiting or repressing distinctiveness in an individual reduces mental health and promotes de-individuation to the detriment of the individual and the collectivity.

A collectivity grows in functioning and perfection as the individuals become more and more individuated. De-individuation consists of being more and more conventional and uniform. A dictatorial and hostile collectivity is formed of individuals who are increasingly de-individuated. Democratic groups are collectivities formed by individuals who are individuating more and more. Undemocratic and tyrannical collectivities put pressure on the individual to become artificial and uniform.

Growing towards greater individuation involves introducing spiritual consciousness into natural consciousness so that the two levels function in synchrony and correspondence. This is accomplished by adopting the principle of loving others as much as self in everyday activities, interactions, and thinking. Such a change raises consciousness from natural thinking to spiritual thinking, which is a precursor to celestial thinking and functioning.

Psychologically there is an inward resistance to moving from stage 1 individuation to stage 2 individuation. Practicing RTS helps you to switch focus and orientation from self to others. People may resolve to be more considerate and less self-centered, but they are unable to stick to the resolution. People make many kinds of resolutions to improve their lifestyle habits and personal productivity. These attempts typically fail and precipitate the individual into still lower states of awareness and functioning. In other words, *where there is no individuation, there is de-individuation.*

The concept of "de-individuation" is well known in social psychology where it is usually defined as the "loss of self-awareness in groups". Examples include the idea of "blind obedience" to authority without consulting one's morality and conscience, and the loss of personal responsibility and identity when being part of a crowd or creed. A society whose population is de-individuating is marked by political intolerance and severe punishment for those who defy the official policies or attitudes.

Mental functioning in stage 1 individuation is such that it is vulnerable to sliding backward into a state of de-individuation. Dominant individuals and "strong" leaders become attractive forces that pull people into the path of de-individuation. Conformity and conventionality acquire dominance in this mental state. There is an attraction and involvement with being part of a crowd, like a concert or sports event. Picnics and parties tend to be loud involving the orientation of "having a good time". Enthusiasm for entertainment idols and celebrities are seen as normal and desirable. Online social networking and face-to-face partying are general practices that sometimes encourage uniformity and conventionality.

Of course everyone is familiar with the picture that I am drawing. Everybody participates in this picture. I am pointing to a connection I see between these familiar daily activities and the notion of *the ego remaining immersed in natural consciousness*. These activities become of little interest to us when we raise our consciousness to the spiritual-rational level, which is stage 2 individuation.

People in stage 1 individuation can make further progress in individuation by adopting spiritual-rational views, a commitment to democratic leadership, and an attitude of watchful respect for the rights of others. This will convert their mental functioning to stage 2 individuation.

Stage 2 individuation is at first driven by the logic of morality and equity. It involves the perception that without respect for one another the community or group cannot survive. Hence it is logical for our survival to respect one another. In this state of thinking, criminality is condemned as a threat to society and its people. Laws are enacted and supported that protect individual rights and freedom, including due process under the law for everyone.

Many common psychopathologies that plague people in stage 1 individuation cease altogether in stage 2 individuation.

The purpose of theistic self-analysis is to liberate the individual from the heavy burden of everyday weaknesses and emotional plagues. When we are immersed in natural consciousness we are completely at the mercy of psychological forces that are active within the human mind of which we are completely unconscious. We can learn about these psychic forces as we become educated in literature and science. But after becoming aware of their existence we forget about them in our daily activities. That knowledge is basically useless unless we learn to apply it to our thinking patterns in daily life.

Entering the level of mental functioning in stage 2 individuation can come only one way. *We must learn to love others as much as we love our own ego.* In stage 2 individuation we actively train ourselves to learn to love others as much as we love our ego. This involves practicing being considerate of others in all our daily interactions and activities. For example, we can no longer party and entertain unrestrictively as before because this creates disturbing noise to our neighbors. We can no longer barbeque in the backyard unrestrictively because we found out that our next-door neighbor is asthmatic and suffers greatly from environmental smoke.

Similarly, we can no longer cheat or lie to gain an unfair advantage over others. We must also endeavor to give up resentment, anger, revenge, violence, and insults. Furthermore, we can no longer continue to approve of being overweight and to practice a harmful diet and lifestyle. As well, we now feel obligated to be an authentic employee who thinks about the good of the employer and customers, rather than what we prefer and feel comfortable doing. We even start examining and regulating our involvement with music, lyrics, jokes, and entertainment to give up and eliminate what is prejudiced, salacious, cruel, and belonging to what is known as the "low life".

In stage 1 we allow ourselves to get angry with others because we love ourselves more than them. We allow ourselves to compete unfairly and even cheat, as long as it gives us victory. We allow ourselves to take advantage of others and to gleefully participate in damaging gossip. At the same time we are blind to our prejudices and to our irrational assumptions, and we are weak by giving in to impulse and "fun". These patterns of competition and conflict brought us the daily plagues of prejudice, dissatisfaction, resentment, hatred, depression, and all kinds of neuroses that are endlessly varied and recurrent. *Our life in natural consciousness is a foretaste of hell.*

In stage 2 individuation we gain much more power and efficacy in managing ourselves positively and effectively. By switching from loving our ego exclusively to loving others as much as our ego, we open up the spigot of will power that is organically or genetically built into every unique individual mind. Failure of self-change or of self occurs when we don't have access to this built-in anatomical spigot. Theistic self-analysis teaches the individual where to find this spigot of will power. Once it is found, the individual can perform what seems like miracles to the former self.

Individuals are led into this psychological power by teaching themselves how to love others as much as one loves oneself. Giving yourself daily homework exercises as practicing activities can facilitate the acquisition of this indispensable skill of love. As you practice being considerate in your behavior and being respectful in your thinking, there gradually takes place a healing and elevation of your mental environment. You now enter into stage 2 individuation and become immersed in it. Everything changes. You now see everything in a new light. You come to wonder why you were so angry or resentful or defensive until now.

In biology growth never ceases. If it does, the organism dies. Constant growth must take place for healthy development. The human personality is built to never stop developing and changing from birth to death to the afterlife in eternity. Settling into stage 2 individuation has a built-in limit. It is only there as a transition stage to stage 3 individuation. Indefinite growth of the human mind without resistance factors can take place in stage 3 consciousness and functioning. Stage 3 is such that no higher stage exists anatomically or is necessary for the human mind. Stage 3 is therefore basically distinct and different from stages 1 and 2, which may be considered transitional and temporary.

If either stage 1 or stage 2 becomes permanent, de-individuation takes over and consequent devolution and dehumanization.

Stage 3 is called celestial consciousness because we enter it fully only after resuscitation when we continue our personality development in the afterlife. In that ultimate human state the lower forms of consciousness in stages 1 and 2 are rendered inactive. We now find ourselves with the capacity to love others *more than ourselves*. Our happiness is now defined by what happens to others. Not only are we considerate in behavior and respectful in our thinking, but our very pleasure and happiness daily depend on our ability and the opportunity to make others happy with our effort, skills, and talents. We would gladly give away what we possess if someone wants it or asks us for it.

We are granted the experience of celestial consciousness when we become parents and spontaneously love our children more than ourselves, ready to sacrifice our comfort and safety for the sake of them. But this feeling does not generalize to our relationship with others, and it only lasts temporarily while our children are small, need our protection, and remain obedient to us. Many animal species are granted by God a semblance of celestial consciousness as the parents ceaselessly look after their offspring and provide for them at the expense of themselves. Without this gift the species would die out.

Spiritual consciousness of loving others more than self creates heaven in eternity. Heavenly societies or collectivities in the afterlife are perfect in form and wholeness. This form is such that every member of a particular heavenly society is a center to everyone else. Further, every happy emotion, every inventive thought and perception of an individual, is communicated instantly to everyone one else in that collectivity. The perfection of that collectivity comes from the fact that each wants to make all others happy. As a result, every individual is enriched by every other individual in an endless aggregation and accumulation of thoughts, perceptions, and feelings. Each individual contributes most when being distinct and different from all other individuals. Hence the individuation of every individual continues endlessly in a heavenly society.

Jung writes:

> The symptomatology of an illness is at the same time a natural attempt at healing. ~Carl Jung, CW 8, Para 312

> My thesis, then, is as follows: In addition to our immediate consciousness, which is of a thoroughly personal nature and which we believe to be the only empirical psyche (even if we tack on the personal unconscious as an appendix), there exists a second psychic system of a collective, universal, and impersonal nature which is identical in all individuals. ~Carl Jung, The Archetypes and the Collective Unconscious, 1936, p. 43

---

22. The Gates of Consciousness

If you always do the next thing that needs to be done, you will go most
safely and sure-footedly along the path prescribed by your unconscious.
~Carl Jung, Letters Vol. I, Pages 132-133

There is constant psychic traffic going on at the organ or membrane that separates the conscious and unconscious layers of the organic mind. This psychic traffic exchange goes on at each of the three anatomical levels of mental and personality functioning. During states of individuation and regeneration traffic goes from the unconscious to the conscious. In states of de-individuation traffic is reversed and goes from the conscious to the unconscious. Selfhood is lost during de-individuation and gained during individuation.

The lost pieces of the self during early childhood include the experiencing of positive mental states of innocence that God protects from being contaminated by ego, and stores them away within the inmost layers of our unconscious personality for later use in regeneration during adulthood. These hidden unconscious positive mental states are called "*remains*". These include states of innocence and love that we experience in infancy such as gratitude and love towards parents, teachers, and friends; also, innocent feelings of pity for the poor, the needy, or the unlucky, as well as endless curiosity and the delight of exploring and learning.

Swedenborg Writes:
These states together with the goods and truths impressed on the memory,
are called remains, which are preserved in man by the Lord and are stored
up, entirely without his knowledge, in his internal man, and are completely
separated from the things that are proper to man, that is, from evils and
falsities. All these states are so preserved in man by the Lord that not the
least of them is lost, as I have been given to know from the fact that every
state of a man, from his infancy to extreme old age, not only remains in the
other life, but also returns; in fact his states return exactly as they were
while he lived in this world. Not only do the goods and truths of memory

thus remain and return, but also all states of innocence and charity. And when states of evil and falsity recur-for each and all of these, even the smallest, also remain and return-then these states are tempered by the Lord by means of the good states. From all this it is evident that if a man had no remains he must necessarily be in eternal damnation.
~Swedenborg, Arcana Coelestia, AC 561

We can see from this description of "remains" that God plays a critical and extensive role in what is transferred from the conscious to the unconscious and the reverse pattern during every moment of the individual's life and regeneration.

Regeneration begins in young adulthood and would not be possible without the assistance of remains that God causes to travel back from the unconscious to the conscious when we experience spiritual attacks and are engaged in spiritual battles against our shadow. These psychic battles are different in the three consciousness layers of our mental anatomy. Hence there are particular remains that God summons from our unconscious in order to come to our rescue during the spiritual temptations and battles of regeneration.

Without these remains with which to fight spiritual temptations we would yield to them. This results in a further tightening of our attachment to the hell states in our mind. Clearly then, without these remains we would inevitably slide into de-individuation and the hells.

There are those who contaminate and foolishly destroy their own remains by deliberately and systematically weakening their conscience through doing whatever they want and feel like, and disregarding all the dictates of their conscience. By preserving our remains from contamination by our ego God saves us from eternal hell. This is only to the extent that we are willing to cooperate.

It is important to understand how God is active in our mind.

Knowing about *remains* and thinking about oneself with the concept of remains brings the person closer to God. Is it possible to be more intimate with a person than we are with God who works our unconscious thoughts, anatomically transposing them from the conscious to the unconscious, and then years later during regeneration, transposes them back into the conscious, one by one so that we may use the power of that affection we once had as a child to now battle our spiritual problems as an adult. God is a participant in our anatomy! God is a part of our anatomy.

The more we know God *rationally* the more we understand the methods by which God brings out every detail of what happens outside around us and inside within our mind. The more we understand this the more we can respond affectively with gratitude and appreciation for God's amazing involvement with the nitty-gritty details of our mind and our feelings.

As we perceive the ubiquitous co-presence of God in every detail of our mental functioning and personal history, we come to a better realization of how intimately and anatomically we are involved with God. The more we realize this in detail, the closer we grow to God and the more we can reciprocate. And the more we can reciprocate, the more we are able to receive talents and happiness from God who is the only source for these positive human states of mind.

Reciprocation with God is the very process of regeneration and individuation.

> What does God want? To act or not to act? I must find out what God wants with me, and I must find out right away." ~Carl Jung, Memories, Dreams, Reflections, p. 38

> Healing may be called a religious problem. ~Carl Jung, CW 11, para. 523

In order to establish self-confidence and balance we need to learn not only that we are immortal, but that we continue to evolve in the other life towards ever more health and happiness:

Swedenborg Writes:
> They who are in mutual love in heaven are continually advancing to the springtime of their youth, and to a more and more gladsome and happy spring the more thousands of years they live, and this with continual increase to eternity, according to the advance and degree of mutual love, charity, and faith.

Those of the female sex who have died in old age and enfeebled with years, and who have lived in faith in the Lord, in charity toward the neighbor, and in happy conjugial love with their husbands, after a succession of years come more and more into the bloom of youth and early womanhood, and into a beauty that surpasses all idea of beauty such as is ever perceptible to the natural sight; for it is goodness and charity forming and presenting their own likeness, and causing the delight and beauty of charity to shine forth from every least feature of the countenance, so that they are the very forms of charity: some have beheld them and been amazed.

The form of charity, as is seen to the life in the other world, is such that it is charity itself that portrays and is portrayed, and this in such a manner that the whole angel, and especially the face, is as it were charity, the charity both plainly appearing to the view and being perceived by the mind. When this form is beheld, it is unutterable beauty that affects with charity the very inmost life of the beholder's mind. Through the beauty of this form the truths of faith are presented to view in an image, and are even perceived from it. Such forms, or such beauties, do those become in the other life who have lived in faith in the Lord, that is, in the faith of charity. All the angels are such forms, with countless variety, and of such is heaven. ~Swedenborg, Arcana Coelestia, AC 553

When the consciousness of people in the afterlife evolves into its higher phase called "celestial" they are called "angels". In lower levels of consciousness they are called "spirits". This transformation from spiritual consciousness to angelic is proportional to the individual's *"mutual love, charity, and faith"*. Swedenborg uses the expression "faith" to refer to people's rational theistic attitude and comprehension of their personal relationship with God. Today people are usually taught by conventional religious doctrine to think of faith as "blind faith", not "rational faith", seeing the latter as a contradiction. Hence it is important to retrain the thinking that goes with faith.

Swedenborg Writes:

The angelic state is such that everyone communicates his own bliss and happiness to others. For in the other life there is a most exquisite communication and perception of all the affections and thoughts, so that each person communicates his joy to all, and all to each, so that each one is as it were the center of all. This is the heavenly form. And therefore the more there are who constitute the Lord's kingdom, the greater is the happiness, for it increases in proportion to the numbers, and this is why heavenly happiness is unutterable. There is this communication of all with each and of each with all when everyone loves others more than himself. But if anyone wishes better for himself than for others the love of self reigns, which communicates nothing to others from itself except the idea of self, which is very foul, and when this is perceived the person is at once banished and rejected. ~Swedenborg, Arcana Coelestia, AC 549

Hollis writes:
> *Individuation is not egotism, rather its opposite. It is the sacrifice of the Ego.*
> *~James Hollis, Lecture on Marie Louise von Franz's Archetypal Dimensions*
> *of the Psyche*

23. Reciprocation to God
in Natural Consciousness or
Individuation Stage 1

Jung writes:
> *God is the mystery of all mysteries, a real Tromendum. Good*
> *and Evil are psychological relativities. And as such quite real,*
> *yet one does not know what they are. ~Carl Jung, Letters*
> *Vol. I, Pages 539-541*
>
> *A physical fact never proves the existence and reality of the*
> *spirit. .. Only physical phenomena .. happen in a distinct*
> *place at a distinct time, whereas the spirit is eternal and*
> *everywhere. ~Carl Jung, Letters Vol. I, p. 566-8*

God is necessarily active in every individual's mind in order to insure that all the essential processes go on. This Divine activity is totally unconscious to the individual, just like the heart keeps beating and the cells throughout the body exchange oxygen, all going on without our awareness. Our mental functions also require this constant organic activity that cannot go on "by itself" but must be managed and moved by God moment by moment.

But in addition to God's essential activity in these unconscious procedures there is also the provision for God's activity in our mind of which we can be conscious. This is the human reciprocation God is seeking from every individual, and the more the individual cooperates in this area of interaction, the more progress in individuation is achieved. God's motive for this interaction is pure love. *Love is such as to desire to make others happy from oneself.* This is God's highest longing: to have a conscious love relationship with every human being that God creates and supervises from birth to eternity.

So our task is to cooperate with God so that we may reciprocate that love. This cooperation is necessary for us to receive the goods that God has for us and with which God wants to benefit us. These goods are very familiar to all of us: happiness, wisdom, inventiveness, vitality, compassion, the capacity to love others as much or more than self, and an endless number and variety of capacities, talents, and satisfactions.

That is why God gives human beings commandments of life to obey and follow. We can receive God's gifts by compelling ourselves as if from self, but knowingly with God's reciprocal assistance, to live and think in compliance with God's commandments. Doing this is called regeneration that gradually produces a new character and personality structure seemingly of our own forming, though knowing it is actually God's forming. If we forget that it is God's forming and come to believe that it is our own forming, then we lose everything that is good in us from God.

When we fail to reciprocate God's desire for a relationship with us then God's love cannot be consummated in us and we remain incomplete human beings. We know this from our own relationships with each other. When we love an individual we desire to benefit that person by sharing and giving everything we own: our talents, skills, and possessions. This is how we love a spouse and our children, family, and compatriots. But our love cannot be fulfilled when the other person fails to reciprocate our love. We cannot benefit that person fully through our love. We must wait until the person is ready and willing to reciprocate. So it is also with God and God's desire to benefit us through reciprocation of love.

Now we also need to understand that reciprocation to God is done differently at each of the three stages of regeneration or individuation.

Reciprocation to God when we are in *natural consciousness* is restricted and limited to outside conceptions of God. Our motivation and ability to reciprocate to God takes the form of group based worship rituals, prayers, recitations of creeds, sermons, study in classes of doctrine from *Sacred Scripture*, and socializings or fellowships. These are all social activities that require mutual conformity in *external* behavior and speech. But there is an absence of perception of God as being *within* the mind. And yet that perception and acknowledgement is essential for regeneration and "salvation", that is, for a happy life in eternity.

All people must undergo regeneration and individuation in order to attain self-realization, balance, peace, and love of others and of God.

Every human mind is born with the idea of God and the ability to initiate a reciprocal relationship with God. No one needs to learn this. It is innate. This idea of God is implanted in the very anatomy of the human mind. No other idea can compete with this idea in importance and power. However, it is yet possible to cover up the idea of God in oneself by wrapping around it all sorts of natural concepts and ways of reasoning and drawing conclusions that apply to the natural world but not to God.

This can be done with such airtight falsifications that nothing of God is left in the conscious natural mind. It is emptied of anything that it is in a separate psychic realm.

So now if one learns about God through family and culture one comprehends it externally, naturally. There is nothing spiritual in that acknowledgment. The spiritual would require the reasoning that God is within our mind, that God is omnipotent, and therefore God determines what happens in our mind. Further, the spiritual would require us to reason that in order to regenerate our character and personality structure we need to expend the effort as-of self and not wait for God to do it for us.

It is through the as-of self effort that God empowers the new personality structure.

God cannot regenerate us by force since doing that would result in our turning into human robots activated by God! If God were forcibly to remove our evil selfish loves we would be left with nothing, with no life to continue. We could not be regenerated that way. We would remain an incomplete human being and an egotistical devil to eternity. Hence we all need to rationally understand that we must change on a purely voluntary basis. *We must compel ourselves. That is true inner freedom.* But this process takes three distinct stages to achieve.

Jung writes:

> *There is no morality, no moral decision, without freedom. There is only morality when you can choose, and you cannot chose if you are forced.*
> *~Carl Jung, Zarathustra Seminar, p. 262*

> In my experience of almost forty years I have seen quite a number of cases who developed either a psychotic interval or a lasting psychosis out of a neurotic condition. Let us assume for the moment that they were really suffering from a latent psychosis, concealed under the cloak of a neurosis.

> What, then, is a latent psychosis exactly? It is obviously nothing but the possibility that an individual may become mentally deranged at some period of his life.

> The existence of strange unconscious material proves nothing. You find the same material in neurotics, modern artists, and poets, and also in fairly normal people who have submitted to a careful investigation of their dreams. Moreover, you find most suggestive parallels in the mythology and symbolism of all races and times.

> The possibility of a future psychosis has nothing to do with the peculiar contents of the unconscious. But it has everything to do with whether the individual can stand a certain panic, or the chronic strain of a psyche at war with itself. Very often it is simply a matter of a little bit too much, of the drop that falls into a vessel already full, or of the spark that accidentally lands on a heap of gunpowder. ~Carl Jung, CW 3, Para 520

Swedenborg writes:

Everyone is regenerated by means of truths and through living by them. It is truths that enable us to know what life is, and life that enables us to practice truths. This is how goodness and truth are united in the spiritual marriage where we find heaven. ~Swedenborg, Divine Providence, DP 83

From the earliest infancy and childhood the natural receives its quality from the things which flow in from the world through the external senses, and by and from these the man acquires an intellectual. But as he is then in the delights of the love of self and of the world, and consequently in cupidities, both from inheritance and from actual life, the intellectual which he then acquires is filled with such things, and whatever favors his delights he then regards as goods and truths, and the result is that the order of the goods and truths in the natural is inverted, or is opposite to heavenly order.

When the man is in this state, the light of heaven does indeed flow in through the rational, for it is from this that he has the ability to think, to reason, to speak, and to act becomingly and as a good citizen in the outward form; but still the things which are of light, and that conduce to his eternal happiness, are not in the natural, because the delights which rule there are repugnant to them, for the delights of the love of self and of the world are in themselves diametrically opposite to the delights of the love of the neighbor, and consequently to those of love to the Lord.

The man may indeed know the things of light or of heaven, but he cannot be affected with them, except insofar as they conduce to his winning honors and gaining wealth, and thus except insofar as they favor the delights of the love of self and of the world.

From this it may appear that the order in the natural is wholly inverted, or opposite to heavenly order, and therefore when the light of heaven flows in through the rational into the natural, it must needs be either reflected back, or suffocated, or perverted. Hence then it is that the natural must be regenerated before it can be conjoined with the rational. For when the natural has been regenerated, the things which flow in from the Lord through heaven, thus through the rational into the natural, are received, because they agree.

For the natural is nothing else than a receptacle of good and truth from the rational, or through the rational from the Lord. By the natural is meant the external man, which is also called the natural man, and by the rational is meant the internal man. These things have been premised in order that it may be known how the case is with what follows, in which the subject treated of is the conjunction of the natural with the rational. ~Swedenborg, Heavenly Secrets, AC 4612

In other words, in natural consciousness or stage 1 individuation, God is but an abstract external concept, not real and immediate in experience. As a result, some people talk themselves out of the existence of God. This denial is the trigger point for arresting one's rational development and beginning the slide downwards into the shadows of de-individuation.

Patients who have gotten lost in their thinking about God need assistance in getting back to rational theistic thinking. *The first recovery step is to see that there is a spiritual reality and that mental health is to have a mind that corresponds to that reality.*

The first step is therefore to acknowledge that God is that reality, and to understand that when we deny God we put ourselves out of step with reality. Natural consciousness is therefore a dangerous mental state in which one is vulnerable on all sides to the attacks of the shadow in our unconscious. The symptoms of this unhealthy mind interfere with human functioning and potential, and are known from the study of psychopathologies, neuroses, and character faults.

It's important to understand the similarity in mental dysfunction for those who deny God altogether, and those who do not deny God but keep God outside the mind. *In either case there is zero reciprocation to God's co-presence in the mind.* Yet this is the necessary condition for achieving mental health and self-realization through individuation and regeneration.

A critically important activity of God in our mind that is totally unconscious to our awareness or perception involves the activation of innocent affections and loves during our personality development in our infancy and childhood. These are called mental states of "innocence" because they are not yet covered over with falsifications spun by the ego. God saves those genuine mental states in the upper layer of consciousness called celestial consciousness or individuation stage 3. These are called *"remains"* as just discussed. More about remains will be said below.

Sometime in adult life, either early or later, we are ready to undergo regeneration of character based on a reciprocal personal relationship with God. At this point we are still in natural consciousness or still very early in spiritual consciousness. We are guided by our serious and respectful study of *Sacred Scripture* where we are told about the commandments that God wants us to obey and follow in daily living and thinking. *Sacred Scripture* is God's "Word" and is how God talks to us. At first in natural-historical terms, but later in spiritual-rational ideas.

Since we are still mostly in natural consciousness, our ideas of God's commandments are still externalized and bound to the physical world. We then experience commandments as restrictive. They forbid just about everything we do and love to do, almost anything we want and identify with, and most of our pleasures and involvements. This is a difficult spot to be in for someone who aspires to a closer relationship to God. It feels like being in a double bind: if I obey God's commandments I lose what I consider worthwhile in my life; if I break the commandments, I am severely punished. This doesn't sound like a good deal! That's the experiencing of regeneration that we have in natural consciousness.

Jung writes:
> The participation mystique by which society contains the individual may be understood as a statement of the fact that individuals are still undifferentiated from each other, that is to say, they have not yet been self-consciously broken up into individual personalities. ~Carl Jung, C.G. Jung Speaking; Interviews and Encounters, p. 205-218

It may seem like character reformation and greater individuation become hopeless abstract goals, hardly attainable by anyone. This is the great danger point, the point of no return. There is a battle going on in the mind between the armies of good called angels and the armies of evil called devils. *Our mind is the battleground.* The angels communicate with the celestial layer of our mind and seek to find remains placed there by God during our states of innocence before the ego took over. The devils are in the natural layer of our mind and seek to find inherited traits of selfism that they can trigger. The battle for our eternity is now on. It is called being in a state of spiritual temptation.

Without spiritual temptations and mental combat, regeneration cannot proceed and individuation is arrested. Without remains in the celestial mind, angels cannot defend us against the activity of the evil psychic forces that attach themselves to our natural mind. To lose in spiritual combat is to become more and more enslaved by our natural emotions and the falsifications of reality that the ego then spins to blind our true awareness. *There is no comeback after that because the individual then refuses and resists.*

This is why God ceaselessly works in our mind to prevent that personal calamity from happening. God does not allow spiritual temptations to those who have willfully destroyed their remains and have nothing to fight with. When people are allowed to give in to spiritual temptations they strengthen their attachment to their evil loves. For them salvation is not possible until they are willing to voluntarily turn and chase their shadow through spiritual temptations. This absolute unwillingness to resist and reject our selfism may persist to eternity! Hence it is that there are eternal hells, not because God punishes and imprisons, but because the individual refuses. Such is the insanity that comes from de-individuation.

Nor does God bring people into states of spiritual temptation when they are sill immersed in natural consciousness. In that lowest of states of consciousness only natural temptations are allowed to occur. This is necessary to strengthen our social and moral conscience. God brings to every person natural events and happenings that test the person's probity, honesty, consistency, and compassion. When we have an opportunity to steal something or to cheat without the danger of being caught, we are experiencing a natural temptation of conscience. If we resist because of our conscience, we strengthen our character and prepare it more and more for activating our spiritual consciousness. When that happens, we are ready to experience spiritual temptations.

Jung writes:

> *Projection means the expulsion of a subjective content into an object; it is the opposite of introjection. Accordingly, it is a process of dissimilation, by which a subjective content becomes alienated from the subject and is, so to speak, embodied in the object. The subject gets rid of painful, incompatible contents by projecting them. ~Carl Jung, Collected Works 6, para. 783*

> *And if you lose yourself in the crowd, in the whole of humanity, you also never arrive at yourself; just as you can get lost in your isolation, you can also get lost in utter abandonment to the crowd. ~Carl Jung, Zarathustra Seminar, p. 1020*

Swedenborg Writes:

> *For a person is born natural, but becomes spiritual through regeneration; and if he does not become spiritual he is in hell. The knowledge which the natural man, that is, a person who has not been regenerated, possesses dwells in the light of the world, whereas the intelligence which the spiritual man, that is, a person who has been regenerated, possesses dwells in the light of heaven. And as long as a person sees things solely in the light of the world he is in hell; but when he sees them at the same time in the light of heaven he is in heaven. ~Swedenborg, Heavenly Secrets, AC 10156*

> *If we abstain from one sin or another that we have discovered in ourselves, this is enough to make our repentance real. When we reach this point, we are on the pathway to heaven, because we then begin to turn from an earthly person into a spiritual person and to be born anew with the help of the Lord. ~Swedenborg, True Christianity TCR 530*

---

24. Reciprocation to God in Spiritual Consciousness or Individuation Stage 2

Swedenborg Writes:

The rational has no life unless the natural corresponds to it. It is the same as with the sight of the eye-unless this has objects outside of itself which it sees, it perishes; and it is the same with the other senses. The case is also the same if the objects are altogether contrary, for these induce death; and it is the same as with the vein of a spring whose waters have no outflow, causing the spring to be choked.

And it is the same also with the rational-unless there is reception of its light in the natural, its sight perishes, for the knowledges in the natural are the objects of sight to the rational; and if these objects are contrary to the light, that is, to the intelligence of truth and the wisdom of good, the sight of the rational also perishes, for it cannot flow into things contrary to itself.

Hence it is that with those who are in evils and falsities the rational is closed, so that no communication with heaven is open through it except only as it were through chinks, in order that there may be the capacity of thinking, of reasoning, and of speaking.

Consequently, in order that the natural may be conjoined with the rational, it must be prepared for the reception of it, which is effected by the Lord by means of regeneration; and then, when it is conjoined, the rational lives in the natural; for as before said the rational sees its objects in the natural, just as does the sight of the eye in the objects of the world. ~Swedenborg, Heavenly Secrets, AC 4618

We can see from this that spiritual consciousness is always active and functioning unconsciously in our mind. It is part of the anatomy of the mental body that we are born with in the spiritual world of eternity. That is why it is also called the spiritual body, or spirit body, and even psychic body and immortal body.

Since nothing spiritual, mental, or substantial can exist in the physical world or form, the mind and our consciousness must have a substantial, spiritual, or mental body.

This is why I made up the term "*mental anatomy*" several years ago when I was trying to find an alternative to the standard view in psychology and neuroscience that the mind is nothing except the pattern of electrochemical "firings" (activity) of the billions of protein cells that make up the brain of our physical avatar (body). The expression *mental anatomy* affirms in our thoughts that our consciousness, thoughts, and feelings are not "nothing but physical information pattern", but real substantive organic fibers and cells – with the sole difference that these fibers and cells in our mental anatomy are not physical or material, but substantive, spiritual, mental.

You may wonder at the idea of your thoughts and feelings being organic objects formed out of mental substance derived from the Spiritual Sun or God's creation point.

Spiritual-rational knowledge and thinking, as exemplified in this book, gives us the clear understanding that since nothing existed before God created the universe, it must logically follow that the universe was created out of God's substance, which in this book we referred to as "love-substance with its truth-substance". Through the emissions of the Spiritual Sun, the first spot of creation, God's love and truth expanded and filled the universe, filling it with His Own mental substance in infinite variety. This then is the inmost frame of any object that exists.

Our consciousness is an activity of our spiritual body born at our birth and formed anatomically and biochemically from the mental substance available in the mental environment that is the composite inner structure of all creation. This spiritual-rational reasoning repairs the detrimental spiritual effects of the standard idea with which we have been educated, that our feelings, thoughts and imagination are not really "really" real, but just a temporary "epiphenomenon" or "emergent phenomenon" that is sourced in the electro-chemical activity of the physical brain. This materialistic one-sided view of the universe and of God is spiritually harmful to the individual.

But when people *are willing* to elevate their consciousness and reasoning to spiritual-rational consciousness, they can see that it is denying reality when denying the creation of two worlds, denying our immortality, and denying the afterlife of eternity. These spiritual denials immerse natural consciousness in un-reality, or spiritual insanity. The idea of our "mental anatomy" disperses the illogical idea that our mind and its mental activity is either physical or emergent from the physical, and therefore only temporal, not permanent.

In spiritual-rational consciousness we think with the idea of the organic mind as an actual body or spiritual body. We think of the physical body as a copy of the spiritual body and constructed out of physical matter. We are thus born into eternity with our immortal spiritual body and simultaneously with a temporary physical body or avatar that is obedient to our mind. Our mind is functionally operating in natural consciousness that restricts our thinking to what we can experience, measure, or move with our avatar. At death, the three-day dying-resuscitation procedure involves the anatomical process of separation and extraction of our consciousness that we had through the avatar.

Upon the completion of the separation process we are instantly operating in spiritual consciousness that is proper for the mental world of eternity. This is where our spiritual body was born, has grown to an adult mind and personality, and is well suited to function in a mental and substantive world. We thus resume our normal social and intimate relationships with those we encounter in the world of the afterlife. In general, we tend to meet people who are compatible to us in thinking and emotions. Many details on the life we experience in the afterlife may be found in Swedenborg's eyewitness reports in his book titled *Heaven and Hell* (available on the Web).

Functioning in natural consciousness is our day-to-day awareness while we are still tied to our avatar. Viewed anatomically, functioning in natural consciousness would be impossible without the concurrent unconscious functioning of our spiritual consciousness. This higher management activity of consciousness is constantly going on anatomically. It influences the syntax of logic and its coherence that is characteristic of our natural consciousness. It is our unconscious spiritual-rational consciousness that influences the direction of coherence in our thoughts and our intelligent abilities. The two layers of consciousness are in perfect synchrony through the laws of correspondences that binds together the natural and spiritual worlds.

Our mental activity influences the activity of our physical body or avatar. The affective system of our spiritual body is governed by the mental organ that we call *the will*. We wish to scratch our head and the avatar obeys. We love to talk to a friend and our avatar executes a phone call. We dictate to the avatar what keys on the keyboard to touch in what sequence so that we can text a message to someone. The avatar does nothing by itself. It is an inert biochemical computer and robot.

In natural consciousness we tend to abuse our avatar by injecting it with chemical poisons and bacterial harm, and foolishly exposing it to risks and dangers that injure the avatar and impair its functioning. When our physical avatar is injured it loses correspondence and synchrony with the mental body. Our natural consciousness is thereby impaired in development and rationality. The reason we injure our avatar is of course mental and spiritual. It is a function of the quality of our consciousness. This mental state receives its quality from the hierarchy of our loves that are established in our affective system.

Everyone is born with genetic and affective pre-dispositions or tendencies to allow the love of self to mount to the top of the hierarchy in our loves. The exclusive love of self above all things becomes the "ruling love" or chief motivational influence in our daily personality. This predominance influences everything in our personality habits and personality structure. As we grow into adulthood our spiritual consciousness becomes active in our awareness. We then engage in the effort of regeneration that involves the reordering of our loves, the dethroning of self-love at the head of the affective hierarchy, and the enshrining of mutual love at the top of the love hierarchy.

Regeneration makes it possible for us to have new loves, new thoughts, and a new higher human rationality.

25. Spiritual and Natural Thinking

Take for instance the idea of heaven and hell. Everyone knows what these two are and, according to many polls, the vast majority of people believe in the existence of both. This idea could not exist in our natural consciousness were it not the case that our unconscious spiritual consciousness also contains this idea but at a spiritual level rather than natural. The natural idea of heaven and hell corresponds to the spiritual idea but is distinctly different. According to the natural idea, heaven and hell are places somewhere where people end up after dying either as a reward for living according to the commandments of God, or a punishment for living contrary to those laws.

And so, it is believed, that there will come a point in time when this corrupted world would be destroyed by God and rebuilt into a pristine one. At that time the dead of all time would awaken and each would be given the physical body back, intact and healthy. Either heaven or hell will then constitute the lot of all. This natural consciousness view of heaven and hell is confirmed in many people's minds because it so written in the Bible and is taught in religions.

Still, we need to be aware that the words and verses of *Sacred Scripture* can be read either in natural consciousness by itself, or in natural consciousness that is in correspondence with the unconscious spiritual consciousness. When some of the verses are read solely in natural consciousness the only meaning we get is natural and historical. All events are interpreted as referring to this world. And in that case we get the idea from the literal historical version that the "resurrection of the dead" will be sometimes in the future and will take place in the reborn and renewed physical world.

But we can also read these verses in a natural consciousness that is open to influence from the spiritual consciousness. We then apply these verses to the spiritual world of the afterlife rather than to the physical world. The idea of "resurrection" then becomes the three-day dying-resuscitation process we undergo at death. And if we pay attention to some passages in *Sacred Scripture* it will be clear that even in the literal sense there is information indicating that every individual resuscitates immediately after dying. This was discussed and shown elsewhere in this book and in my related books (see List at the very end of the book).

I need to point out a critical difference that exists between the rationality of *natural-rational* thinking and *spiritual-rational* thinking and reasoning. In natural-rational thinking our concepts and our logic are time-bound and place-bound. It is very difficult for most people to eliminate or "abstract out" the time-place condition that is inherent in natural-rational concepts. But this can be done with some practice.

When "heaven" and "hell" are places on earth or on some other location in the natural universe, then they remain time-bound and place-bound ideas. About hell, we think of a prison somewhere where conditions are really awful and where "sinners" are burned and tortured by fire and Satan's pitchforks. This kind of fantasy is immersed in natural consciousness and refers to activity in the physical world. We are using natural-rational rules of reasoning to create the place-bound concepts and to think with them when drawing conclusions.

But it is very different when we are using spiritual-rational concepts and reasoning that apply to conditions in the spiritual world, thus apart from time and place in the physical universe, and apart from physical things such as prisons, burning bodies, and iron pitchforks. We instead think of psychic conditions and forces, of psychological and emotional suffering. The descriptions of the "suffering burning bodies in fire" are now seen as "the suffering of spiritual bodies", which is suffering in the minds of people.

Hell is a mental state in which we feel emotional and mental suffering from various spiritual disorders that are specified in Sacred Scripture, and may be summarized as "sinning against God".

For example, experiencing regret or guilt can be most powerful and overwhelming, as if we were in a hell. Experiencing the desire to be worshipped as a god can be very powerful and all consuming, and if it is not happening, the person suffers a mental hell. Moreover, in spiritual consciousness it is perceived and reasoned that *hell may be a state of suffering, but it is not a state of undergoing punishment by God*. Rather, hell is a mental state in which we are unwilling to give up our attachment to egotism. We rather be spiritually insane than accept and admit that our ego is the devil and source of our suffering.

The only reason that those who are in hell stay there, as if they were locked in, which they are not, is that they are unwilling to leave or rise above that negative level of experiencing that we call hell.

Those in hell refuse to leave when given opportunity. Why? Because they hate being heavenly more than they hate suffering in hell. Being heavenly means to reject ego and love others instead, to work for the benefit of the community rather than for one's own benefit, and to acknowledge that without God we have zero power. Those who are in the advanced de-individuation mode that we call hell, violently refuse to love others as much as self, and even more violently refuse to love God more than anything. They intensely hate all people who won't favor them as a god, and they hate God even more violently. God does not keep people in their mental hell, but only their insane love of ego. Additional details regarding this issue may be obtained from Swedenborg's Writings, especially the two titles *Heaven and Hell*, and *Heavenly Secrets (Arcana Coelestia)*.

Swedenborg writes:

> The two spirits adjoined to man cause him to be in communication with hell, and the two angels cause him to be in communication with heaven. Without communication with heaven and hell, man could not live even a moment. If these communications were taken away, the man would fall dead as a stock; for then would be taken away the connection with the First Esse, that is, with the Lord. This has also been shown me by much experience. The spirits with me were removed a little, and then as they were removed I began as it were to expire, and indeed should have expired if they had not been sent back.
>
> But I know that few will believe there is any spirit with them, nor even that there are any spirits; and this chiefly for the reason that at this day there is no faith, because no charity, and thus it is not believed that there is a hell, nor even that there is a heaven, nor consequently that there is any life after death. Another reason is that they do not see spirits with their eyes; for they say, "If I should see, I would believe; what I see, this is; but what I do not see, I do not know whether it is." When yet they know, or might know, that man's eye is so dull and gross that it does not even see many things that exist in ultimate nature, as is evident from microscopes which make them visible.
>
> How then could it see what is within even purer nature, where spirits and angels are? These man cannot see except with the eye of his internal man, for this is accommodated to such vision. But the sight of this eye is not opened to man while he is in this world, for many reasons. From all this it is evident how far distant is the faith of this day from the faith of ancient times, when it was believed that every man had his angel with him. ~Swedenborg, *Heavenly Secrets*, AC 5849

Jung writes:

> *He who wishes to take the Kingdom of Heaven by storm, to conquer and eradicate evil by force, is already in the hands of evil.* ~ Carl Jung, *Conversations with C.G. Jung, p. 47*

> *The Kingdom of Heaven is a primordial condition like Paradise, but it is later in time and cannot be reached by regressing, only be going forward. We do*

not know whether our present order is final. At another level a new creative solution may be required. ~Carl Jung, Conversations with C.G. Jung, p. 39

The Kingdom of Heaven is within ourselves. It is our innermost nature and something between ourselves. The Kingdom of Heaven is between people like cement. ~Carl Jung, Visions Seminar, p. 444

The unconscious is not just evil by nature, it is also the source of the highest good: not only dark but also light, not only bestial, semihuman, and demonic but superhuman, spiritual, and, in the classical sense of the word, "divine." ~Carl Jung, The Practice of Self, p. 364

Individuation is not an intensification of consciousness, it is very much more. For you must have the consciousness of something before it can be intensified, and that means experience, life lived.

You can only be really conscious of things which you have experienced, so individuation must be understood as life. Only life integrates, only life and what we do in life makes the individual appear.

You cannot individuate, for instance, by locking yourself up in a cell, you can only individuate in your concrete life, you appear in your deed; there you can individuate and nowhere else.

Real consciousness can only be based upon life; upon things experienced, but talking about these things is just air. It is a sort of conscious understanding, but it is not individuation. Individuation is the accomplishment through life.

For instance, say a cell begins to divide itself and to differentiate and develop into a certain plant or a certain animal; that is the process of individuation.

It is that one becomes what one is, that one accomplishes one's destiny, all the determinations that are given in the form of the germ; it is the unfolding of the germ and becoming the primitive pattern that one was born with. ~Carl Jung, Visions Seminar, p. 757

One needs death to be able to harvest the fruit. Without death, life would be meaningless, since the long-lasting rises again and denies its own meaning. To be, and to enjoy your being, you need death, and limitation enables you to fulfill your being. ~Carl Jung, The Red Book, p. 275

---

26. Repentance and Regeneration

Regeneration is the method or spiritual discipline by which we raise our consciousness from natural to spiritual to celestial, thus to our full human potential. *Repentance is the initiating operation that allows us to undergo regeneration.* God closely attends and supervises this psychological process and takes great care that the person is psychologically ready to resist spiritual temptations.

The process involves God connecting and disconnecting our mind with particular spirits and angels that are present near out spiritual body to assist in our spiritual effort of resisting temptations by means of spiritual truths and the desire to reform and repent of sins against God. Sins are thoughts, intentions, and acts that we maintain even though we know that they are contrary to God's commandments and to our spiritual conscience and eternal welfare. Hence they are called "sins against God", which means that they cause anatomical injury to our spiritual body or mind, and to our ability to live to eternity in heavenly joy and wisdom.

Swedenborg explains what is spiritual repentance:
True repentance means not only examining what one does in one's life, but also what one intends in one's will to do.

The reason why true repentance means not only examining what one does in one's life, but also what one intends in one's will to do, is that deeds are the product of the understanding and the will. Thought is what makes a person speak and the will is what makes him act, so speech is thought speaking and action is the will acting. Since this is the origin of all speech and action, it follows without a doubt that it is those two which sin when the body does.

A person too can repent of the evils he has physically committed, but still think and will evil. This is like cutting down the trunk of a tree that is no good, but leaving its root in the ground; from this the same tree grows up again and spreads itself around. But it is different if the root too is pulled up; and this is what happens in a person when he examines at the same time the intentions present in his will, and rids himself of evils by repentance.

A person can examine what in his will he intends to do by examining his thoughts, for intentions show up in these. He can do so, for instance, if he thinks about, wills and intends revenge, adultery, theft, false witness and longings for these things, as well as blasphemy against God, the holy Word and the church, and so on. In these circumstances, if he concentrates his mind on this and investigates whether he would do these acts if fear of the law or of losing his reputation did not prevent him, if after investigation he thinks that he does not will these acts because they are sins, then he is truly and inwardly penitent.

Even more does he do so, when he takes pleasure in those evils and at the same time is free to commit them, but still he desists and abstains. If he does this repeatedly, he finds the pleasures he gets from those evils become with repetition unpleasant to him, and he ends by consigning them to hell. This is what is meant by the Lord's words:

If anyone wants to find his soul, he will lose it, and if anyone loses his soul for my sake, he will find it. Matt. 10:39.

A person who rids himself of the evils in his will by this kind of repentance is like the man who at the right time uproots from his field the tares sown by the devil, so that the seeds planted by the Lord God the Saviour find the ground unencumbered and grow into a crop (Matt: 13:24-30). ~Swedenborg, True Christian Religion, TCR 532

27. Repentance and Self-Examination

Swedenborg further writes:
There are two loves which have long been enrooted in the human race, the love of ruling over all, and the love of possessing the goods of all.

The former love, if free rein is given to it, rushes on even so far as to wish to be the God of heaven; and the latter, if free rein is given to it, rushes on even so far as to wish to be the God of the world. To these two loves are subordinated all other evil loves, of which there are hosts; but to examine these two is exceedingly difficult, because they reside most deeply within and hide themselves; for they are like vipers concealed in a cloven rock, which retain their poison, so that when one lies down upon the rock they give their deadly stroke, and again withdraw to their hiding-place. They are also like the sirens of the ancients, who allured men by their song, and by that means slew them.

These two loves also decorate themselves in splendid attire, as a devil by magical hallucinations does among his own, or among those whom he wishes to delude.

But it must be clearly understood that these two loves may bear rule among the humble more than among the great, among the poor more than among the rich, among subjects more than among kings; for the latter classes are born to dominion and wealth, and these they at length come to regard in the same way as any other man, a governor, a director, a sea captain, or even a poor farmer, regards his servants and possessions. It is different, however, with kings who aspire to dominion over the kingdoms of others.

The intentions of the will must be examined, because in the will the love resides, for the will is its receptacle, as shown above.

From the will every love breathes out its delights into the perceptions and thoughts of the understanding, for these act from the will and not at all from themselves, because they wait on the will and consent to and confirm all that pertains to its love. The will therefore is the very house in which the man dwells, and the understanding is the hall through which he goes out and in. This is why it has been said that the will's intentions must be examined; and when these have been examined and removed, man is lifted out of the natural will in which both inherited and actual evils have their seat, into the spiritual will through which the Lord reforms and regenerates the natural, and by means of this again, what is sensual and voluntary in the body, thus the whole man. ~Swedenborg, The True Christian Religion, TCR 533

Those who do not examine themselves, are comparatively like invalids whose blood is vitiated by the closing of the capillary vessels, which causes atrophy, numbness of the limbs, and painful chronic diseases arising from a thickening, tenacity, acridness, and acidity of the humors, and consequently of the blood. But on the other hand, those who examine themselves even as to the intentions of the will, are like those who have been cured of these diseases, and restored to the life they enjoyed in youth. Those who examine themselves properly, are like ships from Ophir laden with gold, silver, and valuables; but before they have examined themselves they are like ships loaded with filth, such as are used to carry off the mud and ordure of the streets.

Those who examine themselves interiorly become like mines, all the walls of which are resplendent with ores of precious metals; but before this, they are like marshes with foul exhalations, containing snakes and poisonous serpents with glittering skins and noxious insects with shining wings. Those who do not examine themselves are like the dry bones in the valley; but after they have examined themselves, they are like these same bones when the Lord Jehovah had laid sinews upon them, caused flesh to come upon them, covered them with skin, and put breath in them, and they lived (Ezek. 37:1-14). ~Swedenborg, The True Christian Religion, TCR 534

You can see that rational theistic self-analysis is the process of self-examination for the purpose of identifying the contaminated intentions in our will and mind by which we love ourselves at the expense of everybody else.

Swedenborg explains further about what kind of repentance is efficacious for regeneration, and therefore for salvation.

Swedenborg writes:
Those Also Repent Who Although They Do Not Examine Themselves, Yet Refrain From Evils Because They Are Sins; An Those Who From Religion Do The Woks Of Charity Exercise Such Repentance.

Since actual repentance, which is examining oneself recognizing and acknowledging one's sins, praying to the Lord and beginning a new life, is in the Reformed Christian world exceedingly difficult for many reasons that will be given in the last section of this chapter, therefore an easier kind of repentance is here presented, which is, that when anyone is giving thought to any evil and intending it, he shall say to himself, "Although I am thinking about this and intending it, I will not do it because it is a sin." By this means the temptation injected from hell is checked, and its further entrance prevented.

It is strange that anyone can find fault with another for his evil intentions, and say, "Do not do that because it is a sin," and yet find it difficult to say this to himself; but this is because the latter touches the will, but the former only the thought nearest to hearing. Inquiry was made in the spiritual world as to who were capable of this [actual] repentance, and they were found to be as few as doves in a vast desert. Some said that they could repent in the easier way; but were not able to examine themselves and confess their sins before God.

All who do good from religion, avoid actual evils, but they very rarely reflect upon the interiors pertaining to the will, for they believe that they are not in evil because they are in good, and even that the good covers the evil. But, my friend, the first thing of charity is to shun evils. This is taught in the Word, the Decalogue, baptism, the holy supper and even by the reason; for how can anyone flee away from evils and banish them without some self-inspection? And how can good become good until it has been interiorly purified? I know that all pious men, and also all men of sound reason, will assent to this when they read it, and will see it as genuine truth; but still, that few will act accordingly. ~Swedenborg, The True Christian Religion, TCR 535

And yet all who do good from religion, not only Christians, but even pagans, are accepted and after death adopted by the Lord; for the Lord said:

> *I was an hungered, and ye gave Me to eat; I was thirsty and ye gave Me to drink; I was a sojourner, and ye took Me in; naked, and ye clothed Me; I was sick, and ye visited Me I was in prison, and ye came unto Me. And He said, Inasmuch as ye did it unto one of My brethren, even the least, ye did it unto Me. Come, ye blessed, inherit the kingdom prepared for you from the foundation of the world (Matt. 25:31 seq.).*

To this I will add the following, which is new: All those who do good from religion, after death reject the doctrine of the present church respecting three Divine persons from eternity, and also its faith as applied to the three in their order. These turn to the Lord God the Savior, and accept with pleasure what belongs to the New Church.

But the rest, who have not exercised charity from religion, have hearts of adamant, that is, hardened hearts. They first approach three Gods, then the Father alone, and finally no God. They look upon the Lord God the Savior as the son of Mary only, born from marriage with Joseph, and not as the Son of God; and then they discard all the goods and truths of the New Church, and straightway connect themselves with the spirits of the dragon, and with them are driven away into deserts or into caverns on the very confines of what is called the Christian world; and after a time, because they are separated from the New Heaven, they rush into crime, and are therefore sent down to hell.

Such is the lot of those who do not do works of charity from religion, because of their belief that no one is able to do good of himself, except such as he claims merit for; consequently they disregard such works, and associate themselves with the goats, who are damned and cast into the eternal fire prepared for the devil and his angels, because they have not done what was done by the sheep (Matt. 25:41-46). It is not there said that they did what is evil, but that they did not do what is good; and those who do not do what is good from religion do what is evil, since: No man can serve two masters; for either he hates the one and loves the other, or he holds to the one and despises the other (Matt. 6:24).

Jehovah says through Isaiah:

> *Wash you, make you clean; put away the evil of your doings from before mine eyes; cease to do evil; learn to do well, then although your sins have been as scarlet, they shall become as white as snow; although they have been red like crimson, they shall be as wool (Isa. 1:16-18).*

~Swedenborg, The True Christian Religion, TCR 536

It must be understood that those who do good from natural goodness only, and not also from religion, are not accepted after death, because there is only natural good in their charity, and not spiritual good also; and it is the spiritual that conjoins the Lord to man, and not the natural apart from the spiritual. Natural goodness belongs to the flesh merely, being acquired by birth from parents; but spiritual goodness belongs to the spirit born anew from the Lord. Those who do the good works of charity from religion, and consequently do not commit evil, before they have accepted the doctrine of the New Church concerning the Lord, may be likened to trees that bear good fruit, although but little, and also to trees that bear excellent small fruit, which are nevertheless cared for in gardens.

They may also be likened to olive trees and fig-trees in forests, and again to fragrant herbs and balsamic shrubs on hills. They are like little chapels or houses of God, where pious worship is performed; for they are the sheep on the right hand, and the rams which the goats assault, according to Daniel (8:2-14). In heaven such are clothed in garments of a red color, and when they have been initiated into the goods of the New Church they are clothed with garments of a purple color, which acquire a beautiful golden glow in proportion as they also receive truths. ~Swedenborg, The True Christian Religion, TCR 537

In other words, a critical distinction must be made between doing good to others from "natural goodness" vs. doing good to others from "religion", that is, from a desire to obey God and the Commandments in *Sacred Scripture.* Only the latter is efficacious for producing rebirth and regeneration of our personality. To think and act from spiritual or "genuine conscience" is a spiritual-rational operation, and therefore it is efficacious. This assumes that "genuine conscience" is possible only from the desire to obey God's commandments and to avoid sinning against God when we disregard the "voice of conscience" that informs us what is doing evil against another.

When we act from our natural and socialized conscience, which may also be called "humanism" or humanist life-philosophy, we are unable to distinguish what is genuine good and truth since what we love, that we call good, and what we believe, that we call truth. When we act and think from natural goodness we are in natural consciousness. To act from spiritual goodness, which is genuine goodness, we must be motivated by our personal relationship to God. This is called doing "good works", bearing "good fruit", doing the "works of charity", and "being purified".

28. Confession and Self-examination

Further, regarding confession and supplication Swedenborg writes:

There are two duties incumbent on man, to be done after examination, namely, supplication and confession.

The supplication should be that the Lord may be merciful, that He may give power to resist the evils that have been repented of, and that He will provide inclination and affection for doing good, Since apart from the Lord man can do nothing (John 15:5). The confession will be that he sees, recognizes, and acknowledges his evils, and finds himself to be a miserable sinner.

There is no need for man to enumerate his sins before the Lord, nor to supplicate forgiveness of them. He need not enumerate them, because he has searched them out and seen them in himself, and consequently they are present to the Lord because they are present to himself. Moreover, the Lord led him to search them out, disclosed them, and inspired grief for them, and together with this an effort to refrain from them and begin a new life.

Supplication need not be made to the Lord for forgiveness of sins, for the following reasons: First, because sins are not abolished, but removed; and they are removed so far as man continues to refrain from them and enters upon a new life; for there are innumerable lusts inherent, coiled up as it were, in every evil, and they cannot be put away instantly, but only gradually, as man permits himself to be reformed and regenerated.

The second reason is, that as the Lord is mercy itself, He forgives all men their sins, nor does He impute a single sin to anyone, for He says, "They know not what they do." Nevertheless, the sins are not thereby taken away; for to Peter asking how often he should forgive his brother's trespasses, whether he should do so seven times, the Lord said: I say not unto thee, until seven times, but until seventy times seven (Matt. 18:21-22). What, then, will not the Lord do?

Still it does no harm for one burdened in conscience to enumerate his sins before a minister of the church, in order to lighten his burden and obtain absolution; because he is thereby initiated into a habit of examining himself, and reflecting upon each day's evils. But this kind of confession is natural, while that described above is spiritual. ~Swedenborg, The True Christian Religion, TCR 539

In other words, regeneration begins with self-examination and is followed by confession and repentance, and afterwards by supplication. We are to ask God to give us the ability to resist doing the evils that we discover in our thinking and activities. God then provides us with the "inclination and affection for doing good". *Of ourselves we cannot stop doing what we love and this keeps us in natural consciousness, thus making regeneration impossible.* Swedenborg explains that we don't need to "enumerate" to God each of our sins because God not only knows them but also leads us to observe them, recognize them, and confess them before God. We do not do this from ourselves but from God who is constantly present and managing our regeneration steps and our inclinations.

Nevertheless, we still ought to supplicate God for forgiveness of our sins because it reinforces the spiritual idea in our mind that our sins are multiple and various. They cannot be "abolished" by God but only "removed" so that they are no longer active complexes in our mind. There is always the possibility for sins that are removed to come back with a vengeance and interrupt our regeneration process. Every evil in our personality contains "innumerable lusts inherent, coiled up as it were, and they cannot be put away instantly, but only gradually" as we permit ourselves to be reformed and regenerated by God.

Continuing with Swedenborg's explanation of repentance and forgiveness in relation to our regeneration:

Actual Repentance Is Easy For Those Who Have Now And Then Practised It, But It Is A Very Difficult Task For Those Who Have Not.

Actual repentance is to examine oneself, to recognize one's sins, to confess them before God, and thus to begin a new life; this is in accord with the previous description of it. To the Reformed Christian world (meaning by this all those who are separate from the church of Rome, and also to those attached to that church who have not practiced actual repentance), this repentance is a very difficult task. This is because some are unwilling and some are afraid to practice it; and continued neglect establishes a habit, induces unwillingness, and at length gains the endorsement of the reasoning intellect, and this with some produces sadness, dread, and terror at the thought of repentance.

Actual repentance is so extremely difficult in the Reformed Christian world chiefly because of their belief that repentance and charity contribute nothing to salvation, but faith alone, from the imputation of which forgiveness of sins, justification, renovation, regeneration, sanctification, and eternal salvation follow. Moreover, their dogmatic writers say that man's cooperation of himself, or as if of himself, is useless, is an obstacle to Christ's merit, and is repugnant and injurious to it. And this idea is implanted in the minds of the common people, although they are ignorant of the mysteries of that faith, merely by the sayings, that "faith alone saves," and who can possibly do good of himself?"

For this reason: repentance among the Reformed is like a nest of young birds deprived of the parent birds, which have been captured and killed by the fowler. To this another reason may be added, that a so-called Reformed Christian is associated in the spiritual world as to his spirit, only with such as are like himself, who introduce such things into the ideas of his thought, and lead him away from the very first step toward self-inspection and self-examination. ~Swedenborg, The True Christian Religion, TCR 561

I have asked many of the Reformed in the spiritual world, why they did not practice actual repentance, when it was enjoined upon them both in the Word and at baptism, as also before the holy communion in all their churches. They made various replies. Some said that contrition with a lip-confession that they were sinners, is sufficient; some that such repentance, because it takes place while man is acting from his own will, is not consistent with the generally accepted faith.

Others said, "How can anyone examine himself, when he knows that he is nothing but sin? This would be like casting a net into a lake filled from bottom to top with mud containing noxious worms." Others said, "Who can look into himself so deeply as to see in himself Adam's sin, from which all his actual evils flow? Are not both kinds of evil washed away by the water of baptism, and removed or covered up by the merit of Christ? What then is repentance but a requirement, which sadly disturbs the conscientious? By the Gospel are we not under grace, and not under the hard law of that repentance?" and so on.

Some said, that whenever they undertake to examine themselves, dread and terror fill their minds as if they saw a monster near their bed in the morning twilight. From all this the reasons are made clear why actual repentance in the Reformed Christian world has become rusty, as it were, and is discarded.

In the presence of these persons I also asked some who adhered to the Roman Catholic religion about their actual confession to their ministers, whether it was difficult. They replied, that after they had been initiated into it they were not afraid to recount their trespasses to a confessor who was not severe, that they gathered them up with a kind of pleasure, telling the lighter ones cheerfully, and the more serious somewhat timidly; also from habit they freely returned annually to their appointed confession, and, after receiving absolution, to festivity; moreover, that they look upon all who are not willing to disclose the defilements of their hearts, as impure. Hearing this, the Reformed who were present hastened away, some deriding and laughing, some astounded and yet commending.

Afterward some drew near who belonged to that same church, but had lived in Protestant countries, who, according to the usage there established, did not make a special confession, as their brethren do elsewhere, but a general confession to one who held the keys for them. These said that they were utterly unable to examine themselves, to trace out and set forth their actual evils and the secrets of their thoughts; and that they felt this to be as repugnant and terrifying as an attempt to cross a ditch to a rampart where an armed soldier stands and cries, "Keep back." From all this it is now clear that actual repentance is easy to those who at times practice it, but is extremely difficult to those who have not practiced it. ~Swedenborg, The True Christian Religion, TCR 562

It is known that habit is a second nature, and that therefore what is easy for one is difficult for another; and this is true of self-examination and a confession of what is thereby discovered. What is easier for a hired laborer, a porter, or a farmer, than to work with his hands from morning till evening, while a gentleman or a delicate person could not do the same work for half an hour without fatigue and sweating? It is easy for a footman with a staff and easy boots to pursue his way for miles, while one accustomed to ride can hardly run slowly from one street to another. Every mechanic who is attentive to his task goes through it easily and willingly, and when he leaves it, longs to return; while another, who understands the same trade, but is indolent, can scarcely be driven to work.

The same is true of everyone, whatever may be his office or pursuit. To one diligent in piety, what is easier than to pray to God? while to one who is a slave to impiety, what is more difficult, and vice versa? What priest, preaching before a king for the first time, does not feel timid? but after doing it frequently he goes through boldly. What is easier for an angelic man than to raise his eyes to heaven, or for a devilish man than to cast them down toward hell? But if the latter becomes a hypocrite, he too can look up to heaven, but his heart is turned away. Everyone becomes imbued with the end he has in view and the habit arising therefrom. ~Swedenborg, The True Christian Religion, TCR 563

One Who Has Never Repented Or Has Never Looked Into And Searched Himself, Finally Ceases To Know What Damning Evil Or Saving Good Is.

As few in the Reformed Christian world practice repentance, this is here added, that he who has not looked into and searched himself, finally ceases to know what damning evil or saving good is, because he has no religion from which to know it; for the evil that a man does not see, recognize, and acknowledge, remains; and whatever remains becomes more and more enrooted, until it obstructs the interiors of the mind, whereby man becomes first natural, then sensual, and finally corporeal, and in such states he knows not any damning evil or saving good. He becomes like a tree growing on a hard rock, which spreads its roots among the crevices and finally withers away from lack of moisture.

Every man rightly educated is rational and moral; but there are two ways to rationality, one from the world and the other from heaven. He who has become rational and moral from the world only, and not from heaven, is rational and moral in word and gesture only, but is inwardly a beast, and even a wild beast, because he acts as one with those who are in hell, where all are wild beasts. But he who is rational and moral from heaven also, is truly rational and moral, because he is so at once in spirit, word, and body; the spiritual being within these two latter like a soul actuating the natural, sensual, and corporeal; it also acts as one with those who are in heaven.

Therefore there can be a spiritual-rational and moral man, and also a merely natural-rational and moral man. These two are not distinguished from each other in the world, especially if the man has by practice become imbued with hypocrisy; but they are distinguished by the angels in heaven as easily as doves from owls or sheep from tigers.

The merely natural man can see good and evil in others, and also rebuke others; but not having looked into and examined himself, he does not see any evil in himself, and if any is discovered by another, he cloaks it by means of his

rationality; as a serpent hides his head in the dust, and immerses himself in it, as a hornet buries himself in mud. This is done by the delight of evil, which encompasses him as a fog does a marsh, absorbing and extinguishing the rays of light. Infernal delight is no other. It is exhaled from hell, and flows into every man, into the soles of his feet, his back, and his occiput; and when it is received by the head in the forehead and by the body in the breast, man is made a slave to hell; and for the reason that the human cerebrum is devoted to the understanding and the wisdom it contains, but the cerebellum to the will and its love. This is why there are two brains. But that infernal delight can be corrected, reformed, and inverted solely by the spiritual-rational and moral.
~Swedenborg, *The True Christian Religion, TCR 564*

In other words, when we are in natural consciousness our morality is "sensual", "corporeal", and "fleshly". This means that all its ideas and rules are based solely on natural ideas that apply to life on earth with the physical body. When we are in this modality of mental operation we "believe nothing but what we can see with our eyes and touch with our hands, calling that something real, and rejecting everything else". In this mentality we deny the life after death, heaven, and the work of regeneration. Our spiritual consciousness is not yet activated hence we can see nothing of spiritual truths.

There are those who say that they have religion and that they believe in God, and yet may be doing this merely as a social posture for status, gain, reputation, or influence, which are not genuinely moral reasons. From this self-centered motive they are calculating, cunning, and malicious to others, thus devoid of genuine charity and concern for them. They permit themselves to be avaricious, unfaithful in marriage, and crafty in dealings with others.

The ancients called this type of person a "*serpent of the tree of knowledge*". Their sub-conscious mind is in telepathic communication with evil spirits who inspire them to act contrary to genuine morality and charity. In the afterlife they drop all pretenses and happily join those hellish spiritual communities that inspired them throughout life on earth. They thus willingly and happily enter hell in eternity. This may be fun at the beginning, but later they suffer harsh things from the action and cruelty of the others with whom they form an evil collectivity.

29. Self-Witnessing
the Evils We Practice

Part of undergoing regeneration is to raise our level of awareness and mental functioning to what is "above" sensual consciousness. We thereby immerse our mental operations in spiritual ideas that give us clear light and understanding where before was nothing but falsity and spurious justifications, and this is to be in "spiritual insanity". Hence Swedenborg encourages us to "look into ourselves" to identify the evils we practice and enjoy.

Swedenborg writes:
> There shall now be given a brief description of the merely natural-rational and moral man, who viewed in himself is sensual, and if he goes on, becomes corporeal or fleshly; but the description shall be sketched in separate statements.

> The sensual is the outmost of the life of man's mind, adherent to and coherent with his five bodily senses. He is called a sensual man who judges of everything from the bodily senses, and believes nothing but what he can see with his eyes and touch with his hands, calling that something real, and rejecting everything else. The interiors of his mind, which have their vision from the light of heaven, are closed, so that he sees nothing of the truth that relates to heaven and the church.

> Such a man thinks in outermosts, and not interiorly from any spiritual light, because he is in gross natural light; therefore he is interiorly opposed to the things that pertain to heaven and the church, although outwardly he can speak in favor of them, even zealously, in proportion to his hope of gaining power and wealth by means of them. Men of learning and erudition, who have confirmed themselves deeply in falsities, and still more those who have confirmed themselves against the truths of the Word, are more sensual than others.

> Sensual men reason acutely and skillfully, because their thought is so near to speech as to be almost in it, as it were, on the lips; also because they ascribe all intelligence to the speech that is from memory alone. Moreover, they can

dexterously confirm falsities, and after confirming them they believe them to be true; but their reasoning and confirmation are from the fallacies of the senses, which captivate and persuade the common people. Sensual men are more cunning and malicious than others.

The avaricious, adulterous, and crafty are especially sensual, although to the world they seem talented. The interiors of their minds are vile and filthy; by these they communicate with the hells; in the Word they are called dead. Those who are in the hells are sensual, and more so the more deeply they are in them; and the sphere of infernal spirits conjoins itself from behind with man's sensual. In the light of heaven their occiput seems hollow. Those who reasoned from sensual things only, were called by the ancients serpents of the tree of knowledge.

Sensual things ought to occupy the last place, not the first; and in a wise and intelligent man they do occupy the last place, and are subordinate to things interior; but in a foolish man they occupy the first place, and are predominant. When things sensual occupy the last place, a way is opened by means of them to the understanding, and truths are perfected by the method of extraction. Such sensual things stand most near to the world, and admit what flows to them from the world, and, as it were, sift it. By means of sensual things man communicates with the world, and by means of rational things with heaven. Sensual things supply what is of service to the interiors of the mind. There are sensual things that supply what is serviceable both to the intellectual and to the voluntary part.

Unless thought is raised above sensual things man has but little wisdom. When man's thought is raised above sensual things, he comes into a clearer light, and at length into heavenly light, and then he has a perception of such things as flow down from heaven. The outmost of the understanding is the natural knowing faculty, and the outmost of the will is sensual delight.
~Swedenborg, The True Christian Religion, TCR 565

As to his natural man, man is like a beast; he acquires the image of a beast by means of life. Consequently in the spiritual world there appear about such a man beasts of all kinds, which are correspondences. For man's natural, viewed in itself, is purely animal; but because there is a spiritual superadded, he can become a man; and if he does not become a man from the capacity to become so, he can counterfeit one, although he is then only a talking beast;

for he talks from the natural-rational, but thinks from spiritual insanity, and he acts from natural morality, but loves from a spiritual satyriasis. His actions, seen by a spiritually rational man, are but little different from the dance of one bitten by a tarantula, or that called St. Vitus' dance, or the dance of St. Guy.

Who does not know that a hypocrite can talk about God, a robber about honesty, an adulterer about chastity, and so on. But unless man had the ability to shut and open the door between his thoughts and his words, and between his intentions and his actions, and unless prudence or cunning were the doorkeeper, he would rush into crimes and cruelties more fiercely than any wild beast. But in every man after death that door is opened; and then what he has been is apparent; but he is kept under restraint by punishments and confinements in hell.

Therefore, kind reader, look into yourself, and find out one or another evil that is in you, and from religion dismiss it. If you dismiss evils from any other purpose or end, you do so only that they may not appear before the world.
~Swedenborg, The True Christian Religion, TCR 566

And now I present below a longer selection of what Swedenborg called his "Memorable Relations". These were detailed reports of various interactions he had with the people of the afterlife. He was able to write them down because he was in dual consciousness, aware of his physical surroundings as we are, and simultaneously aware of his spiritual surroundings, as we will be only after our three-day dying-resuscitation procedure. For the last 27 years of his life in the physical world Swedenborg was given this unique ability that was not granted to any scientist before.

This is why Swedenborg called his permanent dual consciousness the "greatest miracle" that God ever granted to anyone on this earth. The purpose for which Swedenborg was granted this unique privilege is that he may *describe and report as a scientist* the knowledge and conditions of life after death. This knowledge could not have been understood or accepted prior to the age of rationality and science in the 18th century. This is why it was now granted to the world of natural consciousness. Civilization had reached an intellectual stage where spiritual knowledge was explicable in rational scientific concepts.

Swedenborg, the internationally respected Swedish engineer and scientist, was selected for this unique mission by God and guided since childhood to become a respected scientist and recognized for expertise in several scientific fields including mining engineering, crystallography, physics, chemistry, human anatomy, psychology, and monetary legislation. It was his stupendous task to write a scientific ethnography of the life and conditions of the people of the afterlife in eternity. Further, he was to show that this *theistic science* is also available as the spiritual knowledge that one can extract from the correspondences and symbolic representations that make up the literal-historical verses of the Old and New Testaments. To prove this, Swedenborg filled 20 volumes of exegesis that gives a word-by-word and verse-by-verse analysis of the correspondential sense of several books of the Bible. Here are three of the Memorable Relations.

Swedenborg writes:

Memorable Relation: What pious and wise man does not wish to know his life's lot after death? I will therefore set forth plainly some general truths in order that it may be known.

Every man, when, after death, he feels that he is still alive, and that he is in another world, and hears that heaven, where there are eternal joys, is above him, and hell, where there are eternal sorrows, is beneath him, is at first remitted into his externals, in which he was in the former world; and he then believes that he is certainly going to heaven, and talks intelligently and acts prudently.

And some then say, "We have lived morally, we have pursued honesty, we have not done evil purposely." Others say, "We have frequented churches, heard masses, kissed sacred images, and on our knees poured out prayers." Others again, "We have given to the poor, helped the needy, read pious books, and also the Word," with other like things.

But when they have said these things, angels approach and say, "All that you have mentioned you have done in externals, but you do not yet know what you are in your internals. You are now spirits in a substantial body, and the spirit is your internal man. It is this in you that thinks what it wills and wills what it loves; and that is the delight of its life.

Every man from infancy begins life from externals, and learns to act morally and talk intelligently; and when he begins to gain some idea of heaven and its happiness, he begins to pray, to frequent churches, and to observe the solemnities of worship; and yet when evils spring forth from their native fountain, he hides them in his mind's bosom, and also ingeniously covers them over with reasonings from fallacies to such an extent that he does not even know that evil is evil.

And then because the evils are veiled over and covered up as it were with dust, he thinks no more about them, except to guard against their appearing before the world. Thus he endeavors merely to lead a moral life in externals, and thus he becomes a double man, a sheep in externals, and a wolf in internals; and he is like a golden box containing poison, or like a man with a foul breath holding something aromatic in his mouth to prevent those near him from perceiving it; or he is like a mouse's skin that smells of balsam.

You said that you had lived morally, and had followed pious pursuits; but tell me, have you ever examined your internal man and there perceived any lusting after revenge even to murder, after libidinous living even to adultery, after defrauding even to theft, after lying even to false witness? In four of the commandments of the Decalogue it is said, Thou shalt not do these things, and in the two last, Thou shalt not lust after them. Do you believe that in these things your internal man has been like your external? If you do you are perhaps deceived."

To this they replied, "What is the internal man? Is not the internal and the external one and the same? We have heard from our ministers that the internal man is nothing but faith, and that oral piety and a morality of life are the signs of it, because they are its operation." To this the angels answered, "Saving faith is in the internal man, and charity likewise; and from them come Christian fidelity and morality in the external man. But if the above mentioned lusts remain in the internal man, thus in the will and therefrom in the thought, and if in consequence you love these things interiorly, and yet act and speak otherwise in externals, evil is then with you above good, and good below evil; consequently, however you may talk as if from the understanding, and act from love, evil is within and thus is veiled over; and then you are like cunning apes which perform actions like those of men, but the human heart is wholly lacking.

But what your internal man is, of which you know nothing, because you have not examined yourselves and afterwards repented, you will see after a while, when you put off your external man and are let into the internal. When this takes place you will no longer be recognized by your companions, nor even by yourselves. Wicked men, who were moral, I have then seen to be like wild beasts, looking at the neighbor with savage eyes, burning with deadly hatred, and blaspheming God, whom they adored while in the external man." Hearing this they withdrew; and the angels then said, "You will see your life's lot after a little; for your external man will soon be taken away from you, and you will enter into the internal, which is now your spirit. ~Swedenborg, The True Christian Religion, TCR 568

The above report provides empirical confirmation of the distinctly contrastive consequences of living life in natural consciousness, which is called the "external man". This mental state is suitably adapted to life in the physical body and its societal conditions. But it is ignorant and oblivious of anything spiritual, and yet our life in the physical world is almost nothing compared to our life in eternity. Hence it is critical that we modify our everyday way of thinking and acting to bring it into alignment with the conditions of the life that we will experience after death. This is the "internal man" or the mind in spiritual consciousness. Regeneration is the process of opening up our spiritual mind while we are still in the physical world.

By this process, our natural consciousness is gradually and progressively rearranged in the modality of the spiritual laws and truths. This means that the "external mind" can now be obedient and subject to the "internal mind". It is the reborn state in which spiritual consciousness is within natural consciousness and the two act synchronously as one. It is the liberation of the natural mind.

In the next *Memorable Relation* quoted below we find out that sensation and pleasure are not felt in the physical body but in the spiritual body, which is our mind. We are born with the two bodies, one temporary and made of dead physical matter, the other immortal and made of living spiritual substance. When we touch something here we have the subjective illusion that the sensation is in the hand that touches some object. Later, when we become educated in public school we learn that the sensation is not in the hand but in the brain, carried there by nerve fibers. Still later when we learn spiritual truths we realize that the sensation is in the spiritual body, while the physical body is not capable of anything but what are electro-chemical operations in the nerves and brain.

There is therefore a connection between the spirit body and the physical body so that our mind in the spirit body may correspond to the electro-chemical operations in the physical brain. This is how we are aware of the physical environment. Another way I think about this is to call my physical body an "avatar". My mind or spirit body uses the physical avatar to sense and act in the physical world. It is obvious that this avatar is not alive and cannot experience sensation or feeling. When this avatar stops responding to my will it is said to be "dead". Of course, this is just a way of speaking according to appearances since the physical body was never alive to begin with.

It is also explained that the sensations and pleasures we experience in natural consciousness are relatively obscure and weak compared to those we feel in spiritual consciousness. This is good news and something we can really look forward to! Rather than losing or diminishing our sensual life upon death we gain a much enriched sensory awareness and pleasure.

By the same token we are cautioned that the spiritual joys and pleasures that we experience from heavenly loves and thoughts are accompanied by happy odors and scents in the spiritual environment, while selfish and hellish loves are accompanied by the experience of "filthy" and unpleasant odors and environments. Such are the conditions of living in the afterlife that what is in our thinking and feeling are represented outside our spirit body as either a heavenly environment or hellish.

The loves and intentions in our personality are instantiated by correspondence in what is outside in the environment of our spirit body. Hellish cities and environments appear dark, smelly, cave-like or desert-like, and are filled with dangerous and obnoxious animals and vermin. In contrast, heavenly loves and thoughts instantiate a pleasant paradise environment with fragrant gardens of flowers and fruits, and houses or palaces that have super-natural beauty in art and architecture. Knowing these facts about the afterlife can motivate us to continue our daily efforts at self-change and regeneration.

Swedenborg writes:

Third Memorable Relation: Every love in man [still living on earth] *breathes forth a delight by which it makes itself felt. It is breathed forth first into the spirit* [spirit body or mind] *and from that into the body* [physical body]*; and the delight of one's love, together with the pleasantness of thought, constitutes his life.*

This delight and pleasantness are felt by man [in natural consciousness] *only obscurely while he lives in the natural body, because that body absorbs and blunts them; but after death, when the material body is laid aside, and the covering or clothing of the spirit* [spirit body] *thus removed, man has a full sense and perception of these delights of love and pleasantnesses of thought, and, what is wonderful, sometimes even as odors. Because of this, all in the spiritual world are affiliated according to their loves, those in heaven according to theirs, and those in hell according to theirs.*

The odors into which, in heaven, the delights of loves are turned, are all perceived like the fragrances, sweet smells, pleasant exhalations, and delicious sensations that arise from gardens, flower-beds, fields and forests in the mornings in spring. But the odors into which the delights of the loves of those in hell are turned, are perceived like the pungent, fetid and putrid smells that arise from cesspools, dead bodies, and ponds full of rubbish and ordure; and, what is wonderful, the devils and satans there perceive these smells as balsams, aromatics and frankincense, refreshing their nostrils and hearts. In the natural world it is also given to beasts, birds, and worms to be associated according to odors, but not to men until they have laid aside their bodies as exuviae.

On this account heaven is most distinctly arranged in accordance with all the varieties of the love of good, and hell, on the contrary, in accordance with all the varieties of the love of evil. It is owing to this opposition that there is a gulf between heaven and hell which cannot be passed; for those who are in heaven cannot endure any odor from hell, because it excites nausea and vomiting, and threatens them with swooning if they inhale it. The effect is similar upon those who are in hell, if they pass the middle line of that gulf.

I once saw a certain devil [those in the afterlife who are not regenerated]*, who at a distance had the appearance of a leopard (a few days before he had been seen among the angels of the lowest heaven, having the art to make himself an angel of light), who had passed beyond the middle* *line and was standing between two olive trees, yet did not perceive any odor offensive to his life, for the reason that there were no angels present. But the moment they approached he was seized with convulsions and fell down rigid in all his limbs; and then he appeared like a great serpent drawing himself up in folds, and at length gliding down through the opening, from which he was taken by his companions and carried into a cavern, and there by the rank odor of his own delight he was revived.*

Again, I once saw a satan [those in the afterlife who are not regenerated] *punished by his companions. I asked why, and was told that with his nostrils stopped up he had gone near to those who were in the odor of heaven, and had returned and brought that odor with him on his clothing. It has often happened that a putrid odor, like that of corpses, from some open cavern in hell, has painfully touched my nostrils and brought on vomiting.*

From all this it can be seen why in the Word the sense of smell signifies perception, for it is often said that Jehovah smelled a sweet savor from the burnt-offerings; also that the anointing oil and the incense were made of fragrant substances; and on the other hand the children of Israel were commanded to carry out of their camps what was unclean in them, and to dig down and bury their excrements (Deut. 23:12, 13). This was because the camps of Israel represented heaven, and the desert without the camps represented hell. ~Swedenborg, The True Christian Religion, TCR 569

30. Midway Between Heaven and Hell

In the next *Memorable Relation* quoted below we find out that when we arrive in the afterlife of eternity following the three-day resuscitation process we find ourselves midway between heaven and hell. It is in that intermediate mental state that each individual is prepared for life in heaven or in hell depending on the loves that the individual wants to retain above all other loves. If this love is unregenerate then the individual spontaneously sinks down into a hellish mental community that is made of people or "spirits" that share similar loves. It is the love that attracts and binds. No one is "judged" or "punished" contrary to what many people have been told. This impression is derived from many things in the Bible that are said in the literal-historical sense of the verses. But when this sense is penetrated by means of correspondences one can see that *there is no punishment involved but only a free choice.*

This intermediate mental state when we awaken from the dying process is called the "*world of spirits*". This state is in-between the mental states of heaven and of hell. The environment in the "world of spirits" is quite different from that of either heaven or hell. The world of spirits where everyone is awakened from the dying process is adapted to the needs of people who have just arrived and may still partially function in their natural consciousness. *It is critical to know that there is no regeneration possible after death* since our ruling love can no longer be modified by spiritual temptations. Instead, everything that befalls people in that in-between state is designed to have each person become aware of what their internal loves actually are.

There is therefore a gradual growth process at the end of which people become fully conscious of their actual ruling love in their inner personality structure. If this is an unregenerate love it is selfish and the thoughts of the person are spiritually insane. If the ruling love is altruistic and regenerated, God can remove all the other loves to which people may still be subconsciously clinging. Upon the removal of these selfish loves people can at last enter into the undivided heavenly states of mind.

Swedenborg writes:

> *Fourth Memorable Relation: I once talked with a novitiate spirit who, when in the world, had meditated much upon heaven and hell. By novitiate spirits are meant men who have recently died, and who are called spirits because they are then spiritual men.*

> *As soon as this spirit entered the spiritual world, he began to meditate in the same manner on heaven and hell, and when thinking about heaven seemed to himself to be glad, and when thinking about hell to be sad.*

> *As soon as he recognized that he was in the spiritual world he asked where heaven and hell were, what they were, and what was the nature of each. They answered, "Heaven is over your head, and hell beneath your feet; for you are now in the world of spirits, which is intermediate between heaven and hell; but what they are, and what the nature of each is, we cannot describe in few words."*

Then, as he ardently wished to know, he threw himself upon his knees and devoutly prayed to God that he might be instructed. And lo, an angel appeared at his right hand and raised him up, and said, "You have prayed to be instructed about heaven and hell; inquire and learn what delight is, and you will know." As soon as the angel had said this, he was taken up.

The novitiate spirit then said to himself, "What does this mean? 'Inquire and learn what delight is, and you will know what heaven and hell are, and their nature.'" Leaving that place immediately, he wandered around, and asked those he met, "Pray, tell me, if you please, what delight is." And some said, "What sort of a question is that? Who does not know what delight is? Is it not joy and gladness? Delight is delight. One is the same as the other. We know no difference."

Others said, "Delight is the mind's laughter; for when the mind laughs the countenance is merry, the speech is jocular, the gestures are playful, and the whole man is in delight." Others said, "Delight is nothing but feasting and eating rich things, drinking generous wine and getting drunk, and then chatting about various things, especially the sports of Venus and Cupid."

Hearing these remarks, the novitiate spirit being indignant, said to himself, "These answers are boorish, not those of well-bred persons. Such delights are neither heaven nor hell. Would that I could find some wise men." And he went away from these persons and asked, "Where are the wise men?" He was then seen by an angelic spirit, who said, "I perceive that you have an ardent desire to know what the universal of heaven is, and what the universal of hell is; and as this is delight, I will conduct you to a hill where there is a daily meeting of those who inquire into effects, of those who investigate causes, and of those who search out ends.

Those who inquire into effects are there called spirits of knowledge, abstractly, knowledges; those who investigate causes, are called spirits of intelligence, abstractly, intelligences, and those who search out ends, are called spirits of wisdom, abstractly, wisdoms. Directly above these in heaven are angels who from ends see causes, and from causes see effects; from these angels those three companies have enlightenment."

Then taking the novitiate spirit by the hand, he led him to the top of the hill, and to the assembly that was composed of those who search out ends and are called wisdoms. The novitiate spirit said to them, "Pardon my coming up to you; I did so, because from my childhood I have meditated about heaven and hell. I have lately come to this world; and some who were then associated with me said that heaven is here above my head, and hell beneath my feet; but they did not say what either one or the other is or the nature of it; therefore, becoming anxious from constantly thinking about them, I prayed to God; and then an angel came to me and said, 'Inquire and learn what delight is, and you will know.' I have inquired, but thus far in vain. I therefore beg that you will teach me, if it please you, what delight is."

To this the wisdoms replied, "Delight is the all of life, to all in heaven, and to all in hell. To those in heaven, it is the delight of good and truth, but to those in hell, it is the delight of evil and falsity; for all delight belongs to love, and love is the being [esse] of man's life. Therefore, as man is man in accord with what his love is, so is he man in accord with what his delight is. The activity of love is what gives the sense delight; in heaven its activity is with wisdom, and in hell with insanity, but in both cases the activity produces the delight in its subjects. But the heavens and hells are opposite delights; the heavens are in love of good, and the consequent delight of doing good; but the hells are in the love of evil, and in the consequent delight of doing evil. If, therefore, you know what delight is, you know what heaven and hell are, and their nature.

"But inquire and learn still further what delight is from those who investigate causes, and are called intelligences. They are off toward the right." And he left them and drew near to that assembly, and told them the reason of his coming, and begged them to teach him what delight is. And pleased with the question, they said, "It is true that he who knows what delight is knows what heaven and hell are and their nature. The will, from which man is man, is not moved in the slightest degree except by delight; for the will, viewed in itself, is nothing but the affection of some love, thus some delight; for it is some pleasure and consequent satisfaction that causes volition.

And since the will moves the understanding to think, not the least thought is possible except from an influent delight of the will. This is so for the reason that the Lord by influx from Himself actuates all things of the soul, and all things of the mind, in angels, spirits, and men, and in these He actuates by an influx of love and wisdom; and this influx is the activity itself from which comes all delight. In its origin this is called bliss, happiness, and felicity, and in its derivation, delight, pleasantness, and pleasure, and in a universal sense, Good.

But infernal spirits invert everything in themselves, thus turning good into evil, and truth into falsehood, the delight remaining without interruption; for without permanence of delight they would have no will, no sensation, and thus no life. This makes clear what the delight of hell is, and its nature and source; also what the delight of heaven is, and its nature and source."

Having heard this, he was conducted to the third assembly, where those were who inquire into effects and are called knowledges; and they said, "Descend to the lower earth, and ascend to the higher; you will there perceive and feel the delights of both heaven and hell." And lo, at that moment the earth opened at a distance, and through the chasm three devils came up, who seemed to be on fire with their love's delight; and as the angels accompanying the novitiate spirit perceived that these three had come up out of hell providentially, they called out to the devils, "Do not come nearer, but from where you are tell us something about your delights. " They replied, "Know this, that everyone, whether he is called good or evil, is in his own delight, the so-called good man in his, and the so-called evil man in his."

The angels asked, "What is your delight?" They said that it was delight in whoredom, revenge, fraud, and blasphemy. Again the angels asked, "What is the nature of those delights with you?" They said that they were felt by others like the fetid smells from dung, the putrid smells from dead bodies, and the pungent smells from stagnant urine. The angels then asked, "Are these things delightful to you?" They answered, "Most delightful." "Then," said the angels, "you are like the unclean beasts that live in such things."

They replied, "If we are, we are; but such things are grateful to our nostrils." The angels then asked, "What more?" They answered, "Everyone is allowed to be in his own delight, even the most unclean, as they call it, provided he does not infest good spirits and angels; but as on account of our delight, we cannot help infesting them, we are cast into work-houses where we suffer terribly. The prohibition and withdrawal of our delights there is what is called the torment of hell; it is also interior pain."

The angels asked, "Why did you infest the good?" They answered, "We could not help it; it is as if a fury seized us whenever we see an angel, and feel the Lord's Divine sphere about him." To this we said, "Then you also are like wild beasts." Then, as soon as they saw the novitiate spirit with the angels, fury came upon them, which appeared like the fire of hatred; so to prevent their doing harm they were cast back to hell. After this the angels appeared who from ends saw causes, and through causes effects, and who were in a heaven above those three assemblies; these angels appeared in a shining white light, which rolling down in spiral curves brought with it a circular wreath of flowers, and placed it upon the head of the novitiate spirit.

And then a voice issued therefrom, saying to him, "This laurel wreath is given you because you have from childhood meditated upon heaven and hell.
~Swedenborg, *The True Christian Religion, TCR 570*

31. Why Regeneration Is Necessary

Swedenborg writes:
All reason shows that man must be regenerated, for he is born into evils of every kind derived from his parents; and these evils have their seat in his natural man, which of itself is diametrically opposed to the spiritual man. Nevertheless man is born for heaven; although he does not enter heaven unless he becomes spiritual, and he can become spiritual only by means of regeneration.

From this it follows of necessity that the natural man with its lusts must be subdued, subjugated, and inverted, and that otherwise man cannot approach a single step toward heaven, but sinks deeper and deeper into hell.

Who cannot see this, if he believes that he has been born into evils of every kind and acknowledges the existence and contrariety of good and evil, and believes in a life after death, a hell and a heaven, and that evil is what constitutes hell and good is what constitutes heaven?

Viewed in himself the natural man [our states in natural consciousness] *in no way differs in his nature from the nature of beasts. Like them he is wild; but it is as to his will that he is such; in understanding he differs from beasts, in that the understanding can be elevated above the lusts of the will, and not only see but also moderate them; and for this reason man is able to think from understanding, and speak from thought, which beasts cannot do. What man is by birth, and what he would be if not regenerated, can be seen from fierce animals of every kind; that be would be a tiger, a panther, a leopard, a wild hog, a scorpion, a tarantula, a viper, a crocodile, and so on;*

consequently if he were not transformed by regeneration into a sheep, what would he be but a devil among devils in hell?

And in that state, if not restrained by civil laws, would not men from innate ferocity, rush upon one another and slaughter each other, and plunder each other even of the last scrap of clothing? How many are there of the human race who are not born satyrs and priapi or four-footed lizards; and who among these, if not regenerated, does not become an ape? External morality is required, for the sake of covering up their internals; and it does that. .
~Swedenborg, The True Christian Religion, TCR 570

In other words, God is actually doing the regenerating process within the person, but only to the extent that the individual willingly cooperates in that process.

Swedenborg writes:
The Lord is unceasingly in the act of regenerating man, because He is unceasingly in the act of saving him, and no one can be saved unless he is regenerated, according to the Lord's own words in John: Except a man be born anew, he cannot see the kingdom of God (John 3:5-6).

Regeneration, therefore, is the means of salvation, while charity and faith are the means of regeneration. To say that regeneration follows the faith of the present church, which leaves out man's co-operation, is vanity of vanities.

The action and cooperation here described may be seen in everything that is in any state of activity and mobility. Such is the action and cooperation of the heart and of every artery thereof; the heart acts, and the arteries by their sheaths or coats cooperate; hence circulation. It is the same with the lungs. The air acts by its incumbent weight according to the height of the atmosphere, and at first the ribs cooperate with the lungs, and immediately after the lungs with the ribs; from which there is respiration in every membrane of the body.

Thus the meninges of the brain, the pleura, the peritoneum, the diaphragm and the other parts which cover the viscera and enter into their composition, act and are acted upon, and thus they cooperate; for they are elastic; and from this is their existence and subsistence. It is the same in every fiber and nerve, and in every muscle, and even in every cartilage; in everyone of these, as is known, there is action and cooperation.

167

There is such a cooperation also in every sense; for the sensories of the body, like the motor organs, consist of fibers, membranes, and muscles; but to describe the co-operative action of each, is needless; for it is known that light acts upon the eye, sound upon the ear, odor upon the nostrils, and taste upon the tongue, and that the organs adapt themselves thereto; from which there is sensation. Who cannot see from all this, that unless there were such action and cooperation with the influent life in the spiritual organism of the brain, will and thought could not exist?

For life from the Lord flows into that organism, and because of this cooperation, man has a perception of what he thinks, and in like manner of what is there considered, concluded upon, and defined into act. If life were to act merely, and man were not to co-operate as if of himself, he could no more think than a stock, or than a temple while the minister is preaching in it. The temple may indeed, owing to the reverberation of the sound from its doors, have a sense, as it were, of the echo, but not of the discourse. So would man be, did he not co-operate with the Lord in respect to charity and faith. ~Swedenborg, The True Christian Religion, TCR 577

What man would be if he did not cooperate with the Lord, may also be illustrated by comparisons: When he had a perception and sense of anything spiritual pertaining to heaven and the church, it would be as if something distasteful or discordant flowed in, like an offensive smell entering the nose, a discordant sound the ear, a monstrous sight the eye, or a foul taste affecting the tongue.

If a delight of charity or a pleasure of belief were to flow into the spiritual organism of the mind of those whose delight is in evil and falsity, if such delight and pleasure were thrust upon them, they would be in anguish and torture, and finally would fall into a swoon. Because that organism consists of perpetual helices, in such a case it would coil itself up in spirals, and writhe like a serpent on an ant-hill. The truth of this has been proved to me by much experience in the spiritual world. ~Swedenborg, The True Christian Religion, TCR 578

Swedenborg is emphasizing here that no one can be saved who is not regenerated, and no one can be regenerated who is not actively resisting the habitual thoughts and intentions that characterize our mental states in natural consciousness. God cannot regenerate a person by an act of Divine judgment. This would be like turning a lion into a lamb. Their natures are opposed to each other by instinct, constitution, and anatomy. The unregenerate individual is like a lion who preys on others in an attempt to dominate them, control them, and use them for personal benefit regardless of how this will hurt them. God's power of regeneration is attached to our voluntary effort in wanting to change one's personality structure from selfish and loving self exclusively, to loving others as much as self or even more than self. This effort involves resisting spiritual temptations when we feel the impulse to be selfish. This occurs dozens or hundreds of times in a day. Observe your own thoughts and emotions and you'll be convinced!

Swedenborg writes:

Every man may be regenerated, each according to his state; for the simple and the learned are regenerated differently; as are those engaged in different pursuits, and those who fill different offices; those who search into the external things of the Word, and those who search into its internals; those who are principled in natural good from their parents, and those who are in evil; those who from their infancy have entered into the vanities of the world, and those who sooner or later have withdrawn from them; in a word, those who constitute the Lord's external church are regenerated differently from those who constitute His internal church, and this variety, like that of men's features and dispositions, is infinite; and yet everyone, according to his state, may be regenerated and saved.

The truth of this can be seen in the heavens, to which all the regenerate go, in that there are three heavens, a highest, a middle, and a lowest; and those who by regeneration acquire love to the Lord enter the highest heaven, those who acquire love to the neighbor, enter the middle heaven, and those who merely practice external charity, but at the same time acknowledge the Lord as God the Redeemer and Savior, enter the lowest heaven. All these are saved but in different ways.

All may be regenerated and thus saved, because the Lord with His Divine good and truth is present with every man; this is the source of everyone's life and his ability to understand and will, together with freedom of choice in spiritual things; in no man are these lacking. And the means to these are also given, for Christians in the Word, and for Gentiles in their religions, which teach that there is a God, and which furnish precepts respecting good and evil.

From all this it follows that everyone may be saved; consequently that it is not the Lord's fault if man is not saved, but man's, because he does not co-operate. ~Swedenborg, The True Christian Religion, TCR 580

Regeneration Is Effected In A Manner Analogous To That In Which Man Is Conceived, Carried In The Womb, Born And Educated.

In man there is a perpetual correspondence between what takes place naturally and what takes place spiritually, or between what takes place in his body and what takes place in his spirit. This is because man as to his soul is born spiritual, and is clothed with what is natural, which forms his material body. Therefore when this body is laid aside, his soul, clothed with a spiritual body, enters a world where all things are spiritual, and is there affiliated with its like. Since then, the spiritual body must be formed in a material body, and is formed by means of truths and goods which flow in from the Lord through the spiritual world, and are inwardly received by man in such things in him as are from the natural world, which are called civil and moral, the way in which its formation is effected is evident; and since, as before said, there is in man a constant correspondence between what takes place naturally and what takes place spiritually, it follows that this formation is like conception, gestation, birth, and education. It is for this reason that natural births in the Word mean spiritual births, which are births of good and truth; for whatever is mentioned in the sense of the letter of the Word, which is natural, involves and signifies what is spiritual. ~Swedenborg, The True Christian Religion, TCR 583

32. Temptations and Regeneration

Swedenborg writes:
When This Takes Place A Conflict Arises Between The Internal And The External Man, And Then The One That Conquers Rules Over The Other.

A conflict then arises because the internal man is reformed by means of truths; and from truths he sees what is evil and false, which evil and falsity are still in the external or natural man; consequently disagreement first springs up between the new will, which is above, and the old will, which is below; and as the disagreement is between the two wills, it is also between their delights; for the flesh, it is well known, is opposed to the spirit and the spirit to the flesh, and the flesh with its lusts must be subdued before the spirit can act and man become new.

After this disagreement of the two wills a conflict arises; and this is called spiritual temptation. This temptation or conflict does not take place between goods and evils, but between the truths of good and the falsities of evil. For good cannot fight from itself but fights by means of truths; nor can evil fight from itself but by means of its falsities; just as the will cannot fight from itself but by means of the understanding where its truths reside.

Man is not sensible of that conflict except as in himself, and as remorse of conscience; and yet it is the Lord and the devil (that is, hell) that are fighting in man, and they are fighting for dominion over him, or to determine who shall possess him. The devil or hell attacks man and calls out his evils, while the Lord protects him and calls out his goods. Although that conflict takes place in the spiritual world, still it takes place in man between the truths of good and the falsities of evil that are in him; therefore man must fight wholly as if of himself, for he has the freedom of choice to act for the Lord, and also to act for the devil; he is for the Lord, if he abides in truths from good, and for the devil, if he abides in falsities from evil.

From this it follows that whichever conquers, the internal man or the external, that one rules over the other; precisely like two hostile powers contending as to which shall be master of the other's kingdom-the conqueror takes possession of the kingdom, and places all in it under obedience to himself. In this case, therefore, if the internal man conquers, he obtains dominion and subjugates all the evils of the external man, and regeneration then goes on; but if the external man conquers, he obtains the dominion, and dissipates all the goods of the internal man, and regeneration perishes. ~Swedenborg, The True Christian Religion, TCR 596

While it is known at the present day, that there are temptations, hardly anyone knows whence and what they are and what good they effect. Whence and what they are has just been explained, also the good they effect, which is, that when the internal man conquers, the external is subjugated, and as this is subjugated lusts are dispersed, and affections for good and truth are implanted in their place, and are so arranged that the goods and truths which a man wills and thinks he may also do, and may speak them from the heart; and furthermore that by victory over the external man, man becomes spiritual, and is then affiliated by the Lord with the angels of heaven, who are all spiritual.

Heretofore temptations have not been understood, and scarcely anyone has known whence and what they are and the good they effect, because heretofore the church has not been in truths. No man is in truths unless he approaches the Lord directly, rejects the former faith and accepts the new. And this is why no one has been admitted into any spiritual temptation during the centuries that have passed since the Nicene Council introduced a belief in three Gods; for if anyone had been, he would have succumbed immediately, and thus would have precipitated himself more deeply into hell. The contrition which is said to precede the present faith is not temptation. I have questioned very many about it, and they have declared that it is nothing but a word, except perhaps with the simple there might be some timorous thoughts about hell-fire. . ~Swedenborg, The True Christian Religion, TCR 597

When man has passed through temptations he is as to his internal man in heaven, while by means of the external man he is in the world; thus by means of temptations there is a conjunction of heaven and the world effected in man; and then the Lord in him rules his world from heaven according to order. The contrary takes place if man remains natural; he is then eager to rule heaven from the world. Such does everyone become who is in the love of ruling from the love of self. If interiorly examined, such a man believes in himself only and not in God; and after death he believes him to be God who can exercise dominion over others. Such madness prevails in hell, and it even proceeds to such a length that some call themselves God the Father, some God the Son, some God the Holy Spirit, and among the Jews some call themselves the Messiah.

This shows clearly what man becomes after death if the natural man is not regenerated, and therefore to what length his fantasies would carry him if a New Church, in which genuine truths are taught, had not been established by the Lord. This is what is meant by these words of the Lord: In the consummation of the age [that is, at the end of the present church], there shall be such affliction as hath not been from the beginning of the world until now, no, nor ever shall be; and except those days be shortened, no flesh would be saved (Matt. 24:21, 22). . ~Swedenborg, The True Christian Religion, TCR 598

In the conflicts or temptations of men the Lord works a particular redemption; as He wrought a total redemption when in the world. By conflicts and temptations in the world the Lord glorified His Human, that is, made it Divine; in like manner now with man individually, when he is in temptations, the Lord fights for him, conquers the evil spirits who are infesting him, and after temptation glorifies him, that is, renders him spiritual. After His universal redemption the Lord reduced to order all things in heaven and in hell; with man after temptation He does in like manner, that is, He reduces to order all the things of heaven and the world that are in him.
~Swedenborg, The True Christian Religion, TCR 599

A regenerated internal man without a regenerated external also, may be likened to a bird flying in the air with no resting place on dry land except in a marsh, where it is attacked by serpents and frogs, so that it flies away and dies. It may be likened also to a swan swimming in mid-ocean, which cannot reach the shore and make her nest, so that the eggs she lays sink in the water, where they are eaten by fishes. It may be likened also to a soldier on a wall which is pulled down under him, so that he falls headlong and dies amid the ruins.

Again it may be likened to a beautiful tree transplanted into filthy soil where troops of worms eat up its roots, so that it withers and dies. It may also be likened to a house without a foundation, or to a column without a pedestal. Such is the internal man when it alone is reformed and not the external also; for it then has no means of determining itself to doing good. ~Swedenborg, The True Christian Religion, TCR 600

In other words, the center of psychodynamic operation in regeneration is the interaction between the "external man" and "internal man". The "external man" refers to our mind in natural consciousness, while the "internal man" refers to our mind in spiritual consciousness. Our personality structure develops within our experiencing and acting from infancy to young adulthood. This grown up personality is called the "external man" or natural mind.

We are then ready to begin our reformation, regeneration, or rebirth. This is a discretely new beginning for the growth and development of our personality. Our thinking gradually abandons natural-rational reasoning and morality and is replaced with spiritual-rational ideas and explanations. This requires a daily disciplinary attitude and motive that is outlined in this book through the practice of RTS. This spiritual effort must become the center of our life and its focus. Everything we do during the day, from personal to official to public, must be approached and arranged according to the new spiritual truths. These are to rule our mind.

For instance, my research in driving psychology shows that it is common to become angry or furious while driving in traffic, and even to fantasize punishment and torture on the offending motorists. I call it "mental road rage" which sometimes erupts into physical road rage and mayhem. *These negative thoughts and emotions must now be actively resisted on every trip that we use the car.* We are to use spiritual-rational reasoning to oppose the old-brain aggressive approach that is so easy to experience and which leads to angry outbursts and denigrating fantasies.

Time and again, hour-by-hour, all day long our thinking and feeling becomes negative against others or society. In each case we must show resistance to such ideas and emotions, identifying them as illegitimate spiritually, and working out the spiritual consequences in our afterlife of eternity. We are in training to learn to be spiritual-rational beings. This is where our true humanity begins.

But all this effort would fail miserably and return with a vengeance if we tried to do this self-modification alone, that is, without our focus on God. God supplies the guidance, the events, the emotions, and the thoughts. Now all we need to do is to accept it by acknowledging it, and then to love it because it is from God. That's all. Simple. Real. True. If we are sincere in this acceptance then God gives us the experience of successfully resisting our spiritual temptations. This allows us to continue growing through regeneration.

All day long these spiritual temptations will come along as you try to resist this or that negative thought or emotion, doing so because it is evil and from hell. These thoughts will tempt you to go back on your decision to be good. They will arrange themselves in reasonings that appear to you justified. That's the center of the cyclone in the temptation. If you give up your will to resist, you are lost. Next time it will be even harder and even more likely you will give in.

Thus you are lost forever in the cyclone of sin and evil, spiritual insanity and spiritual death. This is serious business. It is not a game. Your eternal future is at stake, either being a spiritually insane person and living with like others in darkness, stink, and fear, or a spiritually rational person and living in eternal bliss, happiness, and wisdom with others who are like-minded, including a spouse that is your true soulmate in eternal marriage.

These spiritual ideas certainly motivate us to resist temptations and to continue to resist them even after occasional failures when we give in to our habitual ways. Each episode of experiencing temptation and giving in to it must be seen as occurring for the last time, and thus the hope for heavenly future is ahead.

> *When This Takes Place A Conflict Arises Between The Internal And The External Man, And Then The One That Conquers Rules Over The Other.* *~Swedenborg, The True Christian Religion, TCR 596*

33. Jung on Individuation and Symbolism

Jung writes:
> *To find out what is truly individual in ourselves, profound reflection is needed; and suddenly we realize how uncommonly difficult the discovery of individuality is. ~Carl Jung, CW 7, Para 242.*

> *In the individuation process, it anticipates the figure that comes from the synthesis of conscious and unconscious elements in the personality. It is therefore a symbol which unites the opposites; a mediator, bringer of healing, that is, one who makes whole.*

> *Because it has this meaning, the child motif is capable of the numerous transformations mentioned above: it can be expressed by roundness, the circle or sphere, or else by the quaternity as another form of wholeness.*

> *I have called this wholeness that transcends consciousness the "self."*

The goal of the individuation process is the synthesis of the self. ~Carl Jung, CW 9i, Para 278

For the alchemists the process of individuation represented by the opus was an analogy of the creation of the world, and the opus itself an analogy of God's work of creation. ~Carl Jung, CW 9i, Para 550

This, roughly, is what I mean by the individuation process. As the name shows, it is a process or course of development arising out of the conflict between the two fundamental psychic facts. ~Carl Jung, CW 9i, Para 522-523

Animals generally signify the instinctive forces of the unconscious, which are brought into unity within the mandala. This integration of the instincts is a prerequisite for individuation. ~Carl Jung, CW 9i, Para 660

If the individuation process is made conscious, consciousness must confront the unconscious and a balance between the opposites must be found. As this is not possible through logic, one is dependent on symbols which make the irrational union of opposites possible. They are produced spontaneously by the unconscious and are amplified by the conscious mind.

The central symbols of this process describe the self, which is man's totality, consisting on the one hand of that which is conscious to him, and on the other hand of the contents of the unconscious. ~Carl Jung, CW 11, Para 755

Individuation appears, on the one hand, as the synthesis of a new unity which previously consisted of scattered particles, and on the other hand, as the revelation of something which existed before the ego and is in fact its father or creator and also its totality. ~Carl Jung, CW 11, Para 400

Individuation is an expression of that biological process—simple or complicated as the case may be —by which every living thing becomes what it was destined to become from the beginning. This process naturally expresses itself in man as much psychically as somatically. ~Carl Jung, CW 11, Para 460

The goal of psychological, as of biological, development is self-realization, or individuation. But since man knows himself only as an ego, and the self, as a totality, is indescribable and indistinguishable from a God image, self-realization—to put it in religious or metaphysical terms —amounts to God's incarnation. That is already expressed in the fact that Christ is the son of God. ~Carl Jung, CW 11, Para 233

The metaphysical process is known to the psychology of the unconscious as the individuation process. In so far as this process, as a rule, runs its course unconsciously as it has from time immemorial, it means no more than the acorn becomes an oak, the calf a cow, and the child an adult.

But if the individuation process is made conscious, consciousness must confront the unconscious and a balance between the opposites must be found. As this is not possible through logic, one is dependent on symbols which make the irrational union of opposites possible. They are produced spontaneously by the unconscious and are amplified by the conscious mind. ~Carl Jung, CW 11, Para 755

The difference between the "natural" individuation process, which runs its course unconsciously, and the one which is consciously realized, is tremendous. In the first case consciousness nowhere intervenes; the end remains as dark as the beginning.

In the second case so much darkness comes to light that the personality is permeated with light, and consciousness necessarily gains in scope and insight. The encounter between conscious and unconscious has to ensure that the light which shines in the darkness is not only comprehended by the darkness, but comprehends it. ~Carl Jung, CW 11, Para 756

---

34. Reciprocation to God in Celestial Consciousness or Individuation Stage 3

Swedenborg writes:

How important it is to have a right idea of God can be seen from the fact that the idea of God forms the inmost element of thought in all who have any religion, for all constituents of religion and all constituents of worship relate to God. And because God is universally and specifically involved in all constituents of religion and worship, therefore without a right idea of God no communication with the heavens is possible. So it is that every nation in the spiritual world is allotted its location in accordance with its idea of God as a person; for this idea and in no other lies an idea of the Lord. ~Swedenborg, Divine Love and Wisdom DLW 13

They who are in mutual love in heaven are continually advancing to the springtime of their youth, and to a more and more gladsome and happy spring the more thousands of years they live, and this with continual increase to eternity, according to the advance and degree of mutual love, charity, and faith. Those of the female sex who have died in old age and enfeebled with years, and who have lived in faith in the Lord, in charity toward the neighbor, and in happy conjugial love with their husbands, after a succession of years come more and more into the bloom of youth and early womanhood, and into a beauty that surpasses all idea of beauty such as is ever perceptible to the natural sight; for it is goodness and charity forming and presenting their own likeness, and causing the delight and beauty of charity to shine forth from every least feature of the countenance, so that they are the very forms of charity: some have beheld them and been amazed.

The form of charity, as is seen to the life in the other world, is such that it is charity itself that portrays and is portrayed, and this in such a manner that the whole angel, and especially the face, is as it were charity, the charity both plainly appearing to the view and being perceived by the mind. When this form is beheld, it is unutterable beauty that affects with charity the very inmost life of the beholder's mind. Through the beauty of this form the truths of faith are presented to view in an image, and are even perceived from it. Such forms, or such beauties, do those become in the other life who have lived in faith in the Lord, that is, in the faith of charity. All the angels are such forms, with countless variety, and of such is heaven. ~Swedenborg, Heavenly Secrets, AC 553

By now you realize why God is the central feature of RTS, and this reinforces the word "theistic" in its name. Swedenborg states in the quote above that "*without a right idea of God no communication with the heavens is possible*". The medical and psychological significance of this statement becomes understandable when we consider the anatomy of the psychic or spiritual body, which is the embodiment of our mind. This is why the spiritual body is also called the mental body.

There are three distinct levels of operation going on simultaneously in the mind, which viewed anatomically is called the spiritual body or the mental body. The three levels of simultaneous operation are arranged in a hierarchy of interdependent functions. All three mental anatomical systems must be operative simultaneously in order for our consciousness to function effectively and in good health.

The hierarchically arranged three levels of consciousness from top to bottom are called celestial, spiritual, and natural.

When we are infants and young children our top two levels are operative only in the unconscious self. Our natural consciousness develops successfully because of the children's dependency on the parents and caretakers. Without the parents or adult caretakers children cannot survive in this world. They move on to their next phase, which is to grow up in a spiritual environment in the afterlife of eternity where they become adult minds.

In this world, as we grow into older childhood and then young adulthood, our spiritual consciousness migrates from the collective unconscious to the individual conscious.

When this second system of mental operation is activated in adulthood, the natural consciousness can continue to grow into healthy maturity. The more the adult person becomes imbued with and attracted to spiritual ideas regarding God, *Sacred Scripture*, and the afterlife, the more conscious becomes the spiritual operation itself, and the more the spiritual ideas and thinking can influence the operation of the natural mental system.

With full development, the two systems – natural and spiritual consciousness -- become correspondences and act in synchrony. The result is that our natural day-to-day living in family and community becomes a true image of spiritual reality. This creates the spiritually enlightened individual who has a loving and intelligent personality with no psychopathological symptoms or dysfunctional weaknesses.

35. The RTS Personality

The title of this book refers to "the RTS personality". This is who we become by living our lives in accordance with RTS principles of understanding and thinking. You are the RTS personality when your natural ideas are re-arranged to correspond to spiritual ideas. In your RTS personality you are kind, forgiving, gentle, compassionate, supportive, loving, caring, rational, wise, inventive, steadfast, community oriented, just and honest, wishing others well and never envious of what others have.

The RTS personality takes care not to hurt others, either their feelings or their reputation and their ownership. This is the first phase of undergoing regeneration. No one can do anything honest or loving as long as he or she is still hurting others. Hurting others is caused by selfish loves immersed in natural consciousness. In that state we are telepathically connected to evil societies in the afterlife. We may "do good" to community and individuals but the motive and ultimate intention is selfish. God uses this selfish motive to benefit others, while the selfish person gets deeper involved and tied to those evil societies. The end result is that immediately after the three-day dying resuscitation procedure, the selfish person joins one of those evil societies and becomes as evil as they are.

36. List of Selfish Things
We Tend to Discount

Our first progress in regeneration is when we compel ourselves to stop hurting others in our daily living exchanges. Here are some memory joggers on how we all frequently hurt others by being selfish. I am making a sufficiently detailed list to help you realize that selfishness is in all things general and small that are part of our personality structure. It is essential that we learn to monitor our selfish loves in action in our daily lives.

** Playing music too loud, not caring about others
** Using the cell phone in a waiting room and talking loud
** Gossiping about someone, revealing private information
** Getting angry with someone due to one's hurt pride, dislike for the person, being in a bad mood, desire for revenge, enjoying being angry, enjoying punishing someone, etc.
** Feeling resentment against someone and condoning it
** Being late for an appointment by not planning right

** Offending someone with judgmental statements

** Swearing, either out loud or to oneself

**Thinking unkind and disrespectful thoughts about someone or some group

** Wishing ill to someone or group

** Exercising unfair discrimination, or condoning it

** Cheating on one's married partner

** Being untidy, unclean, neglectful

** Cheating, stealing, lying to gain an unfair advantage

** Neglecting personal hygiene due to giving in to laziness or due to the love of disorder

** Giving in to the love of rebelling against what is knowingly legitimate

** Wanting to embarrass someone for the sake of amusement

** Letting someone else take the blame for something we did

** Enjoying jokes that are disrespectful of others

** Enjoying entertainment that portray people hurting and betraying each other

** Feeling no responsibility at polluting the environment and the ocean with unnecessary and harmful lifestyle practices

** etc. (can you think of a bunch of others?)

By now you realize that such a list goes on and on. We each have an endless number of ways in which we are being selfish on a daily basis. Getting rid of all of them one by one seems impossible. Indeed so. But God comes to our rescue. God never gives us a task that we cannot perform. God is super-kind and helpful. All we need to do ourselves is to live our daily life of regeneration by compelling ourselves to resist selfish behaviors and thoughts. When these thoughts occur we are to be aware of them. Then we are to disagree with them and reject them because we do not wish any more to be that kind of person who thinks and condones those thoughts.

God does all the rest. God is a Divine Surgeon who repairs our personality structure from within. When we get rid of one selfish love, God can excise a whole clump of them that hang together and usually act together in our mind.

By this daily process, our natural consciousness can incorporate progressively more and more spiritual ideas with which to think in a rational manner about our life in this world and in the afterlife. First our natural consciousness is arranged in correspondence to spiritual ideas. Afterwards, our natural consciousness is arranged to correspond to celestial ideas. The RTS personality can thereby progress still further.

37. Celestial Consciousness

But there is still a higher level of humanity that is "celestial" and which is still stuck in the collective unconscious. The enlightened spiritual person loves others as much as self, loves worship and religious fellowship, compels himself or to avoid sins such as being unfaithful in married life, or hurting hostile others in revenge. The chief motivation that maintains this kind of decent and healthy lifestyle is the motive to obey God's commandments and to refrain from sinning.

The spiritual-natural individual continues to have certain types of weaknesses or psychological complexes that must eventually be consciously addressed by the person, or else there develops a tendency to veer off the spiritual path and even to fall back into mere natural thinking and emoting. If this happens it is a psychological disaster for the individual. From mental health and rational intelligence the thinking and emoting become pathological and spiritually irrational.

But there is an effective method for preventing that danger by allowing the celestial consciousness to become operative in the individual conscious, just as it happened with the elevation from natural to spiritual-natural consciousness.

The very nature of heavenly love is to want what is one's own to belong to another. ~Swedenborg, HH 268

We enter the higher mental state of celestial consciousness when we begin to love others more than self.

Jung writes:

> The unconscious [at times] produces contents which are valid not only for the person concerned, but for others as well, in fact for a great many people and possible for all. ~Carl Jung; The Relations between the Ego and the Unconscious, 1928
>
> The ego is the subject of all successful attempts at adaptation so far as these are achieved by the will. ~Carl Jung, CW 9ii; para 11
>
> Once we have freed ourselves from the prejudice that we have to refer to concepts of external experience or to a priori categories of reason, we can turn our attention and curiosity wholly to that strange and unknown thing we call spirit. ~Carl Jung, Spirit and Life, CW 8, para. 626
>
> From the psychological point of view, the phenomenon of spirit, like every autonomous complex, appears as an intention of the unconscious superior to, or at least on a par with, intentions of the ego. If we are to do justice to the essence of the thing we call spirit, we should really speak of a "higher" consciousness rather than of the unconscious. ~Carl Jung, Spirit and Life, CW 8, para. 643
>
> The individual ego is the stable in which the Christ-child is born. ~Carl Jung, Collected Works, Vol. 11
>
> Only a life lived in a certain spirit is worth living. It is a remarkable fact that a life lived entirely from the ego is dull not only for the person himself but for all concerned. ~Carl Jung, Spirit and Life, CW 8; The Structure and Dynamics of the Psyche, p. 645

Celestial consciousness or individuation stage 3 is a mental anatomical layer that is discretely above spiritual consciousness. The direction of consciousness is downward as the living human flow descends from God where it is perfect and infinite, to the celestial human level of reception that is far above spiritual consciousness.

The idea of loving others more than self seems impossible in natural and spiritual consciousness, but it is self-evident and spontaneous in celestial consciousness.

How can I love the pervert who molests children? How can I love people who deceive others and cheat them of their needs? I can love my parents, wife, children, and country more than I love myself, but how can I love strangers and dangerous people more than I love myself?

Spiritual reasoning hides background assumptions and inconsistencies that influence our conclusions without our realizing it. The motive to love others as much as self because God commands it leads to these errors of thinking. For example, religion from *Sacred Scripture* and doctrine teaches that we must love others and do good to them. Because it is a commandment of God the spiritual-natural person will endeavor to do just that even if it doesn't seem logical. One is taught that God's logic is a "mystery" and isn't understandable to human beings, which is why obeying commandments is called "faith".

However, this kind of puzzlement about God can be repaired when the person backs off from a strictly literal interpretation of God's commandments in *Sacred Scripture*. It is pretty obvious to students of the Bible that many passages and commandments in the *Old Testament* contradict each other. For instance, at one time God is depicted as an angry and cruel tyrant who enjoys taking revenge on those who insult His Glory and He is prompt to punish thousands of people for the disobedience of one or a few of their leaders. Also, God talks at times in certain passages as if He were a racist, distributing rewards and punishments according to one's race, some being identified as favored by God more than others. As well, God elevates men above women in rank and control, and commands the cruel treatment of women such as stoning to death when they are accused by two men of adultery or lewdness.

But then in many other passages God speaks of Himself as being perfect in loving and forgiving, as never punishing or taking revenge, and as longing for recognition not for His Own aggrandizement and glory but for the sake of what He can give and bestow to the person who worships Him and His Glory.

The rational person must take notice of these disturbing contradictions in *Sacred Scripture*, which is the very "Word of God". One type of reasoning that then spontaneously occurs is that the literal-historical description in *Sacred Scripture* reflects not so much God Himself but the natural consciousness of the people to whom the *Sacred Scripture* was given for a religion. This thought allows the celestial consciousness of the individual to begin the migration across the barrier from the collective unconscious to the individual celestial consciousness. It leads the person to notice details and implications in *Sacred Scripture* that were completely missed before.

For instance, when God depicts Himself as vengeful, racist, and cruel against women He is reflecting what people in merely natural consciousness think of God. In ancient times when the *Old Testament* was given to people through the chosen prophets, this is exactly how people thought of God, namely a more powerful version of kings and taskmasters. They would have rejected all of *Sacred Scripture* had it not been written this way. And without *Sacred Scripture* all humanity would be doomed to devolution into bestiality, superstition, and evil magic. In short, there would be no possibility for regeneration of such an insane character.

Every human being would then be born into a community of spiritual insanity and psychological pathology, loving self only and dealing cruelly and savagely with all who did not favor them. Such society could not survive and humanity would end. God prevented this sad fate by giving to each nation and culture a religion based on *Sacred Scripture* that reflected their culture and level of thinking and emoting. In this way they were able to accept that religion and to practice it in natural consciousness.

Once this is well worked out in one's spiritual consciousness, it becomes easier to rationally deal with commandments that order preference to one's own race and to men over women. It becomes a spiritually liberating experience to be able to start loving God as being indeed perfect and loving, always present, and omnipotent. It becomes inconceivable to attribute to God anything that is not loving, forgiving, just, accepting, and rewarding. All things that happen express this loving and human nature of God. One can accept personal misfortune or family tragedy as expressing God's caring and constant provision of our eternal happiness and heavenly communion that is waiting us after death.

For those who trust in the Divine all things are moving towards an everlasting state of happiness, and no matter what happens at any time to them, it contributes to that state. ~Swedenborg, Secrets of Heaven, AC 8478

One can then begin to accept the idea that we are to love others more than self, being fully confident that God is in charge of everything. But at the same time one receives the celestial-rational clarity that tells us that it is foolish to think that God commands us to love our enemy as we love our friends and family. This would be spiritual insanity. We can see that we must love everyone in accordance with the good that is in them from God. It is the good from God in a person that we are to love and not so much the person.

When we are still in natural consciousness we may be called a "dead man" and our life may be called *anti-life*. This is because we are educated to believe in materialistic science. In most school and college courses on human biology and psychology young people are taught that human beings evolved like other animals from lower animals and developed language which allow us to think symbolically and solve problems logically. In comparative psychology research the attempt has been consistent for more than a century to demonstrate that animals can be trained to communicate and to solve problems just like human beings, except that our brain is more complex and therefore we can surpass them in thinking and planning ability.

We may agree with this lowered concept of human beings if it were the case that they remain in natural consciousness and that there does not exist a spiritual consciousness to which human beings may be able to rise above that of animals. Without this spiritual awareness human beings would be nothing but brute animals of a purely physical origin and life. Consciousness would then be a temporary "emergent phenomenon" that ceases into nothing when the physical brain is dead.

But this is not the case. Human beings are born into two worlds with a temporary physical avatar and a permanent psychic or spiritual body. *There is nothing of human mental activity possible in the physical avatar.* Since birth our mind, our emotions, our total personality, are operations of the spiritual body. Nothing whatsoever of our human mental life and feelings are possible in the physical avatar, which only serves to transmit physical or electro-chemical movements of electrons and atoms.

The avatar is designed and connected to the spiritual body by functional laws of correspondences that are built into the biological property of mental operations and physical stimuli. The avatar is connected to our spiritual body operating with it synchronously. Our spiritual body, which is our mind, receives the information from the avatar by reacting mentally to everything that is going on physically. The two are connected virtually through the laws of correspondences that are built into everything physical and everything spiritual or mental.

This is the dualist biology of human life that science and psychology courses might be teaching one day when the stubborn armor of materialism cracks and makes room in education for scientific dualism and theistic science.

Animals are not anatomically built to be able to operate at a conscious spiritual level. It is certain that animals have an "animal soul" which is a spiritual organ and therefore immortal. But the nature of an animal soul is distinctly different from that of a human soul. This spiritual reality may be seen in the difference in form or anatomy between a human being and any other animal. Conscious spiritual operation is experienced only by the human mind in the spiritual body.

But although all human individuals are born with the capacity to experience conscious spiritual activity it is by no means a mental process that develops by itself without conscious attention. It is not uncommon for people to lead a productive and happy life and pass on without ever having experienced conscious spiritual thoughts, perceptions, and feelings.

––––––––––––––––

Jung writes:
> The more you cling to that which all the world desires, the more you are Everyman, who has not yet discovered himself and stumbles through the world like a blind mind leading the blind with somnambulistic certainty into the ditch. Everyman is always a multitude.

> Cleanse your interest of that collective sulphur which clings to all like a leprosy. For desire only burns in order to burn itself out, and in and from this fire arises the true living spirit which generates life according to its

own laws, and is not blinded by the shortsightedness of our intentions or the crude presumption of our superstitious belief in the will. ~Carl Jung, CW 14, Para 192

Not until after we are awakened from the three-day dying-resuscitation procedure that we can experience celestial consciousness directly in our awareness. At that point our natural consciousness shuts down and we function with spiritual consciousness that is enlightened by correspondence with celestial consciousness.

Jung writes:

No man can change himself into anything from sheer reason; he can only change into what he potentially is. ~Carl Jung, CW 5, Para 533

Swedenborg writes:

Those who lack all kindness . . . want to examine and in fact judge everyone and crave nothing more than to find evil, constantly bent as they are on condemning, punishing, and torturing others. Those who are guided by kindness, on the other hand, hardly even notice evil in another but pay attention instead to everything good and true in the person. When they do find anything bad or false, they put a good interpretation on it. This is a characteristic of all angels—one they acquire from the Lord, who bends everything bad toward good. ~Swedenborg, Secrets of Heaven HH 1079

---

38. Ego-self vs. As-of-Self

The word "theistic" in *theistic self-analysis* refers to the premise that God takes an active role in all self. This premise follows from the definition of God as omnipotent. The assertion that God is "omnipotent" means that God has all power in the universe and in the human mind. The expression "all power" does not allow any exceptions. In other words, whatever and wherever power or activity is being exercised it is done from God and by

God. For an atom or particle to move or to hold together with other atoms, there must be power exerted. This activity is God's power in action, or in the field of creation. It takes power for some information to be cognized, to be stored in memory, and then to be recalled to awareness.

This power is God's power by which God sustains our mental activity, as when we are willing or intending something (affective system), feeling pleasure, reasoning (cognitive system), making our muscles move (sensorimotor system), turning our gaze, listening to a sound, etc. These are mental activities and they require anatomical organs that are made of mental substance, or "spiritual substance", since everything that is spiritual is made of mental activity.

Add to this explanation the idea that "God's power" is actually love-substance filling the mental world and the physical universe. God's love-substance is the only power and therefore it is infinite, omnipotent, omnipresent, and omniscient. From this you can understand that love-substance is God's omnipresence since all things were created of love-substance. God is conscious of His Own love-substance everywhere all the time, and before place and time were created.

If this premise is accepted then one can see immediately that all self is theistic self-analysis in actuality.

In order to be consistent with this actuality, theistic self-analysis needs a spiritual alternative to the concept of "ego" or "self" as viewed traditionally in psychology. This new psychological concept may be called *as-of self*. The difference between "self" or "ego" and "as-of self" is like the difference between natural consciousness and spiritual consciousness. We begin intellectual life with the notion of "self", but as we embark upon regeneration, we continue with the reborn concept of "as-of self".

The traditional concept of self is not possible in theistic self-analysis because the idea of self assumes that the self is free to act and to think from itself. This is how people are taught to define individual identity and inner freedom. This traditional idea no doubt came about due to the actual experience of being alone in one's own mind. We do not see God, ghosts, angels, or devils outside of us, and only those see them inside of us who are mentally abnormal. The normal state of mind is to attribute to ourselves everything we see within ourselves. It is known in traditional psychiatry that hearing voices within ourselves is a symptom of serious mental disturbance and personality disorder requiring urgent therapeutic intervention.

The concept and experience of the independent and free inner self is well established and solid in every normal human mind.

But now I need to note that every "normal" human mind in natural consciousness is immersed in negativity, dysfunctions, and psychological neuroses or complexes of all sorts that reduce happiness and productivity, and increase emotional conflict and despondency. This is the process of de-individuation immersed in natural consciousness. It will continue an organic downward path that reduces our humanity and robs us of our innate human capacities. The end of de-individuation is eternal life in a state of mental hell or spiritual insanity. The individual is incapable of reversing course because of a relentless unwillingness to let go of some particular hellish love that occupies the center of the personality structure.

People can change personality structure only when they agree to it. Those in hell refuse to agree to a personality restructuring in which the old ruling love of self is dethroned. People can refuse to let go of this love to eternity, thus endlessly. This is the actual situation in the expression "eternal hell" that offends many people as "excessive and inhuman punishment".

When we function with the concept of the self we are consistent with delusion and inconsistent with actuality. We therefore lack the power to reverse course. *Every individual can reverse this process by adopting the concept of as-of self.* This requires that we acknowledge the omnipotent God who is acting within and without. To "acknowledge God" refers to understanding that God is the only source for our power to modify ourselves.

Theistic self-analysis helps us to understand the concept of *as-of self*. It is not effective to merely impart this new notion by rote or by a persuasive creed, or by encouraging conformity to a peer group. It is absolutely necessary that the new concept of as-of self be incorporated in a consistent worldview that explains the relationship of God to the individual and the world.

Some people will see theistic self-analysis as a "religious" endeavor because its basic concepts assume that God exists, that God is a person, and that God is active in our mind and environment. But these are not a religious creed. These belong to all religions, and if you allow me to say it, to no religion. Indeed, *God does not belong to any religion!* And especially is this true in science.

Theistic self-analysis is a scientific approach. It introduces God into science. It seems to me that there is no need to discuss religions, creeds, and belief systems in self. Clients of all religions will not find anything in theistic self-analysis that is contrary to their religion since every religion acknowledges an omnipotent God. Theistic self-analysis merely draws out the rational implications of this acknowledgment.

Therapists who study the works of Jung and Swedenborg will be better prepared to understand, apply, and teach the new psychology of the as-of self.

Readers who are interested in more details may consult my other books on this topic that are listed at the very end of this book.

The principle of ego-self vs. as-of self is at the center of all other principles in RTS. A useful method is to observe your own relationship with a pet. In the United States and some other countries in Europe and in Japan, the majority of families own a pet such as a dog or cat, a bird or any other tamed animal that forms a personal relationship with the owner.

Jung writes:
> You can only know yourself if you get into yourself, and you can only do that when you accept the lead of the animal. ~Carl Jung, Visions Seminar, p. 458

Swedenborg writes:
> Then the angels said, 'We have been chosen from heaven to instruct newcomers from the lands of the natural world, since all who come here from there have foolish beliefs about heaven, and even about salvation. Therefore, unless these foolish ideas are dispersed, which is done by lessons, their rational faculty would be shut off. This faculty is above the memory as the result of the reception of the light of heaven, and makes men wise; if it were shut off, men would turn into animals, the only

difference being that they could use their external senses to think, and could speak from that kind of thought alone. ~Swedenborg, In: Five Memorable Relations, n. 12

---

39. Self and Pets

It is well known in psychology and in popular knowledge that people's involvement with a pet is beneficial to them mentally and physically. Most people have a deep compassion for animals in general and are extremely upset when they witness callous and cruel treatment of animals. You can gain an overall glimpse of the field of pet psychology by looking it up in Wikipedia or Web search on such phrases as "pet psychology", "animal behavior", "animal psychopathology", and so on.

For instance, in the Wikipedia entry for "human-canine bond" is presented as relating to the idea of "anthropomorphism", which has to do with how human beings think of their pets as thinking, loving, wanting, and planning, all as if they were human. The article also has a section on "benefits" where it cites the American Veterinary Medical Association asserting that *"the human–canine bond is influenced by emotional, psychological, and physical interactions that are essential to the health and well-being of both people and dogs"*. This "human-animal" psychological bond applies to any animal that one relates to as being a pet. The article also makes reference to *"Animal-assisted therapy* (AAT) and activities that demonstrate this human–canine bond and this interaction with an animal; in most cases a dog helps improve the quality of life".

In the perspective of RTS pet bonding can help us to understand better our relationship to God. Think about your relationship to your pet in a way that is analogous to the bond and relationship that exists between you personally and God. You love your pet and there is a personal bond between you and your pet. This bond is unique and special. You are human and therefore you can take care of the pet by protecting it and creating a home environment in which the pet can be happy and healthy throughout its life. God has a personal and unique bond with you as well.

You are God's human pet and you need God to provide you with safety and ability to manage your daily life. You can better understand God's love and caring for you by considering your own love for your pet.

> *I am personally of the opinion that not only people, but even animals have souls. ~Carl Jung, ETH Lecture III, p. 18*

Now notice how what you do on a daily basis to achieve this bond with your beloved pet and to protect and nourish it. You are concerned about the pet's health so you take your pet to the veterinarian on a regular basis and take advice from experts on what is the best diet to feed your pet. God is concerned about your health and diet from the moment you are born and afterwards to eternity. God is involved in making sure you are fed both ways: in the physical body and in the spiritual mind. God brings you specific experiences through events and guides your cognitive and affective reactions to these events. In this way God is constantly building up the content and structure of your personality.

You are also concerned with the happiness and emotional development of your pet. You try to keep things away from the pet, things that are scary and disturbing to your pet, such as certain noises and the presence of other animals and people. You provide your pet with plenty of touching, petting, and loving talk. This makes the pet feel self-confident, secure and content. God constantly looks to maintaining a personal relationship with you. God wants you to relate and reciprocate so that the bond between God-Human and mere human be allowed to grow, deepen, and influence the life of the human being more and more.

Once we begin to maintain this personal daily relationship with God we are in a position in which God can guide us and provide us with all our needs for regeneration, thus for becoming spiritual and happy forever. God can repair us and we can recover from our ills so that we may become healthy and whole. God can do this when we reciprocate; we cannot do it on our own. You cannot wait for your pet to "allow you" to take it to the vet or to alter its diet or to administer some drug. You just do these things because they issue from your love and your understanding.

God has to be pro-active in protecting and leading you. Our own ego is our greatest mortal enemy. Note that at the beginning we would not accept this relationship with God if we perceived that God has all the power and we have none. Your pet needs to feel that it is free to live and do, to explore and react, even at times to stubbornly and irrationally refuse you and resist your effort on the pet's behalf. We do this with God. We refuse to obey and follow. We irrationally insist that we can do it on our own, or that we need more freedom to be happy.

As a result of this foolish self-insistence and self-elevation we run into trouble. God cannot prevent some of these negative things from happening to you without injuring your mind. You understand this when you are training your pet to do something new. You do not take the either/or attitude, which is to make the pet responsible for his failure in learning the new task fast enough. Your love for the pet and your rationality inform you that the pet is such as to need to learn something gradually, not all at once. So you tolerate in your mind intermediate stages during which you are happy even though the pet has not learned to perform the new behavior consistently. Your love gives you the wisdom and motivation to provide for your pet.

When you train your pet you realize that you need to use rewards. Sometimes you also need to use punishment that is appropriate and easy for the pet to connect to its response or lack of it. So the punishing stimulus or the reward needs to come close enough to the pet's behavior in order for them to be connected in the expectations of the animal.

God provides for you many negative experiences and disappointments, as well as many daily rewards and happinesses. Some of these you can perceive are from God, and that makes you happy and feeling reassured that God is looking after you all the time. And some of the rewards you enjoy the benefits thereof but do not think at the time that it was God who gave it to you. People often talk about "having luck" when they win something unexpectedly. Or they may think they have "bad luck" when something unpleasant and disappointing happens. But there is no luck in itself. If luck actually existed then God would no longer be omnipotent since some things will happen by "luck" not by God's will and wisdom. So if you feel lucky you need to attribute it to God as a caring gift under the guise of chance.

An important perception that we obtain through our relationship with our pet is the feeling of co-presence. When we are with our pet we do not feel alone. This is well known by many and it is not unusual for people to acquire a pet for that reason when they feel lonely without a meaningful relationship at the time. *This feeling of co-presence with God is the central beam that upholds the edifice of our future life in eternity.*

Observe this peaceful state of co-presence with your pet. You like to clarify this state of co-presence by doing little things that confirm co-awareness of each other. This is what feels right and healing in the human-animal relationship. You reach out and touch the animal while you smile or say things in a soothing way. The pet responds in its own manner: dogs lick you and jump on you, cats bump you and rub up against you while purring loudly, birds peck your fingers and fly on your shoulders, horses nuzzle you, monkeys hug you, whales or fish come up to see you up close, and so on. All these interactions also occur between animals and they indicate their need and pleasure in the mutual awareness of co-presence.

Once you acquire this feeling of constant co-presence with God, and it does not take much time to learn this, you will never be lonely, despondent, anxious, worried, or scared – not for very long when you do have these feelings. Negativity cannot survive co-presence with God.

There are times when you need to do things to your pet that the pet dislikes and strongly objects by refusal and resistance. For example, when you have to give your pet some medicine that the vet prescribed to take care of a pesky problem the animal is having. You discovered that it's useless to try to reason with your pet by explaining the bad stuff that will happen unless the medicine is swallowed. So you need to trick or compel the pet to get the medicine swallowed.

God uses multiple approaches to deal with our recalcitrance and resistance to doing the right thing. When we do the right thing then God can protect us and provide for all our needs, pleasures, and wishes. Often God has to trick us into doing the right thing when we refuse out of foolishness and spiritually insane self-reliance. When bad and unhappy things befall some people they blame God for it, or else they deny God altogether.

If this happens to you it is necessary to remember that God is in charge of the bad as well as the good. And that God provides the bad *for our sake*, not because God cannot control events. God can prevent any particular bad thing that happens to you. Yes, that's correct. So then why did God allow this horrendous thing to happen to you, or to your loved ones?

People never get to find a satisfactory answer to this situation if they blame God and ask for an explanation. In this mental state understanding anything about God is impossible. Everything gets distorted to fit the self and to make God to be wrong or not worthy of loyalty.

If you come to love and trust God through your personal daily relationship you will feel in God's co-presence all the time. There will be no lapse. God insures this as long as you reciprocate. In this co-presence mentality of mutual love with God, you are able to perceive and understand that the horrendous upsetting bad thing that happened to you or someone, is an act of love. This is what your pet needs to accept and stay loyal to you personally when you try to make the pet swallow the medicine. Sticking to God by being loyal and co-present is the solution to all your problems, weaknesses, and psychopathologies in daily life.

Rationality tells us that God would not provide negative experiences to the children that God created and is raising to become eternal citizens of heaven. So when God provides any negative event to befall us, it is not due to lack of control or lack of love. Observe how you provide negative experiences to your beloved pet, when seen from the perspective of the animal. You force the pet to swallow bad tasting stuff. You leave the pet for many hours. You object when the pet is too rough or too loud or too aggressive. You stop the pet from exploring where it wants to even if it is dangerous. You provide a pet-sitter when you take a trip even if the pet doesn't like that person. And so on. From the pet's perspective many of the things you do for the pet's sake are negative. Thinking about this helps us accept the spiritual rational idea that all things that befall us are necessary for our future happiness in eternal heaven. When you train your pet to acquire some new behavior you do not punish the animal for not doing what you want immediately.

Everything we discussed about pets also applies to infants and children. Think about toddlers excitingly practicing their new ability of moving around, crawling, walking. The mother or other adult watches over the toddler to make sure the child does not get injured. The mother's role with the child is analogous to God's role to the mother. The mother continuously guides the child away from dangerous things by gently turning the toddler's body to face another direction. The child is not aware of this guidance. The child feels entirely free and thinks that it is responsible for avoiding injury.

The mother also feels free and thinks that she is responsible for her ability to protect her child and to take care of the family's domestic needs. Meanwhile however God is the power and the intelligence that guides the mother away from foolish decisions that would hurt herself and her family. The mother may not acknowledge God's moment-by-moment intervention role in her actions and decisions, nevertheless it is the reality and the truth.

You can see rationally why God proceeds this way for the sake of the woman and her family. What would happen if God were to let the woman perceive and experience God's interventions directly? She would no longer be able to function normally. God wills that the individual feels free and not compelled by God or any other force. To feel as-if one is free is essential for being a rational and independent individual who acknowledges responsibility for one's own actions, plans, and intentions.

The mother also proceeds in a similar way with her child. She wills that her child feel free by intervening in the child's stream of behavior and keeping this intervention outside the awareness of the child. Now think about what would happen if the mother directly prevented the child from touching something or walking into something. The child would then perceive this direct intrusion and see it as taking away the child's freedom to move around and go to whatever looks attractive and delightful. You can see the result when the child protests, tries to do what it wants, and when you prevent, it cries and is no unhappy. Even worse, the child stops practicing walking and exploring. This would be a disaster.

Now think of God's parallel role relationship to the mother. God is guiding and training the regenerating individual. What would happen if God now removed from the individual's personality all motives and ideas that are contrary to the commandments? The result would be a disaster for the individual. The experience would be that all delight and joy of life has gone out. Almost all the things one likes to do that make us feel alive would now cease altogether. We would be sitting with our hands in our lap, wanting nothing, thinking nothing, and doing nothing.

God would not initiate such a disaster but protects us from it by intervening without our consciousness and by leaving in place what is contrary to the commandments of life. Eventually, by gradual growth and change, we become motivated to desist from what is contrary to the commandments. In this way our personality structure is gradually regenerated.

It is critically important that we understand rationally God's management approach in everyone's daily lives. It bothers people to see bad things happening everywhere and to ourselves. The insistent question poses itself in our mind: Where is God? Why is God allowing this to happen? A rational approach is needed to understand this fundamental issue. The analogy with the pet and the child may help the person figure it out. God takes into account the fact that when we start regeneration almost all of our delights and joys of life are spiritually unlawful. This is due to being born with selfish and self-centered tendencies that are inherited from the parents, which they inherited from their parents, and so on. The result is an accumulation of selfish traits that suffuses and immerses our personality in what is evil and antisocial.

God does not remove our evils all at once, but only gradually, allowing us to continue having enjoyments and pleasures in our daily lives. God exerts constant pressure on our motivational system to veer us off the selfishness and turn us more and more toward mutual love and love of God. This happens to the extent that we cooperate and reciprocate.

It is again critical for all of us to understand rationally that God's ability to assist us in personality change depends on our as-of self effort. *God's power to effect change in our personality is through the as-of self effort that we are willing voluntarily to expend.* Without that effort God cannot remove the evil traits. *This is why God provides natural and spiritual temptations in the process of regeneration to allow us to perform that as-of self effort.* This as-of self effort involves resisting our desire or intention to perform a selfish act or thought.

God provides us with a conscience that gives us a warning signal when we are contemplating acting on some selfish desire or thought. In natural consciousness (individuation stage 1), the temptations we experience are natural and the conscience that gives us perception and warning is also natural. For example, we may experience the desire to cheat or lie, knowing that no one will find out about it. Our conscience warns us that we don't really know if no one will find out. We should not do it in any event for that is the safest. As well, that will give us a solid personality that others will admire and reward. So to resist cheating and lying is always the safest and best policy.

Later in regeneration God gives us spiritual temptations if we have gathered for ourselves the rational arguments to resist for the sake of spiritual good and truth that we acknowledge as being God's good and truth. This motivation is spiritual-rational, not merely natural-rational. It allows the build up of a spiritual conscience. This at last has full power and efficacy in spiritual regeneration. Now the reasons or motives for which we resist doing certain selfish things are motives of mutual love and love of God's good and truth. Resisting from this perspective brings us fully into individuation stage 2 and its spiritual consciousness.

Jung writes:
> The ego is a province, merely an administrative centre of a great empire. Man is an indescribable phenomenon because his self cannot be completely grasped. The self is the light of the world; it is the full realization of everything in consciousness. Every animal and every plant is a representation of the self... Thus the whole world enters consciousness. We would call the self a multiple consciousness in God, or a spiritual Olympus, or an inner firmament. ~Carl Jung, ETH Lectures, Page 36

---

40. Will Our Pets Be Present With Us In the Afterlife?

It is nearly impossible to consider the spiritual experience of owning a pet without also thinking about the pet's presence with us in the afterlife of eternity. In natural consciousness we may confess to a desire to have an afterlife in which our pets are present with us. But we actually do not believe that this is possible or real. Later in spiritual consciousness we can rationally understand that for us to be in heaven in the afterlife means that our loves will be with us, otherwise what kind of heaven is it? And so we think of our pets, children, and favorite people to be with us in eternity.

But as we continue to proceed in our understanding to celestial consciousness we see additional things not yet understood before. The afterlife of eternity is the mental world in which we exist since birth. We understand that our mental world is substantive or spiritual. It is not a vast empty space in which we each have our thoughts, feelings, and experiences. The mental world is anatomical and organic made of love-substance and truth-substance that creates and fills the mental world of humanity.

All things that exist in the mental world must be made of the human anatomy. Consciousness is the anatomical form of the human mind. Everything that is consciousness must therefore be human or part of human anatomy. But animals do not have a human anatomy. An animal has consciousness or a "soul" due to the animal's anatomy being modeled after the human anatomy. To the extent that the animal anatomy overlaps with the human anatomy it can have consciousness. But this is the animal's own consciousness. It is not human consciousness. The co-presence of consciousness with our pets here on earth is the consciousness that gives us co-presence in the afterlife of eternity.

Swedenborg writes:

> So far as influx and correspondences are concerned, it is similar with animals as with men. That is to say, with an animal there is an influx from the spiritual world and an afflux from the natural world which hold it together and give it life. But the actual operation of that influx and afflux varies according to the forms which animals' souls take and consequently which their bodies take. It is like the light of the world which flows into varying objects on earth to the same degree and in the same way yet acts in differing ways within differing forms. In some it produces beautiful colours, in others horrid colours. Thus when spiritual light flows into the souls of animals its reception is completely different, and the effect it therefore has on the activity of their souls is different from its reception and the effect it has when it flows into the souls of human beings.

> [2] For the souls of human beings exist on a higher level and in a more perfect state, and are such that they are able to look upwards, and so to heaven and the Lord. Consequently the Lord is able to join them to Himself and grant them eternal life. But the souls of animals are such that they cannot do other than look downwards, thus merely to earthly things, and so can be joined only to these. This is also why they perish together with the body. It is their ends in view that show what the life possessed by man is like and what that

possessed by a beast is like. Man is able to have spiritual and celestial ends in view, and to see, acknowledge, and believe them, and to have an affection for them. But beasts can have none but natural ends in view. Thus man is able to dwell in the Divine sphere of ends and purposes which exist in heaven and which constitute heaven, whereas beasts can dwell in no other sphere than that of ends and purposes which exist on earth. Ends are nothing else than loves, for the things which people love they have as an end in view.

[3] The reason why most people do not know how to distinguish their own life from that of beasts is that the two are externally alike. Both are interested in and set their hearts solely on earthly, bodily, and worldly objects. Such people also believe that their life is similar to the life which beasts possess and that like these they are going to become nothing at all when they die. For what spiritual and celestial things may be they do not know because they are not interested in them. From this comes the insanity of our own times of people comparing themselves to animals and not recognizing any internal distinction. But anyone who believes in the existence of celestial and spiritual things, that is, who allows spiritual light to flow in and influence him, sees quite the reverse, and also sees the extent to which he is superior to animals. The life of animals however will in the Lord's Divine mercy be dealt with as a separate subject.
~Swedenborg, Heavenly Secrets, AC 3646

In other words, animals are not immortal in the same sense that people are immortal due to human consciousness being of a different quality than animal consciousness. The immortality of our individual consciousness is due to its ability to be co-present and conjoined with the consciousness of God. This conjunction creates our immortality. But animals cannot be conjoined to God through conscious awareness as are human beings.

But now we need to understand further that in the mental world love has the power to create, not physical animals, but substantive animals. Altruistic or mutual loves create animals of good disposition and capable of loving us. This means that people who will themselves to retain their love for their pets in the interior levels of their personality have this love with them in the afterlife.

With this love they can "recreate" their pets to have them with them. Their pets in eternity will not be physical pets, but mental pets. These are just as real, and more real, than the physical pets they had on earth. The personality of their particular pets and the pets' feelings for their owners will be there unimpaired, since this is based on all the experiences they ever had with each pet.

And further, our substantial or mental pets are just as capable to enjoy new experiences and new learning, so that there is a normal evolution and growth of the relationship, as they enjoyed with each other back on earth.

41. Spiritual Nature of Pets

The spiritual nature of pets is visible to the owners that love them and protect them.

The owners are spiritually attached to their pet, which is an object of their love. Love is spiritual. Therefore the human-pet love interaction is a spiritual relationship to the extent that the pet is able to reciprocate the human approaching it with love and care, by in turn approaching the human with involvement and mutual care.

In natural consciousness, we see our pets as individuals, as "like our children", and as loyal friends. In spiritual consciousness, we see our pets as objects of our love that dwell deeply within our consciousness. Few things parallel or approach the intensity of our affection and the closeness in friendship, that we experience with our pets. This unbreakable attraction is a spiritual activity. It is the conjunction of love. Our spiritual love for our pets, when reciprocated, elevates the consciousness of the pet above itself. This involves a new experience for the pets.

The relationship of love with a human elevates the pet closer to the human level of consciousness.

For the pet this is the spiritual benefit that God provided through the human-animal love relationship.

Pet owners know that pets love rituals. My two cats are about five years old now and the following is a partial list of daily rituals that they invented or taught us to perform with them:

- Walking to the dish together and putting fresh pellets into the dish
- Turning on the sink water faucet to dribble level
- Walking together, following, stopping, looking around
- Sitting with (chair, floor, bed, grass)
- Grooming, scratching, rubbing, combing, trimming nails
- Talking to with soft voice modulation
- Playing, learning tricks
- Walking to bed together or sleeping area
- Carrying and walking around, stopping, walking more
- Greeting by elaborate and tailor made reciprocal rubbing rituals
- Calling and coming (or not!)
- Congratulating by vigorous taps and modulated voice
- Visiting the vet
- Looking out of the window together
- "Suckling" (clothes, cashmere blanket)
- Offering cuttings from lemon grass and catnip plants
- Sharing breakfast papaya scrapings

Each ritual has a special meaning to the animal and performing it enriches the animal's life, happiness, health, and consciousness level. I often feel guilty and painful remorse when I think that I have neglected the cats by skipping rituals. I think that they have hardly anything of life with us without those human-animal rituals. The rituals are the things that make their life to be a worthwhile "elevated" experience. How can I rob them of the little they have? And I feel terrible, vowing to myself and to God that I will stop skipping rituals with the cats because of this or that other thing I need to do. So, now I better stop typing right here and walk to the dish with one of them who is sitting right there looking at me with patience.

To an animal doing something over and over again, every day, and the same way at the same time, means a world of confidence and order that is predictable, safe, meaningful, and fun. The reason pets love rituals with humans is because our beloved pets are *spiritual animal souls*.

Our pets are in their natural consciousness when they experience and enjoy the outward form of a ritual with humans. *But above the animal's natural consciousness level, there is a spiritual level of animal anatomy and functioning that can be activated through a human-animal love relationship.*

It is good to know that *animal souls are immortal spiritual loves that seek animal embodiments over and over again.*

Each type and species of animal love seeks and attains an embodiment in the form of a unique individual physical "avatar" in a species that is specifically equipped with size, function, and abilities to allow its species-love to be satisfied and consummated, thus differently for a bird than for a chipmunk. Every animal species in the physical universe represents some particular species of spiritual love that exists in animal consciousness from the beginning of creation. *This is their inner, collective consciousness.* We are aware of this when we spontaneously speak about an animal's "instinct". Our love makes us aware that our animals know things without learning them. This rationally proves to us that animals are not just physical. They therefore have a spiritual nature.

Many owners are unaware that their animals can function at this spiritual level of consciousness and awareness. Of course, the animal's level of spiritual consciousness is not a sharing at the same level as human spiritual consciousness. Nevertheless, the sharing is spiritual.

Your pet's soul is immortal because God creates all living souls to be immortal.

Swedenborg writes about animal instinct:

That all things in the world come into existence from the Divine, and are clothed with such things in nature as enable them to exist there and perform a use, and thus to correspond, is clearly evident from individual things seen in both the animal and vegetable kingdoms. In both there are things that anyone, if he thinks interiorly, can see to be from heaven.

For illustration a few things out of a countless number may be mentioned, first some things in the Animal Kingdom. Many people are aware what knowledge there is implanted as it were in every animal. Bees know how to gather honey from flowers, to build cells out of wax in which they store their honey and thus provide food for themselves and their own [hive] even for the coming winter. That a new generation may be born, their queen lays eggs, and the rest take care of them and cover them. The whole hive live under a certain form of government which all in the hive know by instinct. They preserve the working bees and cast out the drones, depriving them of their wings, besides other wonderful things which they have from heaven for the sake of use. For, throughout the world, their wax serves the human race for candles, and their honey for sweetening food.

[2] And what happens in the case of caterpillars (vermiculus), the meanest creatures in the animal kingdom? They know how to get food from the juice of leaves suited to them, and afterwards at the appointed time to invest themselves with a covering and place themselves, as it were, in a womb and so hatch out an offspring of their own kind. Some are first changed into nymphs and chrysalides which spin threads; and this travail being over, they come forth clad with a different body and, furnished with wings, fly in the air as in their heaven. They celebrate marriages, lay eggs and provide for themselves a posterity.

[3] Besides these specific instances, all creatures that fly in the sky know in general the food suitable for their nourishment, not only what it is but even where to find it. They know how to build nests for themselves, each species different from any other, to lay eggs in the nest, to sit upon them, hatch their young and feed them, and to turn them out of the home when they are able to be independent. They also know their enemies that they have to avoid and their friends with whom they may associate, and this from earliest infancy; not to mention the wonders in the eggs themselves in which all things lie ready in their order for the formation and nourishment of the embryo chick, besides innumerable other things.

[4] Who, thinking from any rational wisdom, will ever say that these things are from any other source than the spiritual world to which the natural world is of service in wrapping around it a body that is derived from it or for presenting as an effect that which is spiritual in its cause? The beasts of the earth and the fowls of the air are born into all this knowledge while man, who is superior to them, is not. The reason is that animals are in the order of their life and have not been able to destroy what is in them from the spiritual world, because they have no rational [faculty]. Man, on the other hand, who thinks from the spiritual world, having perverted what is in him from that world by a life contrary to order, which his rational faculty has favoured, must needs be born into mere

ignorance and afterwards be led back by Divine means into the order of heaven. ~Swedenborg, Heaven and Hell, HH 108

42. The Souls of Animals and Plants

In the following selection we have confirmation of the cross-cultural notion that both animals and plants have souls. *Now I know that all souls are created immortal.* An animal has an immortal soul and so does a plant! I started thinking differently about plants after thinking about this explanation in the Swedenborg Reports.

The 'big news' for me was that animals and plants have *the same soul!*

Did you know these things about plants and animals?

1) Plants have a soul that is immortal
2) Animals have an immortal soul
3) Animal soul and plant soul are the same soul in different embodiment
4) Animal souls or plant souls have their origin in some human love and affection that people experience in natural consciousness
5) Plants are connected to human beings through the plant's soul, which is a component of human affection
6) Animals are connected to human beings through the animal's soul, which is a component of an affection in the human mind
7) In the mental world of the afterlife in eternity plants and animals appear suddenly and are active the environment of the spiritual body. The type of plant or animal that appears to view corresponds to the moods and interests of the people in that state. Bad moods and selfish plans bring around poisonous plants and pesky or dangerous animals. Mutual love brings around beautiful and scented plants and docile and affectionate animals.
8) In the mental world of the afterlife we can inspect and reflect on the plants and animals around us and as a result discover in them deeper layers of our loves and thoughts. The objective outside that is clearly seen becomes a picture of the subjective inside that is only seen in

obscurity. Collective consciousness in the mental world creates images or maps of itself so that we may know what is in our personality that is still unconscious to us.

Here is the selection from the Swedenborg Reports:
Continuation Concerning the Vegetable Kingdom

Both animals and plants have the same origin, and thence the same soul; the difference being only in the forms into which the influx is received.

That the origin of animals, which is also their soul, is a spiritual affection, such as pertains to man in his Natural, was shown above. That the same affection is also the origin of plants is evident, especially from plants in the heavens; in that they appear there, for instance, according to the affections of the angels, and also represent them; so much so, that the angels behold and learn in them, as in their own types, the quality of their affections; and further, in their changing according to their affections; this, however, occurs out of the societies.

The only difference is, that it is from the Spiritual in its intermediates, that the affections appear under the form of animals, and from the Spiritual in its ultimates which are the lands there, that they appear under the form of plants. For the Spiritual, from which they are, in its intermediates is living, but in its ultimates it is non-living, retaining in the latter case no more life than is sufficient to produce a resemblance of life. The case is almost the same as in the human body, whose ultimates, produced from the Spiritual, are the cartilages, the bones, the teeth, and the nails, the life, which is from the soul, terminating in them.

[3] It does not at the first view appear that the vegetative soul is from the same origin as that of the beasts of the earth, the birds of heaven, and the fish of the sea, in consequence of this difference, that the one lives and the other does not. That this is the case is nevertheless manifestly evident from the animals, as well as the plants, that are seen in the heavens and in the hells. In the heavens there appear beautiful animals, and plants of a similar quality; in the hells, on the other hand, noxious animals, and plants of a similar quality appear. From the appearances also of the animals, and similarly from those of the plants, angels and spirits are known; for there is a

perfect agreement between their affections and these appearances. The agreement is even of such a nature, that an animal may be changed into a plant in agreement with it, and similarly a plant into an animal in the same condition.

[4] The angels of heaven know the degree of affection represented in both the one and the other. I have heard and also perceived that it is in each case similar. I have been permitted to understand clearly the correspondence, not only of animals, but also of plants, with the societies both of heaven and hell, and thus with the affections of these societies; for societies and affections in the spiritual world make one. Hence it is that in so many passages in the Word mention is made of gardens, groves, forests, and trees, as well as of plants of various kinds; and that they there signify spiritual objects according to their respective origins, which all have reference to affections.

The difference, therefore, between plants in the spiritual world, and those in the natural world is, that in the former world they-both the seeds and the germinations from them-exist, in a moment, according to the affections of the angels and spirits there; while in the latter their origin is implanted in the seeds, from which they spring every year.

There are moreover two properties of nature, namely, time and consequent succession, and space and consequent extension, but these do not exist in the spiritual world as properties of it; they are there the appearances of states of life in those who are there. It is also for this reason that from the lands there, which exist from a spiritual origin, plants spring up in a moment, and also in a moment disappear. This however occurs only when the angels retire, for when they remain, the plants continue.

Such is the difference between plants in the spiritual and those in the natural world. ~Swedenborg, Apocalypse Explained, AE 1212

43. Animals in the Spiritual World of the Afterlife

Pet owners and animal lovers who are practicing the RTS point of view will be very interested in what Swedenborg saw in the spiritual world, in which he was living every day for 27 years as a dual consciousness person, active simultaneously in his functions here on earth as a Swedish citizen and scientist, and at the same time active as a spiritual anthropologist who was interviewing the inhabitants of the afterlife of eternity where all humanity gathers at death.

Swedenborg writes:

For true and just are his judgments.- That this signifies that the laws of the Divine Providence, and all the works of the Lord, are of the Divine Wisdom and Divine Love, is evident from the signification of true and just, when said of the Lord, as denoting those things which pertain to His Divine Wisdom, and also those which pertain to His Divine Love, of which we shall speak presently; and from the signification of judgments, when said of the Lord, as denoting the laws of His Divine Providence (concerning which see above, n. 946). By judgments, therefore, are signified works, since all the works of the Lord are from His Divine Providence, and according to its laws; the reason is, that everything which the Lord does has regard to eternity, and those things which have regard to eternity are of His Divine Providence. The reason why truths signify those things which are of His Divine Wisdom, and just things those which are of His Divine Love, is, that from the Lord as the Sun proceed heat and light; the light is His Divine Wisdom, and the heat is His Divine Love. Light therefore signifies Divine Truth, from which angels and men derive all their intelligence and wisdom, while heat signifies Divine Good, from which angels and men derive all their love and charity. Such are this light and heat in their essence.

[2] Continuation [concerning the Life of Animals].- No one can understand the nature of the life of the beasts of the earth, of the birds of heaven, and of the fish of the sea, unless he is also acquainted with the nature and quality of their soul (anima). That every animal has a soul is a well-known fact; for animals live, and life is the soul; for this reason they are also called in the Word living souls. That this soul in its ultimate form, which is corporeal, such as it appears before the sight, is an animal, cannot be better known from any other source than the spiritual world. For in the spiritual world, just as in the natural, beasts, birds, and fishes of every kind are seen, and in form so similar that they cannot be distinguished from those which are in our world. But the difference is this, that in the spiritual world they have an apparent existence from the affections of angels and spirits, so that they are appearances of affections. For this reason they also vanish as soon as the angel or spirit departs, or his affection ceases. It is therefore evident that their soul is nothing else; and consequently

that there are as many genera and species of animals as there are genera and species of affections.

It will be seen in what follows that the affections, which are represented in the spiritual world by animals, are not interior but exterior spiritual affections, which are called natural; and further that there is not a hair or thread of wool on any beast, not the smallest portion of a quill or feather upon any bird, nor the point of a fin or scale upon any fish, which is not formed from the life of their soul, and thus which is not from the Spiritual clothed with the Natural. But something shall first be said concerning the animals which appear in heaven, in hell, and in the world of spirits, which is between heaven and hell. ~Swedenborg, Apocalypse Explained, AE 1199

Because the whole of heaven, the whole of hell, and the whole world of spirits are each divided into societies, and the societies arranged according to the genera and species of affections, and because the animals there are appearances of affections, as was just observed, therefore one genus of animal with its species appears in one society and another in another, and all the genera of animals with their species in the societies taken together. In the societies of heaven gentle and clean animals appear; in the societies of hell savage and unclean beasts, and in the world of spirits beasts of an intermediate kind.

In the heavens I have seen lambs, sheep, goats, so similar to those in the world that there is no difference whatever; also turtle-doves, pigeons, birds of paradise, and many others, beautiful in form and colour; fish also in the waters, but these were in the lowest parts of heaven. In the hells on the other hand there are seen dogs, foxes, wolves, tigers, swine, mice, and many other kinds of savage and unclean beasts, besides poisonous serpents of many species, also crows, owls, and birds of night. But in the world of spirits are seen camels, elephants, horses, asses, oxen, stags, lions, leopards, bears, also eagles, kites, magpies, peacocks, and quails. I have also seen compound animals there, such as were seen by the prophets, and are described in the Word, as in the Apoc. xiii. 2, and elsewhere.

[4] Since there is such a resemblance between the animals that appear in that world and those in this world that they cannot be at all distinguished; and since the former derive their existence from the affections of the angels of heaven, and from the lusts of the spirits of hell, it follows that natural affections and

lusts are their souls, and that these, being clothed with a body, are animals in a corresponding form.

But what affection or lust forms the soul of this or that animal, whether a beast or wild beast of the earth, a bird of day or of the night, a fish living in clear or foul water, does not belong to this place to explain. Animals are frequently mentioned in the Word, and they have there a signification according to their souls. The signification of lambs, sheep, she-goats, rams, kids, he-goats, heifers, oxen, camels, horses, asses, stags, and also of certain birds, may be seen explained in the Arcana Coelestia. ~Swedenborg, Apocalypse Explained, AE 1200

Those who lived in the most ancient times thus signified the things relating to the understanding and to the will; and therefore in the Prophets, and constantly in the Word of the Old Testament, the like things are represented by different kinds of animals. Beasts are of two kinds; the evil, so called because they are hurtful; and the good, which are harmless. Evils in man are signified by evil beasts, as by bears, wolves, dogs; and the things which are good and gentle, by beasts of a like nature, as by heifers, sheep, and lambs. The "beasts" here referred to are good and gentle ones, and thus signify affections, because it here treats of those who are being regenerated. The lower things in man, which have more connection with the body, are called "wild animals of that earth" and are cupidities and pleasures. ~Swedenborg, Heavenly Secrets, AC 45

In the world of spirits various representatives manifest themselves. On many occasions animals too manifest themselves before the eyes of spirits [people in the afterlife], such as horses wearing varying decorative trappings, oxen, sheep, lambs, and different kinds of other animals; and sometimes animals such as have never been seen on earth but are purely representative. Such animals seen also by the prophets and mentioned in the Word had the same origin. Animals which appear in that world are representative of affections for good and truth, and also of affections for evil and falsity.

Good spirits have full knowledge of what those animals mean, and also when they see them, they gather what it is that angels are discussing with one another, for when the conversation of those angels passes down into the world of spirits it sometimes manifests itself in this manner. For example, when horses appear, the spirits know that the angels are talking about matters of the understanding; when oxen and young bulls appear, that they are talking about natural goods; when sheep appear, about rational goods and about integrity; when lambs appear, about still more interior goods and about innocence; and so on. ~Swedenborg, Heavenly Secrets, AC 2179

A careful distinction is made in the Prophets [Old Testament] between beasts and wild animals of the earth, and between beasts and wild animals of the field. The practice of calling goods 'beasts' extends to calling people in heaven who are nearest to the Lord 'living creatures' ~Swedenborg, Heavenly Secrets AC 46

Regarded in itself eating animal flesh is something profane, for in most ancient times people never ate the flesh of any beast or bird, but only different kinds of grain, especially wheaten bread, also the fruit of trees, vegetables, milk, and milk products such as butter. Slaughtering living creatures and eating their flesh was to them abominable, akin to the behaviour of wild animals. Service and use alone was demanded of those creatures, as is clear from Gen. 1:29, 30.

But in the process of time when mankind began to be as savage as wild animals, indeed more savage, they first began to slaughter living creatures and eat their flesh. And because man had become such, he was permitted to do so and is still permitted today. And insofar as he does so from conscience, it is quite legitimate, for his conscience is given form from all those things he presumes to be true and so legitimate. Consequently nobody nowadays stands in any sense condemned because he eats meat. ~Swedenborg, Heavenly Secrets, AC 1002

44. Spiritual Meaning of Animal Species

In the first brief selection that appears below, Swedenborg gives an analysis of the expression "And right flank" that belonged to a sacrificial animal that was commanded for their religious rituals in order to make the ritual spiritual in significance.

Swedenborg writes:
'And the right flank' [Old Testament, Exodus 29:22] means inmost good.

'The right flank' means inmost good because animals' flanks have the same meaning as the loins and thighs on a human being; a human being's loins and thighs mean conjugial love and consequently the good of celestial love, which is the good of the inmost heaven; and the right side of the loins and the right thigh mean the inmost good there.

For by virtue of their correspondence the parts on the right side of a human being mean good from which springs truth, and those on the left side truth through which comes good; and those in the middle therefore mean the joining together of the two, that is, of good and truth. From this also it becomes clear that the flanks are the hindquarters of an animal where its genital organs reside, but not the forequarters, for these are called its breast. ~*Swedenborg, Heavenly Secrets, AC 10075*

In other words, the animals used for their religious rituals were specified by God in their books of *Sacred Scripture*. Different species and sub-species and variations of animals were to be observed and chosen in order to validate the spiritual significance of the rituals that they performed from obedience to the "Word of God". If they had used an animal of a different species, age, gender, or color that was specified in the "Word of God" there would have occurred a spiritual profanation because there was a spiritual clash between the substitute animal and the celestial correspondences that made the ritual holy.

The people who worshipped together as a nation at that historical time shared the same spiritual fate with each other. Hence for anyone of them to ritually profane the holy would have brought physical hardships and suffering on all its people. This is of course not the situation today in our modern culture. What they saw as normal, namely a joint spiritual fate as a nation, we see today as irrational and unjust, therefore not possible. We think and behave in the consciousness of individual independence, and our spiritual rationality relies on *Sacred Scripture* verses that say:

"The soul who sins shall die. The son shall not suffer for the iniquity of the father, nor the father suffer for the iniquity of the son. The righteousness of the righteous shall be upon himself, and the wickedness of the wicked shall be upon himself." Ezekiel 18:20

In those days they shall say no more, The fathers have eaten a sour grape, and the children's teeth are set on edge. But every one shall die for his own iniquity: every man that eateth the sour grape, his teeth shall be set on edge.' Jeremiah 31:29-30

From these two passages among many, we can see that *Sacred Scripture* always contains the prophecy of the future, of the regenerated personality that has its three levels of consciousness activated. Here we simply see validated and justified our modern civilization's love and respect for individual freedom, independence, and justice through due process for the protection of every individual.

45. The Birds of Consciousness

Swedenborg writes:

One *morning after sleep, my thought was deeply engaged on certain arcana of conjugial love, and finally, on the following: In what region of the human mind does love truly conjugial reside, and hence in what, conjugial cold?*

I knew that there are three regions of the human mind, one above the other, and that natural love dwells in the lowest region, spiritual love in the higher, and celestial love in the highest;

also that in each region there is a marriage of good and truth; and because good pertains to love and truth to wisdom, that in each region there is a marriage of love and wisdom, and that this marriage is the same as the marriage of the will [affective system] *and understanding* [cognitive system], *the will being the receptacle of love* [affective system] *and the understanding the receptacle of wisdom* [cognitive system].

[2] While in deep thought concerning this, lo, I saw two swans flying towards the north, and presently two birds of paradise flying towards the south, and also two turtle-doves flying in the east.

As I followed their flight with my sight, I saw that the two swans bent their northerly course to the east, as likewise did the two birds of paradise on their southerly course; and that, joining the two turtle-doves in the east, they flew with them to a lofty palace there, around which were olive trees, palms and beeches.

The palace had three tiers of windows, one above the other; and, directing my attention to them, I saw the swans fly into the palace through open windows in the lowest tier, the birds of paradise through open windows in the middle tier, and the turtle-doves through open windows in the highest tier.

[3] As I was looking at this, an angel stood by my side and said, "Do you understand these sights?" I replied, "Partly." He then said: "That palace represents the abodes of conjugial love as they are in human minds. Its highest part into which the doves betook themselves represents the highest region of the mind where conjugial love with its wisdom dwells in the love of good;

its middle into which the birds of paradise betook themselves represents the middle region where conjugial love with its intelligence dwells in the love of truth; and its lowest part into which the swans betook themselves represents the lowest region of the mind where conjugial love with its knowledge dwells in the love of what is just and right.

[4] Moreover, the three pairs of birds signify these same things--the pair of turtle-doves, the conjugial love of the highest region, the pair of birds of paradise the conjugial love of the middle region, and the pair of swans the conjugial love of the lowest region. The like are signified by the three kinds of trees around the palace--the olive, the palm, and the beech.

In heaven, we call the highest region of the mind celestial, the middle spiritual, and the lowest natural; and we perceive them as abiding places in a house, one above the other, and the ascent from one to the other by degrees, as being made by stairs. In each story are two rooms, as it were, one for love the other for wisdom. In front is a bedchamber, as it were, where love with its wisdom, or good with its truth, or, what is the same thing, the will with its understanding, consociate in bed.

In that palace stand forth as in effigy all the arcana of conjugial love.

[5] On hearing this, being kindled with a desire to see the palace, I asked whether, being a representative palace, it was granted any one to enter in and view it. He answered: "To none save those who are in the third heaven, because to them every representative of love and wisdom becomes real.

It is from them that I heard what I have reported to you, and also this, that in the highest region love truly conjugial dwells, in the chamber or room of the will, in the midst of mutual love, and in the chamber or room of the understanding, in the midst of the perceptions of wisdom; and that, in the bedchamber which is at the front and in the east, they are consociated in bed.

To my question, "Why are there two chambers?" he said, "The husband is in the chamber of the understanding and the wife in the chamber of the will."

[6] I then asked, "Since conjugial love dwells there, where then does conjugial cold dwell?" He answered: "This also dwells in the highest region, but only in the chamber of the understanding, the chamber of the will there being closed; for the understanding with its truths can ascend by a spiral stairway into its chamber in the highest region whenever it wills; but if the will with the good of its love does not at the same time ascend into the neighboring chamber, the latter is shut and in the other chamber it becomes cold; and this cold is conjugial cold.

When there is such cold towards the wife, then from this highest region the understanding looks down to the lowest, and if fear does not restrain it, it also descends thither that it may there grow warm from an illicit fire.

After saying this, he wished to recount still further particulars concerning conjugial love on the basis of its effigies in that palace, but he said: "Enough for the present. Inquire first whether these things are above the common understanding. If they are, why more? but if not, more will be disclosed.
~Swedenborg, Conjugial Love, CL 270

Here again, as I mentioned in another place, some people see the Swedenborg selection above as written in the style of allegory, rather than being objective reporting of ongoing external events. These are critics who may be unfamiliar with Swedenborg's integrity and loyalty to objective science. This was in his mind a key feature of his mission that he was given by God, namely, to report objectively and empirically as a scientist, and with integrity and accuracy as an eyewitness reporter, of the spiritual world of the afterlife.

The story description gives us spiritual *information about the afterlife*. For instance:

1) that there are animals to be seen there
2) that every species of animals carries a spiritual meaning, e.g.,
   turtle doves represent our celestial consciousness
   birds of paradise represent our spiritual consciousness
   swans represent our natural consciousness
3) that there are houses there with three stories, each with a
   spiritual representation for the three levels of anatomy in our
   consciousness
4) that our affective and cognitive systems work together through
   mutual interdependency in function and activity
5) that the cognitive system, or our understanding, can be
   activated in all its levels to give us new consciousness and
   understanding at each higher level
6) that we are unable to elevate the functioning of our affective
   system in the same way that we do with our understanding, and
   therefore our higher understanding remains abstract knowledge
   or "cold" because it is unable or unwilling to practice the things
   of higher understanding
7) that our higher consciousness is produced in actuality not by the
   understanding or cognitive system, but by our will, or affective
   system.

> *Nothing can exist except from something else, and so
> at last from Him, who is and who exists in Himself; and
> He is God. ~Swedenborg, Apocalypse Explained, AE
> 1206*

46. Love of Self:
Good and Bad

Jung writes:

> But if you hate and despise yourself—if you have not accepted your pattern— then there are hungry animals (prowling cats and other beasts and vermin) in your constitution which get at your neighbours like flies in order to satisfy the appetites which you have failed to satisfy. ~Carl Jung, Zarathustra Seminar, p. 502

Swedenborg writes:

> The love of self is the source of all the evils that destroy civic society. ~Swedenborg, Heavenly Secrets, AC 2045

> As the love of self is the source of hatreds, revenges, cruelties, and adulteries, it is the source of all things that are called sins, wickednesses, abominations, and profanations, and therefore when this love is in the rational part of man, and is in the cupidities and phantasies of his external man, the influx of heavenly love from the Lord is continually repelled, perverted, and contaminated. It is like foul excrement, which dissipates, nay, defiles, all sweet odor; it is like an object that turns the continually inflowing rays of light into dark and repulsive colors; and it is like a tiger, or a serpent, which repels all fondling, and kills with bite and poison those who offer it food; or like a vicious man who turns even the best intentions of others, and their very kindnesses, into what is blameworthy and malicious. . ~Swedenborg, Heavenly Secrets, AC 2045

> They who are in the loves of self and of the world cannot possibly believe that they are in things so filthy and unclean as they actually are in, for there is a certain pleasure and delight that soothes, favors, and allures, and causes them to love that life, to prefer it to all other life, and thereby to suppose that there is nothing of evil in it; for whatever favors anyone's love and the life thence derived is believed to be good. Hence also the rational consents, and suggests falsities which confirm and cause such blindness that they see nothing of the nature of heavenly love; and if they were to see it they would say in their hearts that it is a wretched affair, or a thing of naught, or something of the nature of a phantasy that takes hold of the mind, as in sickness.

But that the life of the love of self and of the world, together with its pleasures and delights, is filthy and unclean, may be seen by everyone who is willing to think from the rational faculty with which he is gifted. The love of self is the source of all the evils that destroy civic society. From it as from an unclean pit spring all hatreds, all revenges, all cruelties, nay, all adulteries; for he who loves himself, despises, vituperates, or hates, all others who do not serve him, or do him honor, or favor him; and when he hates, he breathes nothing but revenges and cruelties, and this in proportion to the degree in which he loves himself, so that this love is destructive of society and of the human race. ~Swedenborg, Heavenly Secrets, AC 2045

It is common to hear the advice from both professionals and others that you need to love yourself and that this is both a good thing and healthy thing to do. Some historical quotes from respected writers also give this advice, sometimes adding the argument that if you don't love yourself you cannot thrive in happiness and mental growth. Or, if you must love yourself before you can love others. I am reminded of a teaching from the saintly Rabbi Hillel often quoted as, *"If I am not for myself, who will be for me? Yet if I am for myself only, what am I? And if not now, when?"*

This maxim contains a deep spiritual truth about the love of self that most people would readily understand and accept. Swedenborg points out that everyone needs to take care of one self, or else one cannot take care of others or to perform useful things to community and society. He mentions such things as a healthy lifestyle, enjoyment of entertainment and socializing, gathering and safeguarding one's wealth, whether rich or poor, and accepting and enjoying receiving honors and rewards.

It is possible to call these daily normal activities as "love yourself" in the sense of care for yourself, do not neglect or injure your body or your mind. Also I would add, don't let others take advantage of you or exploit you inappropriately because this will reduce your ability to be useful in your job and other responsibilities. Hence Hiller's maxim that if I don't do this for myself no one else is going to do it, or can do it.

At the same time this cannot be separated from the idea of taking care of yourself, namely, that if I love myself only and do not love others equally, then I am in the wrong and cannot be a real person who is growing and developing in a positive and commendable direction. Swedenborg says that spiritual consciousness is acquired when we switch over from loving myself only, to loving others *as much* as I love myself.

This is a part that may not be well understood by many people. It is common to think and say that if we love others at times, it proves that we don't just love ourselves only. People cite such things as giving charity donations, volunteering for free services to the needy, cutting down on noise and parties to just a few a year, not being rude, and so on. These are mentioned as indications or proof that we don't just love ourselves only. But this is an error.

Swedenborg writes:

The love of self is wishing well to oneself alone, and to others only for the sake of self, even to the church, one's country, or any human society. It consists also in doing good to all these solely for the sake of one's own reputation, honor, and glory; and unless these are seen in the uses he performs in behalf of others he says in his heart, How does it concern me? Why should I do this? What shall I get from it? and therefore he does not do it. Evidently, then, he who is in the love of self does not love the church or his country or society, nor any use, but himself alone. His delight is solely the delight of the love of self; and as the delight that comes forth from his love is what constitutes the life of man, his life is a life of self; and a life of self is a life from what is man's own, and what is man's own, regarded in itself, is nothing but evil. He who loves himself loves also those who belong to him, that is, in particular, his children and grandchildren, and in general, all who are at one with him, whom he calls his. To love these is to love himself, for he regards them as it were in himself, and himself in them. Among those whom he calls his are also all who commend, honor, and pay their court to him.

What love of self is can be seen by comparing it with heavenly love. Heavenly love consists in loving uses for the sake of uses, or goods for the sake of goods, which are done by man in behalf of the church, his country, human society, and a fellow-citizen; for this is loving God and loving the neighbor, since all uses and all goods are from God, and are the neighbor who is to be loved. But he who loves these for the sake of himself loves them merely as servants, because they are serviceable to him; consequently it is the will of one who is in self-love that the church, his country, human societies, and his fellow citizens, should serve him, and not he them, for he places himself above them and places them beneath himself. Therefore so far as any one is in love of self he separates himself from heaven, because he separates himself from heavenly love. ~Swedenborg, Heaven and Hell, HH 556-7

Swedenborg points out that it is common for people to do things for others as a strategy to benefit oneself, so that if one no longer sees a benefit to doing something for others or community, then the desire to do care for the others is gone. This is an instance of loving others for the sake of self only and not for the sake of these others. For instance, we may give charity donations in order to make ourselves feel better, not because we are being responsible for the sake of the community and country. Of course such donations do good to needy causes, but it does not do any good to the donor.

Another example is when people are friendly to some other person but become immediately rude and unfriendly when that person no longer favors them or rejects them. A common instance occurs with the love of parents for their children. It is a biological love that affects everyone who is in natural consciousness. This love is strengthened even more when parents perceive their own traits in their children, such as appearance of face and types of things they enjoy in common with parents.

Swedenborg points out that parenting love at this merely natural level of thinking and feeling leads people to indulge their children, even when this is not good for them, but worse, leading them to excuse their children's negative and selfish traits, not considering or wanting to consider that this kind of "unconditional love" is detrimental to the healthy growth and development of those children. And at the same time, when their children get older and show signs of obstinate independence and differences from the parents, there is a spontaneous withdrawal of their love for those children. This too indicates that their love for their children is a selfish love that is for the sake of themselves more so than for the sake of the children.

Parents in spiritual consciousness are contrastively different. They tend to love the positive and creative traits of each of their individual children, rather than the individual as an unconditional person. Parents in spiritual consciousness refrain from indulging their children because it is bad for them. Neither is their love for the individual child unconditional, loving both good traits and bad. In other words, the spiritual love of parents is for the sake of the child and not for the sake of themselves. If the child is obstinate and selfish, and refuses to be morally guided, the love of the parent is diminished for that child. Instead, there remains a sense of duty and responsibility for continuing to provide the necessary needs for that child, just as one would help a stranger or a neighbor's child who is in want of protection and provision.

Spiritual consciousness focuses and responds to the quality and motive of any individual's actions, children or strangers. The motive of a persons' action towards others or community may be recognized by adding the phrase "*for the sake of*" for every action being considered. Here are some examples that will help you clarify this complex issue.

1. I forced myself not to be rude for the sake of staying out of trouble.
2. I forced myself not to be rude for the sake of being considerate of their feelings.
3. I am motivated to do a good job as an employee so that I may get ahead of the others for my own sake.
4. I am motivated to do a good job as an employee so that I may be a responsible person.
5. I am motivated to do a good job as an employee so that I may get promoted, earn a higher salary for the sake of my family.
6. I drive carefully to avoid destroying my car or injuring me.
7. I drive carefully to avoid hurting or injuring another motorist.
8. I tell my guests to keep the noise down because someone might call the police.
9. I tell my guests to keep the noise down because it bothers my neighbors and it's unfair to them.
10. I love my country so I'm not to criticize it for anything.
11. I love my country but for the sake of everyone I must criticize those who abuse their power.

You can see the distinction that I am making when you examine the various statements and how they differ with respect to doing things for the sake of self only versus for the sake of others as well as self.

Swedenborg explains:

As regards the affections of truth and of good the case is this: The genuine affections of truth and of good which are perceived by man are all from a Divine origin, because from the Lord; but on the way, as they descend, they diverge into various and diverse streams, and there form for themselves new origins; for as they flow into affections not genuine but spurious, and into the affections of evil and falsity in the man, so are they varied.

In the external form these affections often present themselves like the genuine ones; but in the internal form they are of this spurious character. The sole characteristic from which they are known is their end; if as regards their end they are for the sake of self or the world, then these affections are not genuine; but if as regards their end they are for the sake of the good of the neighbor, the good of societies, the good of our country, and especially if for the good of the church and the good of the Lord's kingdom, then they are genuine, because in this case they are for the sake of the Lord, inasmuch as the Lord is in these goods. ~Swedenborg, Arcana Coelestia, AC 3796

See other details at http://www.soc.hawaii.edu/leonj/theistic/mental-anatomy.htm

> *I could say just as well that you could never attain the self without isolation; it is both being alone and in relationship. ~Carl Jung, Zarathustra Seminar, p. 797*

47. Loving Others As Much as Loving Oneself

The content of Background Principle 1 was the ego-self vs. the as-of-self. It was there explained why there was a need for the new theistic as-of self concept, namely, the rational idea that if God is omnipotent then the power needed for the organic activity of the mind must be given by God. Nor can God give some of that power to us, no matter how tiny, because then God would no longer be omnipotent. In other words, God is an active participant in our mental activity and personality growth.

God is therefore a key figure in all self. Whatever it is that the therapist wants the patient to think or do, that it is that God has to agree to and supply the power and the know-how. No self-change or recovery can take place without God's active involvement and participation.

The problem of therapy and recovery is to practice a personal relationship with God on a daily basis. To undergo this practice patients or trainees need to understand what God wants with them and why God has allowed them to slip into mental states where they became patients needing help.

Patients or trainees can begin by exploring the process described as background principle 2: loving others as much as loving oneself. This is the therapeutic power tool! Understanding this principle pulls the mind out of mere natural consciousness and into rational consciousness where mental power tools become available for use.

Both patients and therapists need to undergo this process of experiencing the lift in consciousness when practicing the principle of loving others as much as loving oneself. And along with this raise in consciousness there comes the perception of the power tool God provides.

It is an arduous process to individuate, especially when one has been growing in the wrong direction. Our personality is dominated by loves, intentions, and behaviors that put the ego into self-centered mode of functioning. We can hide this and pretend otherwise for the sake of reputation, gain, and security. When the ego is at the center of our personality we de-individuate. We enter a state of suffering and pain, plagued by daily inadequacies, negativity, neuroses, and a variety of debilitating psychopathologies.

The as-of self can love others more than oneself.

Carrying out a personal and healing relationship with God means to involve God in our life and moment to moment consciousness. God is omnipresent and therefore present with our mind all the time. It is strange and abnormal to life with someone 24/7 and never acknowledge each other's presence. One of the roommates may acknowledge the other but if the other does not reciprocate there is no co-presence. Each remains in their own world apart.

Acknowledging God's co-presence is therefore a critical step in the individuals recovery.

48. How To Know What Is Selfish

There is a difficult paradox to figure out when we try to solve the spiritual issue of how I know when I am being selfish. This problem is made more difficult by the normal practice of calling "good" whatever we love or enjoy, and calling "bad" whatever we dislike or fear. This way of thinking is normal when we are immersed in our natural consciousness. There is no objective or rational principle that is used for deciding what is good or bad. Hence we are unable to judge rationally when something we think or do is selfish or is from mutual love or love of others as much as we love ourselves. It is hard for us to label as selfish what we love and enjoy. This is because what we love we perceive as good and good does not belong to selfishness.

These are the entangled threads that obscure our understanding of what is selfish in our personality.

To cut through the tangled cords, we can stop resisting input from the activity our spiritual-rational consciousness. Our natural or material ideas oppose the inflow of spiritual ideas. Yet to understand our selfishness we must use spiritual ideas. We can stop resisting spiritual ideas when we understand that the resistance is nothing but the aftereffects in our mind of the materialistic society in which we grew up. Now we can make the decision to disconnect ourselves from these aftereffects, which we have not chosen out of free will. They were implanted in our way of thinking before we understood that there are alternatives such as "theistic science" or "rational faith".

The context for understanding selfishness is that it is a way of thinking and interacting that is noxious to self, noxious to others, and noxious to society as a whole. This is a fundamental property of selfishness, namely, that it is out of order with spiritual reality and with creation.

To understand selfishness we need to see it in its organic context. Selfishness is actually an unhealthy organ in our mental anatomy. When selfishness is absent mutual love can be present. Mutual love is in the order of creation. The human mind cannot survive on its own. It is not born that way. Minds in the human species are anatomically interconnected, never alone. A mind alone that has been disconnected from other minds, does not function, does not give us consciousness, nor thinking or intelligence.

We can learn to identify selfish thinking and acting by adding the expression "for the sake of" to the activity in question. For instance

Selfishness refers to motive. It is for the sake for which we do or think something. Doing something "for the sake of self only" is a selfish motive. It is a an anatomical malfunctioning of the affective system that consists of our loves. Doing something for the sake of self only is not a legitimate or healthy motive. It is contrary to creation and spiritual order, which is that God creates every soul and mind for others who will benefit from the new soul or mind. When the mind is selfish it no longer functions for others. Hence it cannot function in a healthy manner.

This is easier to understand when you recall that in the afterlife we live in collective consciousness, not individual consciousness, which is the way we do now in natural consciousness. When we join a spiritual society in the afterlife we become immersed in the collective consciousness of that society as a group. In positive societies of mutual love there cannot be individuals who are selfish. The orientation and attitude of selfishness is instantly communicated telepathically to everyone else in the society. Everyone suddenly feels attacked to the core, rejected, disrespected, injured. Everyone's love would jointly act to isolate and contain the source of this selfishness amongst them. The offending individual would instantly and violently be ejected from their sphere.

Once you understand that selfishness is an anatomical threat to survival you still need to acquire the spiritual ability to identify selfishness in your thinking and feeling.

We also need to understand what it is to do something for the sake of self only. What is the difference between these:

- Doing something for the sake of self
- Doing something for the sake of self only
- Doing something for the sake of self and others

- Doing something for the sake of others

The answer may surprise you: The first three are selfish. Only the last is from mutual love.

In natural consciousness we define selfishness as *"Doing something for the sake of self only"*. And then we add: *"And only if it hurts others."* It is the philosophy of our generation that it is good to regularly do something "just for yourself". This is legitimate from a spiritual understanding. Swedenborg reports that angel couples in the heaven of mental eternity are most happy to be engaged in useful work for the sake of others, both in their heaven and those still on earth. Nevertheless they enjoy doing things for themselves and if they don't do this their happiness decreases.

From a spiritual perspective it's OK to do things just for yourself. Some people call that being selfish and try to make others feel guilty about it. But from the spiritual perspective there is a distinct difference between being selfish and doing things "just for yourself", or as some people say, "pampering" yourself. And in fact we can include doing anything for yourself as spiritually legitimate. Someone once mentioned to me that she was feeling exhausted from trying to meet the demands that her grandparents were putting on her every day. She could not do her own work and she had no time for her friends. At the same time she said she was feeling guilty for resenting them for it and for all sorts of other negative thoughts and emotions. What would she do if she was practicing RTS?

First she would immediately think that her having those feelings of resentment towards her grandparents was a spiritual temptation that God provided for her regeneration and for her salvation from the hells in her mind. As soon as makes this first step her feelings of guilt vanish. And this would provide her with the ability to make the second step, to be mentioned below.

When she defines what she feels as resentment against her grandparents, whom she greatly respects by tradition, she is embroiled with herself and falls into the traps that the self sets for the self. Self-entrapment is a characteristic way of behaving in natural consciousness. This is the process of devolution, or backwards evolution, that organically occurs in our natural consciousness when it rejects the order and arrangement that flows in by correspondence from the activity going on in our spiritual consciousness. This is how God created us as an operator of consciousness at three levels.

Anatomically this mental operation requires three distinct levels of operation: celestial, spiritual, and natural. God created them to operate in perfect synchrony. All three are active and there is a downward command cycle from celestial, to spiritual, to natural. It is the celestial consciousness that is closest to God and sets the order for everything else in creation.

The order and arrangement in our natural mind is to be dictated or set by the activity going on in our spiritual mind. When the Fall happened the natural mind began to choose its own arrangement, and finally rejected totally all incoming correspondences from the spiritual mind. At that point in human history on this planet the devolution or negative evolution began for the human race. This Fall necessitated the incarnation of God as an ordinary human being on earth. In that human state God repaired His own inherited natural mind by undergoing regeneration and experiencing temptations. When God's natural mind was anatomically repaired through regeneration it became the model for all human beings in their natural mind.

From that moment onward all human beings could be saved if they were willing to undergo regeneration. This is why the incarnated God is called the Savior.

So from an RTS perspective her first step is to realize that her resentment and other negative feelings were spiritual temptations with which God was facing her. This realization would eliminate her resentment and guilt. Her second step would be to figure out that she was not being selfish or disrespectful to her grandparents for defining limits to her availability to them. It is spiritually legitimate for her to be engaged in taking care of her life and its activities. This includes her time with friends and enjoying recreational activities, including the pursuit of her interests.

So from a practical point of view all she had to do is to make it clear to them when she will be available for carrying out their errands or taking them to certain places. This person's feelings of resentment and guilt were caused by the self entrapping itself. All the psychological dysfunctions and mental suffering that plague most people in our world are caused by self-entrapment. Jung's psychotherapy was always concerned with helping patients to free the self from the captivity by the self. Undergoing regeneration frees the self from its entrapments, seductions, compulsions, and viciousness.

I pointed out that "doing something for self and others" is still selfish, while "doing something for others", is mutual love. We need to understand why it is still selfish when people do things that serve both self and others?

Here again are the four options I listed just above:

- Doing something for the sake of self
- Doing something for the sake of self only
- Doing something for the sake of self and others
- Doing something for the sake of others

Consider the difference between the last two items. Doing something for the sake of others does not involve the self as part of the motivation. For instance, a neighbor needs something from a certain store but his car is in repair. I offer the neighbor to pick up the item for him next time I am at that store. This means that I am doing it for the sake of self and others. But if I offered to go pick it up right away even though I don't need to go there, then I am doing it for the sake of others.

The same logic would apply to giving away clothes to a charity organization when I decided to get rid of those clothes. An altruistic motivation may be involved in the decision to give the clothes to charity instead of throwing them away, especially if it's somewhat inconvenient to store the clothes for a few days while it is being picked up.

We also need to understand the difference between "doing something for the sake of others" and "doing something for others". It is always helpful to specify "for the sake of" to keep things clear about the motivation. For instance:

- Doing something for another person for the sake of that person

- Doing something for another person for the sake of self

The second item involves self-interest. The first item is altruistic.

49. The Ten Commandments
and Regeneration

The *Ten Commandments* are taught to children and everyone knows about them. Only a few people can identify all ten. In the spiritual sense the number "10" signifies "all", similarly to the number "12". So the Ten Commandments contain within themselves all the Commandments that God gives in *Sacred Scripture*. The style of the Commandments is "Don't do this forbidden thing". Don't lie. Don't profane God's Name. Don't steal. Etc. In the following selection, Swedenborg explains why this style is used for the *Ten Commandments* in the *Old Testament*.

Swedenborg writes:
> The evils enumerated in the Decalogue [Ten Commandments] include all the evils that can ever exist; therefore the Decalogue is called the ten commandments, because "ten" signifies all. The first commandment, "Thou shalt not worship other gods," includes not loving self and the world; for he that loves self and the world above all things worships other gods; for everyone's god is that which he loves above all things. The second commandment, "Thou shalt not profane the name of God," includes not to despise the Word and doctrine from the Word, and thus the church, and not to reject these from the heart, for these are God's "name."

> The fifth commandment, "Thou shalt not steal," includes the shunning of frauds and unlawful gains, for these also are thefts. The sixth commandment, "Thou shalt not commit adultery," includes having delight in adulteries and having no delight in marriages, and in particular cherishing filthy thoughts respecting such things as pertain to marriage, for these are adulteries. The seventh commandment, "Thou shalt not kill," includes not hating the neighbor nor loving revenge; for hatred and revenge v witness," includes not to lie and blaspheme; for lies and blasphemies are false testimonies.

> The ninth commandment, "Thou shalt not covet thy neighbor's house," includes not wishing to possess or to divert to oneself the goods of others against their will. The tenth commandment, "Thou shalt not covet thy neighbor's wife, his man-servants,"

and so on, includes not wishing to rule over others and to subject them to oneself, for the things here enumerated mean the things that are man's own. Anyone can see that these eight commandments contain the evils that must be shunned, and not the goods that must be done. ~Swedenborg, Apocalypse Explained, AE 935

There are amplifications of meaning of each Commandment that we should take note of.

The First Commandment, "Do not worship other Gods" signifies in the spiritual sense, not to love ourselves more than anything since what we love more than anything is a god to us. As well, it signifies not to love anything in the physical world more than the things in the spiritual world.

The Second Commandment, "Do not profane the Name of God" signifies in the spiritual sense, not to deny the Word of God, and not to disrespect people's worship rituals and beliefs about God.

The Fifth Commandment, "Do not steal" signifies that we must shun all frauds and financial deceits or cheating.

The Sixth Commandment, "Do not commit adultery" signifies in its extension that we must not give in to adulterous and pornographic thoughts and interests. We must fight them as sins against God and breaking the Commandments.

The Seventh Commandment, "Do not kill or murder" signifies in its extension that we must no hate or love revenge because hatred and revenge desire to murder.

The Tenth Commandment, "Do not covet the neighbor's wife and his possessions" signifies in its extension that we must not dominate others and try to subject them to our rule

The Ten Commandments tell us the evils that we must shun, instead of saying the goods that must be done. Why is this?

It is because of the order of progression in regeneration. Regeneration is firstly the process of learning *how to stop doing and thinking selfish things*, which are also called "bad" and "evil" things. In the Ten Commandments *God tells us that we need to stop doing bad things to others before we can start doing good things to them.*

Mutual love is to withhold oneself from hurting others, and to do this from a desire to protect them from all harm.

We can inhibit ourselves from aggressing others when we don't want to get into trouble. This is a selfish motive. The evidence for this will show up in your thoughts and feelings if you examine them. Most people have learned to routinely put on an acceptable appearance and conduct when interacting with others. The "put on" of being nice while thinking bad thoughts cannot be counted as mutual love. But when we are being nice to others because we want to love and appreciate them, we are doing it out of mutual love.

Learning to do and think from mutual love is the second phase of regeneration, after we succeeded in inhibiting being disrespectful or nasty. We must stop being nasty before we can be respectful. This is the reason that God in the Ten Commandments tells us what we must not do since this is the start of undergoing regeneration. It is remarkable that every single chapter and verse in Sacred Scripture contains a spiritual meaning in which God talks to us about regeneration.

God in "the Word" designates the central topic and issue in human life, namely, the issue of regeneration.

Human beings are created to be born for heaven. But since the "Fall" of consciousness from spiritual to natural, human beings are born with a strong predilection for hell through their clinging to selfishness more than to anything else. Unless we undergo regeneration we are headed to a life of hell in the afterlife of eternity. This is because when we complete the three-day dying-resuscitation process we are immersed in spiritual consciousness as our only reality to eternity. Here is where love determines our mental state.

Selfish loves keep us in natural consciousness. Trying to survive with material ideas in a spiritual environment is disastrous for the individual. Reality does not make sense. We cannot adapt to anything real. Reality is spiritual. To survive well we must allow ourselves spiritual loves of mutual love, which are called heavenly loves.

We can live in heaven when our personality reacts spontaneously from mutual love. We then experience only good will towards all others. We experience horror at the thought of hurting someone for our benefit. We maintain a personal relationship with God by keeping God present in our mind all the time, never deviating from this rule. Swedenborg reports that when we are in our heavenly state we see God present before our eyes no matter which way we walk or turn.

This is the outward effect of the inner striving of each person to cling to God from love and appreciation. Most people who are in the heavenly mental state see before them who appears as Sun. The Sun of the spiritual world of eternity is God's love-substance with its truth–substance streaming from God's mind into the created and finited universe. This streaming creates the atmospheres and spaces of the mental world of humanity. Our mental body contains organs of reception for love and truth substance. It is the never ending continuous source for the flow of all our mental activity and consciousness.

Love of self is therefore the unwillingness to stop doing bad things to others because we don't want to give up its delights and enjoyments.

This includes thinking badly about others, such as ridiculing them, disrespecting them, gossiping about them, or objectifying them sexually. These are instances of thinking badly about others. God says, Make yourself stop doing that and I can heal you by regeneration of your personality structure.

Swedenborg writes:
> Our purpose is what we love above all else. We focus on it in each and every thing we do. It exists in our will like a hidden current in a river that moves and carries things along, even when we are doing something else, because it is what motivates us. ~Swedenborg, True Christianity, TCR 399

50. How Good and Truth
Act in Our Mind

Swedenborg wrote that nothing is more important for us to know than how our will and our understanding act together in our mind. You no doubt observed this with yourself, that you could be a better person, a happier individual, more productive and more useful to others and society, if you could always act the way you rationally decide it would be best. The problem is, as we can all observe with ourselves, that we break our rules, promises, resolutions, plans, and considered intentions. Why do we practice these self-defeating routines?

Answering this requires that we know how our will and our understanding act together to produce actions and speech. The will is an operation of the mind's affective system while the understanding operates in the cognitive system. So the issue is to understand how the affective and cognitive systems work together in the mind's anatomy.

The affective system operates through loves that are very powerful biological and psychic energy bundles. Our affective system receives these love-substance bundles from the psychic atmosphere that surrounds the mind and from which we absorb psychic nutrients needed for our mind to operate. When we are born our mind is in natural consciousness, which is a level of mental operation that absorbs love-bundles from two opposite sources: the loves of the people in heaven and the loves of the people in hell.

The entire humanity of individuals is connected anatomically through these love-bundles. In natural consciousness we absorb "good loves" from heavenly societies that give our affective system the ability and inclination to love others as much as self, and to love God more than self, and these are spiritual loves or connections. We also absorb "evil loves" from infernal societies that give our affective system an inclination to love ourselves above everything, including others and God.

Swedenborg writes:
I have talked at times with spirits that had recently come from the world about the state of eternal life, saying that it is important to know who the Lord of the

kingdom is, and what kind and what form of government it has. As nothing is more important for those entering another kingdom in the world than to know who and what the king is, and what the government is, and other particulars in regard to the kingdom, so is it of still greater consequence in regard to this kingdom in which they are to live to eternity.

Therefore they should know that it is the Lord who governs both heaven and the universe, for He who governs the one governs the other; thus that the kingdom in which they now are is the Lord's; and that the laws of this kingdom are eternal truths, all of which rest upon the law that the Lord must be loved above all things and the neighbor as themselves; and even more than this, if they would be like the angels they must love the neighbor more than themselves.

On hearing this they could make no reply, for the reason that although they had heard in the life of the body something like this they had not believed it, wondering how there could be such love in heaven, and how it could be possible for any one to love his neighbor more than himself. But they were told that every good increases immeasurably in the other life, and that while they cannot go further in the life of the body than to love the neighbor as themselves, because they are immersed in what concerns the body, yet when this is set aside their love becomes more pure, and finally becomes angelic, which is to love the neighbor more than themselves.

For in the heavens there is joy in doing good to another, but no joy in doing good to self unless with a view to its becoming another's, and thus for another's sake. This is loving the neighbor more than oneself. They were told that the possibility of such a love is shown in the world in the marriage love of some who have suffered death to protect a consort from injury, in the love of parents for their children, as in a mother's preferring to go hungry rather than see her child go hungry; in sincere friendship, in which one friend will expose himself to danger for another; and even in polite and pretended friendship that wishes to emulate sincere friendship, in offering the better things to those to whom it professes to wish well, and bearing such good will on the lips though not in the heart; finally, in the nature of love, which is such that its joy is to serve others, not for its own sake but for theirs. But all this was incomprehensible to those who loved themselves more than others, and in the life of the body had been greedy of gain; most of all to the avaricious.
~Swedenborg, Heaven and Hell, HH 406

The psychic energy bundles of good loves are kept in a separate anatomical structure than the evil loves since putting them together would neutralize and destroy the quality of the good loves. Thus it is that we alternate in different situations between being considerate and generous to being selfish and greedy in accordance with the love-bundle that is being activated in each situation. This alternation and balance gives human beings maximum freedom in favoring the one or the other type of love.

In the absence of external coercion we can choose according to our loves. We thus become our loves in effigy. In the following selection Swedenborg discusses this psychodynamic operation in terms of the good and the truth, or their opposites. The good refers to good-substance streaming into our affective system where it can stay genuine good, or be turned into selfish evil. In one case the individual has mental energy to think and act well, in the other to think and act badly.

Further, there is a power differential between good-substance and truth-substance. Good activates the will or affective system, while truth activates the understanding or cognitive system. Considered anatomically the will is higher, more powerful, and more perfect than the understanding. It is not generally known that the loves in our will select the formation of our thoughts in our cognitive system. What we think is dictated by what we love or intend. Thinking is subject to feeling and serves it. This is why our ability to think logically and observe accurately is diminished when our will is exploding with anger or panic.

People have many "blind spots" which are things they don't see that others do see. The difference is the variation in love. Good loves associate with true understanding and keen perception, while evil loves produce obscure understanding and irrational thinking. When you change your love you change yourself.

Swedenborg writes:
> The truths that are from good are said to be the forms of good because they are nothing else than goods formed. He who conceives of truths in any other way, and especially he who separates them from good, does not know what truths are. Truths do indeed appear as if separate from good, thus as a form by themselves, but only to those who are not in good, or to those who think and speak otherwise than as they will and thence act.

Our thinking is done through the use of truth-substance. This has a built-in property of rationality so that the sequences of thoughts or ideas that are produced form a coherent unit. Good loves produce rational sequences of thinking but evil loves produce distorted and irrational sequences. Hence good loves produce correct and realistic conclusions but bad loves generate falsities and hypocrisies.

Swedenborg writes:

For man is so created that his understanding and will may constitute one mind, and they do constitute one mind when the understanding acts as one with the will, that is, when the man thinks and speaks as he wills and thence acts, for in this case the things of his understanding are forms of his will. The things of the understanding are what are called truths, for truths are properly of the understanding, whereas the things of the will are what are called goods, for goods are properly of the will. From this it follows that regarded in itself the understanding is nothing but the will formed.

But as the term "form" savors of human philosophy, the matter shall be illustrated by an example, from which will be seen that truths are the forms of good. In civil and moral life there exist what is honorable and what is becoming [decorum, appropriateness]. What is honorable is to will well to others from the heart in the affairs of civil life, and what is becoming is to testify this in speech and gesture.

Thus regarded in itself what is becoming is nothing but the form of what is honorable, for this is its origin, and therefore when what is honorable shows itself by what is becoming (that is, in a becoming manner by speech and gesture), that which is honorable appears in every detail of that which is becoming, insomuch that whatever is uttered in the speech or shown in the gesture appears honorable, and is the form or image through which that which is honorable shines forth. In this way the two things make a one, like an essence and its form, or like what is essential and what is formal.

But if anyone separates what is honorable from what is becoming, that is, if anyone wills evil to a companion, and yet speaks well and behaves himself well toward him, there is then no longer anything of what is honorable in the speech and gestures, however much he may study to make a show of the form of what is honorable by what is becoming; for it is really dishonorable, and every discerning person so calls it, because it is either feigned, or fraudulent, or deceitful.

From all this we can see how the case is with truths and goods; for truths in spiritual life are circumstanced as is what is becoming in civil life; and hence it is evident what is the quality of truths when they are the forms of good, and what when separated from good; for when they are not from good they are from some evil, and are its forms, however much they may counterfeit the forms of good. ~Swedenborg, Heavenly Secrets, AC 4574

In other words, when we act from selfish loves we become deceitful and hypocritical. One might say that truth is not in us. Instead of rationality, insanity is in us. When we are in this deteriorating or unhealthy natural consciousness it is impossible to undergo regeneration and the healthy process of individuation is arrested and distorted. Now the unconscious psychic love bundles from the societies who are in evil loves bombard us with endless more evil loves so that instead of our character becoming healthier it progressively becomes sick and dysfunctional.

Jung writes:

Did you ever think of the evil in you? ~Carl Jung, Liber Novus, p. 274

Great is he who is in love, since love is the present act of the great creator, the present moment of the becoming and lapsing of the world. ~Carl Jung, Liber Novus, p. 253

I live in my deepest hell, and from there I cannot fall any further. ~Carl Jung. Quoted by Marie Loise Von Franz, Jung: His Myth in Our Time, p. 174

We are the origin of all coming evil. ~Carl Jung

Swedenborg writes:

After death we each become our love, and our spirit is nothing but the emotions that embody our love. Once we become a spirit, then, it is from our emotions that we think and speak, and it is from our emotions that we form an intent and carry it out. Whatever we respond to emotionally, or love, is what we then long for and absorb, and whatever we do not respond to, or love, we oppose and reject. In fact our face gradually becomes the face of our emotions, or our love. From that point on, our face tells others who we are. So do the words we speak, and the sound of them is the sound of our emotions. In short, after death we become our love (or emotions) in tangible form. ~Swedenborg, Apocalypse Explained, AE 837

It should be recognized that by his own endeavour a person is able to simulate what is actually Divine and to present himself before others as an angel of light. But what is seen by the Lord and by angels is not the outward form he presents but the form that exists inwardly, which is foul when the proprium is the source of it. With people like this everything within them is merely natural and not at all spiritual. They see everything in natural light alone and nothing in the light of heaven; indeed they do not know what the light of heaven is, nor what anything spiritual is. All their inner powers are turned to things of an external nature, in almost the same way as those of living creatures are; nor do they allow themselves to be raised by the Lord to anything higher. Yet the human being, superior to animals, has a special ability, namely the ability to be raised by the Lord towards heaven and the Lord, and so be led by Him. All those are raised in this manner who love goodness and truth for their own sake, which is the same thing as loving the neighbour and God since in a general sense the neighbour means that which is good and true, and in a lower sense that which is right and fair; and also God constitutes what is good and true, and what is right and fair, since God is the source of them. AC 10284

Angelic life consists of worthwhile, thoughtful actions, actions that are useful to others. ~Swedenborg, Heaven and Hell 403

The unconscious is not just a receptacle for all unclean spirits and other odious legacies from the dead past—such as, for instance, that deposit of centuries of public opinion which constitutes Freud's "superego." ~Carl Jung, CW 4, Para 760

---

51. Spiritual Rationality and Rational Spirituality

When I was a young man and searching for spirituality I received the impression from my readings that spirituality is above human rationality. I concluded that what is spiritual cannot be explained but must be achieved by experiencing and by consciousness. The promoters of this idea associate God with "conversion experiences of being one with God" rather than with rational understanding of God. But RTS offers a different explanation.

First, there is no true rationality without spirituality. Second, there is no spirituality without true rationality. This is easier to understand as soon as we make a distinction between two types of rationality in our mental functioning, a lower and a higher.

The lower rationality develops first and is immersed in natural consciousness. Hence it is called natural-rational consciousness. This type of thinking and reasoning is adapted to what we can use effectively when we are working our physical avatar to act and manage social life and citizenship here on earth. The entire structure of our ego-personality is composed of natural ideas that are tied to or immersed in the pragmatics of physical properties. These are the only ones we need for manipulating our physical avatar. These natural ideas are called material ideas because they involve matter, quantity, cause-effect, time, space, location, measurements, and systems. Perhaps you might want to take a few minutes to try to find a concept, idea, or principle that you know of and that does not contain these physical qualities either directly or indirectly.

We have been taught the difference between concrete things and abstract things. And abstract things are presented as being non-physical. For instance a tree is a concrete thing, while the principle of "freedom for all" is abstract. You can think of many more such examples. But if we examine both concrete and abstract concepts from the perspective of spiritual-rational consciousness we can realize that abstract concepts such as freedom, government, scientific principles, or respect for your neighbor, and so on, are constructed to be applied to the physical world and to the people interacting in that world. It would not make rational sense to suddenly introduce ideas that are contrary to this practical approach.

Our conscious lower rationality, called natural-rational consciousness, is completely opposed to our unconscious higher rationality called spiritual-rational consciousness. It makes sense that the two types of rationality would be opposed to each other before we begin our regeneration process. When we try to apply natural rationality to spiritual ideas, we conclude that there is no proof of God's existence, and that there is no proof for the existence of an afterlife world in eternity.

With RTS thinking we can see through this bogus objection. When we ask for "proof" of God's existence, or "proof" of life after death, we are asking for something self-contradictory and impossible. To not see this is a consequence of the limits imposed on natural-rational reasoning.

It is common in lower rationality to reason that if God really existed we would be able to prove it, just like all other things in science that need to be proven before being accepted. It is the same with the afterlife of eternity. Spiritual facts and ideas cannot be proven to materialistic reasoning. This is impossible due to logical self-contradiction since the requested "proof" is something physical that can be measured and defined in relation to other physical things. This is a logical contradiction since the spiritual is defined as separate from the natural.

How can something that is separate from the natural be given a natural proof of its existence? If a natural or physical proof were possible for the existence of something, then the thing would not be something spiritual. This is by definition when we say that the natural and the spiritual are discretely different or separated.

Swedenborg reports that there are individuals in the afterlife of eternity who are unable to think in spiritual rationality. In consequence their natural thinking becomes illogical and non-adaptive to the For instance, they may believe themselves to be god and that they have omnipotence. Their fantasies are such that they see themselves ruling over all things as a god, with the power to kill or save, to free or enslave. They can fantasize that the rocks in the ground are gold nuggets and the entire wealth in the universe belongs to them. Swedenborg documents many such mentally deranged people in the afterlife. This is the consequence in the afterlife of having refused in this life to learn to think in a rationality that is not merely natural and material.

Rational theistic self-analysis (RTS) is based on the spiritual principle that mental health depends on the successful integration of the two types of rationality. Those who arrive in the afterlife with an unintegrated ego-personality are mentally ill and incapable of successfully adapting to the realities of the psychic world of eternity. It is completely feasible for an individual to be successful with their physical avatar in this life and appear competent and healthy mentally. And yet, if they do not develop their skills in spiritual rationality they are unable in the afterlife to integrate and stabilize their personality structure.

Many people experience inner dissonance and sometimes despondency and are searching for a more satisfying life. They are known in the historic literature as "seekers of truth".

Those who allow themselves to be led by inner strivings for a higher life are led by God to spiritual rationality and thence to the integration of their lower and higher ego-consciousness.

The practice of RTS can assist people to be open to God's leading them. Learning the higher rationality is one component of mental health. The other is acquiring new habits of love or loving. Selfish love leads to strengthening the ties to lower rationality. Mutual love or spiritual love for the sake of God leads to strengthening the ties to higher rationality. *Spiritual love and spiritual rationality are thus tied to the same organic function.*

Perhaps the most startling aspect of moving from natural to spiritual rationality is to feel comfortable with the spiritual reality of the vertical community to which we belong. In natural rationality we feel terrified at the notion that we are never alone in our mind and that we are constantly in the company of spirits and angels. It is best to reject this notion altogether if one withdraws from spiritual rationality. *There is a psychological danger in accepting the vertical community in natural consciousness alone.*

Spiritual rationality develops gradually as one is being regenerated by God. The pace of regeneration depends on the individual's cooperation by striving to resist selfish pleasures and concerns for the sake of being a better human being. This striving is the opposite of the motivation that occupies us when considering self-benefit before benefit to others. We can see this clearly when we consider our children and those of other parents. Children quite naturally focus on their own fun, preferences, and needs. What happens when we try to teach them to be more considerate of the needs of others? They deeply resist and resent that rule. They feel it as a loss of their happiness and freedom in life.

Still, as children get older they are compelled by consequences to act like they care about others and not just about themselves. This is a put-on for the sake of themselves. Many things and circumstances of daily life teach them how to get away with thinking of themselves as number one and acting that way whenever punishment or disapproval can be avoided, and when not, to simulate caring for others, which they do not feel and which they abhor. *They quickly latch on to false principles that teach them that it is healthy to love themselves.*

It is to be known that God never forces anyone to love others or to stop loving themselves. It would be useless for mental development to be forced to do anything. The only way possible to change personality from natural to spiritual is to choose in total freedom. *The individual must experience choosing in freedom.* When this is done God can re-awaken innocent feelings of love for others in which there is no thought or calculation of self-benefit. Infants and children spontaneously experience such love in total freedom. This innocent or spiritual love is immediately captured by God and miraculously put aside for use by the individual in building up the new ego-personality during the regeneration process. There is no power for regenerating our personality without these innocent forms of love that are untainted by selfish intent.

It is to be noted that children readily accept the idea of God, God's omnipresence and humanity, and the connection that God provides us with in the form of angels. Children in their innocence love angels. They understand angels and God. But later as the self-centered and self-motivated ego-structure grows in power they begin to doubt that angels exist or that God is really omnipresent, human, and all-powerful.

There cannot be any spiritual development when an individual rejects the reality of our vertical community. It may not be necessary at first to know that angels and spirits with whom we are connected are actually people who had lived on earth and are now in their afterlife. And yet it is a fact that eventually must enter the individual's spiritual rationality. The reality is that no human mind can live or survive alone. Our psychic body, from the instant it is born in the psychic world, is immediately surrounded by other psychic bodies or minds in the afterlife. The human mind cannot operate on its own, just like ants or bees can do nothing on their own and if separated from other ants or bees they die. *To think thoughts and to feel emotions are completely impossible on our own.*

Swedenborg writes:

> *Such being the nature of heaven, no angel or spirit can have any life unless he is in some society, and thereby in a harmony of many. A society is nothing but a harmony of many, for no one has any life separate from the life of others.*
>
> *Indeed no angel, or spirit, or society can have any life (that is, be affected by good, exercise will, be affected by truth, or think), unless there is a conjunction thereof through many of his society with heaven and with the world of spirits. And it is the same with the human race: no man, no matter who and what he may be, can live (that is, be affected by good, exercise will, be affected by truth, or think), unless in like manner he is conjoined with heaven through the angels who are with him, and with the world of spirits, nay, with hell, through the spirits that are with him.*
>
> *For every man while living in the body is in some society of spirits and of angels, though entirely unaware of it. And if he were not conjoined with heaven and with the world of spirits through the society in which he is, he could not live a moment. The case in this respect is the same as it is with the human body, any portion of which that is not conjoined with the rest by means of fibers and vessels, and thus by means of functions, is not a part of the body, but is instantly separated and rejected, as having no vitality.*
>
> *The very societies in and with which men have been during the life of the body, are shown them when they come into the other life. And when, after the life of the body, they come into their society, they come into their veriest (truest) life which they had in the body, and from this life begin a new life; and so according to their life which they have lived in the body they either go down into hell, or are raised up into heaven. ~Swedenborg, Heavenly Secrets, AC 687*

God wills to constantly unify all individuals together so that the entire human race stands out like one universal individual called the Grand Human. In other words, God wills to integrate all human beings into one functioning unit. For an individual to think of himself or herself as an independent individual is to be immersed in unreality or ignorance. Of course we can easily acknowledge that we could not survive on our own without parents and the community. We are thinking then of the physical body and we do not wish to extend this acknowledgement to the mind or psychic body. In our mind we are alone. We are taught that only "crazy people" feel others in their mind.

But the point is precisely that. *We do not feel others in our mind, unless we are crazy.* God carefully prevents any individual in natural consciousness to have the feeling of not being alone in our mind. This is necessary so that we may feel free and independent in our mind. Even after we fully come to accept the reality of the vertical community, we still do not consciously experience the presence in our mind of spirits and angels, or even of God. It is to protect that feeling of freedom that God makes sure the vertical community does not break through into our consciousness. But it is different in spiritual consciousness here and in the afterlife.

And yet people like Jung and Swedenborg have been allowed to experience that breakthrough. Jung met and had relationships with many of these people in the collective unconscious. But this permission is not necessary or advantageous for most people.

Jung writes:
> If there were no consciousness, there would be no world; the whole world, as far as it enters into our consideration, depends upon that little flame of consciousness, that is surely the decisive factor. ~Carl Jung, Visions Seminar, p. 898

> It is in very truth the eternally living, creative, germinal layer in each of us, and though it may make use of age-old symbolical images it nevertheless intends them to be understood in a new way. ~Carl Jung, CW 4, Para 760

---

52. Conjugial Love

Swedenborg writes:

> *Those that are in heaven are continually advancing towards the spring of life, with a greater advance towards a more joyful and happy spring the more thousands of years they live; and this to eternity, with increase according to the growth and degree of their love, charity, and faith. Women who have died old and worn out with age, if they have lived in faith in the Lord, in charity to the neighbor, and in happy marriage love with a husband, advance with the succession of years more and more into the flower of youth and early womanhood, and into a beauty that transcends every conception of any such beauty as is seen on the earth.*

> *Goodness and charity are what give this form and thus manifest their own likeness, causing the joy and beauty of charity to shine forth from every least particular of the face, and causing them to be the very forms of charity. Some who beheld this were struck with amazement. The form of charity that is seen in a living way in heaven, is such that it is charity itself that both forms and is formed; and this in such a manner that the whole angel is a charity, as it were, especially the face; and this is both clearly seen and felt. When this form is beheld it is beauty unspeakable, affecting with charity the very inmost life of the mind. In a word, to grow old in heaven is to grow young. Such forms or such beauties do those become in the other life who have lived in love to the Lord and in charity towards the neighbor. All angels are such forms in endless variety; and of these heaven is constituted. ~Swedenborg, Heaven and Hell, HH 414*

We have discussed many wonderful spiritual ideas throughout this book. Some readers may wonder why I have left to the end of the book the discussion on romance and sex when viewed in spiritual consciousness. Perhaps it's because this is the most wonderful of all the spiritual ideas I have discussed and requires some prior spiritual knowledge to be understood, believed, and appreciated.

You already know that the universe is made of love-substance that is a conscious part of God's infinite and eternal mind. I have taken occasion earlier to express my amazement and overwhelming awe at the realization that God is Human and omnipresent. God's human nature, which is the original human, is love! How wondrously fortunate or blessed I feel that this is the God we have and know. Every human being can say, "God loves me", and it is true. Or, "God is my Father and provider of everything that is good for me that gives me pleasure, happiness, and inner satisfaction and fulfillment."

Now this awesome God of love has created one thing in human experiencing that is special, so special that by itself it outweighs the goodness and happiness of all other spiritual things put together. This most precious and wonderful jewel of life is called "conjugial love", an expression coined and used by Swedenborg. The extra "i" after the "g" contrasts with the more usual "conjugal". My usage is to use "conjugal" for marriages in which the partners are in natural consciousness, and to use "conjugial" for marriages with both partners in spiritual and in celestial consciousness.

In natural consciousness we think of sex, romance and marriage as temporary things, lasting either a short time, or longer, or a lifetime. Yet all of these are limited experiences, not eternal and endless. When we are immersed in the experiencing of passionate romantic love we want it to go on forever. This is called the honeymoon state and is given though our unconscious celestial consciousness. We are threatened and devastated at the thought that this mutual entanglement of mind is going to end and disappear some day.

But as we begin our regeneration process *we begin to perceive from God that the mental state of romantic pair-hood (or pairdom) is immortal and continues on forever.*

In the afterlife, people in love with each other cannot be kept apart, unlike the situation on earth where lovers can be kept apart through geographic distance, socio-cultural distance, age, or centuries. But in the mental world of eternity God's love-substance is the supreme power and influence in the afterlife (as indeed it is everywhere). The anatomical definition of love is that it is the celestial consciousness of itself longing to be *consummated*. Love is the inmost and most forceful vital energy that explosively seeks out its partner who is known as truth-substance.

Truth-substance is the outer covering of love-substances. This is similar to the idea of a burning fire at night. We see the light from it and realize that it is the heat that streams out and fills the environment that appears like light. It helps to understand this profound human mystery if you imagine that love and truth make up the universal and Divine marriage in God's mind.

This is the ultimate marriage that God longs to give us! Our spiritual body in the mental world of eternity is immersed in the abundance of love-substance and truth-substance. Our mental anatomy absorbs this Divine-Human substance with our three systems of functions. We absorb love-substance with the receptor organs in our affective system, which includes the mental organ of the heart and its mental circulation. We absorb truth-substance with the receptor organs of our cognitive system, which includes thinking, reasoning, and understanding.

Love-substance in our affective-motivational system seeks out with explosive passion truth-substance in our cognitive system that is compatible for forming a celestial pair.

This is the experiencing in romantic pairs when falling in love and mutually loving each other.

Mutual love is the anatomical marriage of love and truth. This anatomical conjunction must go through two steps. First, we must discover or create that marriage in our own consciousness. Second, we must experience it though the consciousness of the other.

In the title RTS, "Rational" pertains to the cognitive system in our mind, while "Theistic" pertains to the affective system. Our mental anatomy is built in a form to receive into our consciousness love-substance and truth-substance *separately*. Yet love and truth in God's mind are *united as one*. It is called the "*Divine Marriage of Good and Truth*".

So when love is separated from its truth it passionately keeps seeking through our cognitive system and its knowledge database until it finds its true partner. The passionate search of love for its truth is the very basis of creation. God creates things by separating love and truth that are united in God. When love-substance and truth-substance are separated in Divine creation they each are absorbed by independent systems of the mind's organic body. Now love and truth exist in our mind as two single things, each having its own independent ability and life.

We are born in this natural consciousness in which the love-substance lives independently and separately from its conjugial partner, the cognitive system. *Both love and truth in our consciousness long to reconnect and rejoin to be one again, as they are in the mind of God.* This union is called "*the marriage of love and truth*", also expressed as the "*the marriage of good and truth*". The equivalence of the two expressions makes sense since love-substance is the origin of all good, all powers, functions and abilities in the human mind.

Love-substance in our affective system gives us an endless variety of motivation and enjoyment. We would lie in a coma without love-substance streaming into our motivational system on a continuous basis. With truth-substance continuously streaming into our cognitive system, we can have thoughts and intelligence that direct our activities to the demands and pleasures of our affective system. Hence love and truth conjoined is our very life and consciousness.

This tension of love longing for its truth is the celestial romance that creates human minds and a world filled with things that are useful and pleasing to the human mind. *Love and truth are our anatomical parents.* As infants we experience reaching for a desired object and obtaining it through our reaching. This is the first step in the marriage of love and truth that creates our consciousness. All first steps in higher human development take place in infancy. We are then in a mental state that is open to reception and open to the experiencing of the union that is effected in the act of will of reaching and the act of obtaining.

We want a glass of cold water and suddenly we feel ourselves getting up and walking to the refrigerator. This is the marriage of love and truth in our consciousness. Without this marriage we could not have gotten that glass of cold water. Our love to satisfy the momentary desire for drinking cold water would remain unsatisfied and would keep tormenting us until satisfied. Now this love finds its truth with which it immediately forms a passionate union achieving the new existential status of pair-hood.

The path to the refrigerator and the memory of its functions is an event occurring in the cognitive system, which is also our rationality and intelligence. Our affective longs for a sensorimotor consummation (e.g., cold water), but it is helpless in the single or independent state. The love (desire for drinking cold water) must find and marry its truth (the path to the refrigerator). This explanation may seem to some readers as naïve and poetic rather than scientific. But if you stick with the literal of it, you remain within your understanding of mental anatomy and biology.

Our life moment by moment is therefore an expression of love and truth continually and ceaselessly engaged with each other. It is called a "return" because love and truth are married in God's mind but separated in the mind of our natural consciousness. This is why we love our self more than anything. This is why we need to be saved through regeneration. Our personality in natural consciousness is composed of loves that have entered into a pretense marriage, not a love marriage, with versions of truth and masses of unrestrained and spiritually insane cognitions. No health and wholeness can exist in such false marriages.

53. Love-substance, Truth-substance and Eternal Salvation

Natural light in the physical world exists from spiritual light in the mental world of eternity. Natural or physical light is made for our physical avatar on earth by which we can see the objects of the physical environment. Natural consciousness is in natural-spiritual light. These are ideas within our cognitive system that are restricted to material principles.

When we undergo our regeneration we enter in our consciousness the spiritual layer of anatomical functioning. Now we see ideas from spiritual light. Ideas are mental objects and their quality and power is created by the anatomical level involved: natural, or spiritual, or celestial. Our consciousness is tied to its proper anatomical level of functioning.

In the following passage Swedenborg explains that spiritual or celestial light is actually wisdom from rationality, which is from the truth-substance that is absorbed by our cognitive anatomy. I inserted explanations in square brackets [ ].

Swedenborg writes:

Light is mentioned many times in Sacred Scripture, and in the internal sense it means truth springing from good. In the highest internal sense however 'light' means God since He is Good and Truth itself. He Himself is also in actual fact the light in heaven, but this is infinitely brighter than the light on earth.

In that light spirits and angels [those already living in the afterlife] *behold one another, and by means of it all the glory* [beautiful and useful things] *that exists in heaven* [the celestial anatomy of our consciousness] *is clearly visible. In brightness that light seems to be much the same as the light in the world, but this is not the case, for it is not a natural light but a spiritual one. It holds wisdom within itself, so much so that it is nothing else than wisdom that shines in this manner before the eyes of those in heaven. Consequently the wiser the angels are* [those who live in the celestial regions of the mental world of eternity], *the brighter the light surrounding them.*

This light also enlightens the understanding of man [our cognitive system], *especially of one who is regenerate* [loves others more than self and God above all things], *but man* [in natural consciousness] *does not discern it during his lifetime* [on earth] *because the light of the world reigns at that time.*

Evil spirits too in the next life [those who arrive in the afterlife still loving self more than anything] *behold one another, and also behold many representatives which manifest themselves in the world of spirits. They do so indeed by the light of heaven. Yet it is an inferior light like that coming from a coal fire, for when the light of heaven reaches them it is turned into this inferior light* [corporeal consciousness, which is the lowest of the natural].

As for the source itself of light, this from eternity has existed from God alone, for Divine Good itself and Divine Truth itself, the source of light, is God. The Divine Human which existed from eternity, John 17:5, was

that actual light. Because such light was unable any longer to influence the human race which had retreated so far from good and truth, and so from the light, and had cast itself into darkness [natural consciousness that denies or resists its own spiritual consciousness], God was therefore willing to be born and assume the [physical] Human itself [incarnation into a Divine human avatar]. Indeed in so doing He was able to bring light not only to man's rational concepts but also to his natural ideas. For God made Divine within Himself both the Rational [spiritual] and the Natural [physical] so that people who were in such gross darkness [natural consciousness] could have light.
~Swedenborg, Heavenly Secrets, AC 3195

In other words, the idea and reality of God can enter our natural consciousness only because God incarnated in the physical avatar. Natural consciousness can accept a God that exists at the natural level. By having incarnated with God's own physical body, God can enter into our natural consciousness today. *Those who stick to the idea of God as the "Divine Natural Human" can be impressed and influenced by God through that spiritual-natural idea of God.* This occurs in our natural consciousness, which was not possible prior to God's incarnation. Our natural consciousness is materialistic, and hence God could have no meaning except in a Divine Physical Human body.

This was the purpose of the incarnation, namely to allow materialistic consciousness to be aware of God in a natural body.

Clearly then, the Incarnation of God when the time had arrived, was part of the continuing creation of human life on earth.

When we regenerate our understanding of God, our personal relationship to God deepens and becomes spiritual, that is, spiritual-natural, and not merely natural. Beginning our regeneration marks the turnaround in our personality from loving self more than others, to loving others as much as self or more than self, and loving God above everything.

When we accept and practice this principle of spiritual love, we enter deeper into our spiritual-rational consciousness, which is above that of the natural and the spiritual-natural. Now in spiritual consciousness itself, we enter into the *collective unconscious* and the portion of it that is called *individual unconscious*. These are "psycho-geographic" spheres or zones in the mental world in which you live along with everyone else. "To think" is to move around in the mental world. Our love chooses the direction on any occasion. Our loves and our thoughts form a conjoined pair that is called the *spiritual marriage* within individual consciousness. This union is between our "motivational" system, also called affective, and the thinking organ, called the cognitive system.

All our conscious thoughts come from the marriage of love and truth in our mind, which anatomically considered is the integrating action of the heart and lungs, that is, of our motivation and our thinking. Love drives us onward and its truth manages the required direction. Together they achieve the consummation of the love and its beneficial effects.

There are thoughts that are not in our individual consciousness. Each time we elevate our consciousness, our thoughts acquire a new quality, a new power for our human use. Our reasoning and our conclusions are enhanced in a distinct way. On the lower level is the "crude" model of the materialistic version of reality. This zone of human consciousness always progresses downward into still lower materialistic thinking, such as the denial of God, of life after death, and of the immortality of our personality. When we function in this lowest level of human consciousness we may be called spiritually insane.

54. Chaste Sexual Love

Swedenborg writes the following in his book titled *Conjugial Love*:

> *I shall add here two accounts of experiences, of which this is the first.*
> *I once heard from heaven the sweetest music. There were wives there together with girls, who were singing a song. Its sweetness was like the affection of some love, pouring forth in a harmonious stream. Songs in heaven are nothing but affections in audible form, that is, affections expressed in modulated sounds, for just as thoughts are expressed by speaking, so are affections by singing. Angels [those in celestial*

consciousness] *can grasp the subject of the affection by the regularity and fluency of the modulation.*

There were a number of spirits [those in spiritual consciousness] *around me, some of whom told me that they could hear this very sweet music, and it was the music of some affection, but they did not know what its subject was. They made various guesses, but without success. One guess was that the song expressed the affection of the bridegroom and bride on plighting their troth* {pledging loyalty to each other], *another that it was their affection on entering wedlock, another that it was the earliest stage in the love of husband and wife.*

[2] Then an angel from heaven suddenly appeared among them, and said that they were singing about chaste sexual love. The bystanders enquired what chaste sexual love was. The angel replied that it was a man's love for a young woman or a wife of lovely appearance and good manners, free from any idea of lewdness; and the similar love of a woman for a man. With these words the angel vanished.

The singing continued, and since they then knew the subject of the affection it expressed, they began to hear it in many different ways, in each case depending on the state of their own love. Those who looked on women chastely heard the singing as harmonious and sweet. But those who looked on women unchastely heard it as inharmonious and depressing, and those who looked on women with distaste, heard it as discordant and harsh.

[3] The ground on which they were standing was suddenly changed into a theatre, and a voice was heard, saying, 'Discuss this love.' Spirits then quickly appeared from various communities, and among them some angels dressed in white, who said, 'In the spiritual world we have made enquiry into all the kinds of love, not only the love of a man for a man and a woman for a woman, and the reciprocal love of husband and wife, but also a man's love for women and a woman's love for men. We have been allowed to work through communities checking, and we have not yet found any shared chaste sexual love, except among those endowed with constant potency by truly conjugial love; and these are in the highest heavens.

We have also been allowed to feel the influence of that love on the affections of our hearts, and our feeling was that it surpassed in sweetness every other love, except the love of a married couple whose hearts are one. But we should like you to discuss this love, since it is a new and unfamiliar one to you. Since it is the height of loveliness, we in heaven call it the sweetness of heaven.

[4] So in the discussion the first to speak were those who were unable to think of chastity in connexion with marriage. 'Can anyone,' they said, 'on seeing a lovely or loveable girl or wife so control the ideas he thinks about and keep them so untainted by lust, as to love her beauty and yet not wish, if he were allowed, to taste it? Can anyone turn the lust innate in every man into such chastity as to make it what it is not, and still go on loving? Can sexual love, when it passes from the eyes into the thoughts, stop at the woman's face? Does it not instantly go down to the chest, and beyond? The angels were talking nonsense when they said that there is a chaste form of that love, which is none the less the sweetest of all; a love which is only possible for husbands who have truly conjugial love, so that they have extraordinary potency with their wives. Are these so much above others that on seeing lovely women they can keep the ideas they think about uplifted and as it were in suspense, to prevent them coming down and proceeding to what makes that love?'

[5] The next speakers were those who felt both heat and cold, coldness towards their wives, but heat towards the other sex. 'What is chaste sexual love?' they said. 'Surely to add chastity to love is a contradiction in terms. Can you add a contradiction without taking away what is predicated of a thing, so making it non-existent? How can chaste sexual love be the sweetest of all loves, when chastity robs it of its sweetness? You all know where the sweetness of that love is located. So when the idea of union is thrown out together with that, where is its sweetness, and where is it to come from?'

Then some others intervened, saying, 'We have been with the loveliest women without desiring them. So we know what chaste sexual love is.' But their companions, knowing their lewdness, replied, 'You were then reduced to loathing the other sex as the result of impotence, and this is not chaste sexual love, but the depth of unchaste love.'

[6] On hearing this the angels were angry and asked those who stood on the right, that is, to the south, to speak. 'There is,' they said, 'the love of two men for each other, and the love of two women for each other, and the love of a man for a woman and of a woman for a man. These three pairs of loves are completely different. The love of two men is like the love of two intellects, for man was created and therefore is by birth designed to become an intellect. The love of two women is like the love of two affections for man's intellect, for woman was created and is designed by birth to become the love of a man's intellect. These loves, those between two men or two women, do not sink far into the breast, but stay outside, making merely superficial contact and not leading to any inner union of the two. This too is the reason why two men fence with reasoned arguments on either side, like boxers; and two women sometimes with lusts on either side, like actors pretending to fight with fists.

[7] But the love of a man and a woman is the love of the intellect and its affection, which sinks in deep and leads to union. That union is love; but the union of minds, and not of bodies at the same time, or an impulse towards that union and no other, is spiritual love, and so a chaste one. This love is only possible for those who possess truly conjugial love, and thus have abundant potency, because these people's chastity does not allow them to feel any influence of love from the body of any woman other than their wife.

Being in this state of surpassing potency, they cannot help loving the other sex and at the same time loathing unchastity. As a result they have chaste sexual love, which regarded in essence is an inner spiritual friendship; this gains its sweetness from their abundant, but chaste, potency. That abundant potency is the result of a total forswearing of promiscuity, and, since the wife alone is loved, it is chaste. Now since that love in their case does not partake of the flesh, but only of the spirit, it is chaste; and because their innate attraction makes the woman's beauty at the same time enter the mind, it is delightful.'

[8] On hearing this many of the bystanders clapped their hands over their ears, saying, 'Your remarks offend our ears, and we regard what you have said as nonsense.' They were unchaste. Then the singing from heaven was heard again, and it was even sweeter than before. But to the ears of the unchaste it sounded such a discordant din, that to avoid the

racket they rushed out of the theatre and took to their heels, leaving a few behind, whose wisdom made them love chastity in marriage. ~Swedenborg, Conjugial Love, CL 55.

In the above selection, Swedenborg presents his spiritual explanation of the anatomy of human pair-hood.

The anatomy of spiritual marriage is not physical but mental. Swedenborg's explanation is not about physical marriage as practiced on earth. The people in the afterlife with whom Swedenborg has this conversation, are aware of different types of marriages or unions, such as that between a man (male) with a man (male), a woman with a woman, and a man (male) with a woman or woman with a man. These different types pair-hood unions each specialize in different types of consciousness environments.

The explanation indicates that the "spiritual marriage" we discussed in previous pages, is the integrated function or "union" between our cognitive system ("intellect") and our affective system ("affection"). In individual consciousness the spiritual marriage is between our affective and cognitive systems of anatomical functioning. In collective consciousness the union or marriage is between the two individuals of the marriage pair.

More on this topic may be read in Swedenborg's book *Conjugial Love*, available freely on the Web.

Swedenborg writes:

For people who desire true married love, the Lord provides similar partners, and if they are not found on earth, He provides them in heaven. ~Swedenborg

The inner self is as distinct from the outer self as heaven is from earth. ~Swedenborg

In proportion as man is in the love of self, he is in hell, for in hell is the love of self. ~Swedenborg

55. The Celestial Couple
In the Third Heaven

We must have a psychic image of the body, in order to become conscious of it; we must translate the physical fact of the body into a psychic experience. ~Carl Jung, ETH Lecture IX, p. 221

God calls our individual consciousness a "heaven". And therefore there are three heavens in the human mind called the Natural-Spiritual Heaven, which is the lowest in spiritual-rational consciousness. When we think and feel in spiritual-rational consciousness we are in our second heaven. This genuine spiritual-rational consciousness is called "pure" because it is untainted by any natural-based ideas. Our second heaven anatomy is vastly superior in functioning to the first heaven thinking that is with spiritual-natural ideas. Still higher or closer to God in perfection is the anatomy of our celestial consciousness. Our thinking and feeling in this highest of human consciousness is so far superior to the spiritual consciousness that nothing from the third heaven ideas are comprehensible to our second heaven thinking and understanding.

We must always keep in mind that our individual consciousness operates in accordance with the quality of the anatomical layer whose activity provides us with consciousness at that level.

The expression "elevating our consciousness" or "raising" it, or when we use the expression "highest consciousness", all imply that we have to "go somewhere" we are not now. This is a physicalistic or materialistic view of consciousness. In spiritual-rational thinking we can figure out that since consciousness is the activity of anatomical layers and organs, all levels or functions of consciousness are present all the time as an anatomical feature of the human mind.

Our physical avatar conforms to this rule from our general awareness and knowledge of the head and brain, the torso with the heart and lungs, the legs, and the feet. The head is uppermost on the human body frame and contains the complex organs than the torso or feet. The heart and lungs in the middle of the frame are more complex in function than the legs and feet. This rank ordering of complexity in the body's frame is the result of its correspondence with the rank ordering of mental consciousness in the mental body.

So instead of thinking about movement such as "rising" and "achieving" a more perfect consciousness, we need instead to strive to activate the levels we already have. We are performing this required striving when we desire higher truth and rationality, but not until then. It is the love for truth that makes truth available to our experience and consciousness. We already have the ability to experience all our consciousness levels from natural to spiritual, to celestial.

Spiritual knowledge tells us that in the mental world of eternity, our loves are the rulers of our consciousness and of experiencing our full potentials.

The beginning of regeneration is the start of becoming spiritual and thinking in spiritual consciousness. This beginning requires two steps. First, becoming theistic, which is *to maintain a constant daily personal relationship with God.* Second, accepting the idea and fact that natural consciousness is produced by the love of self, while spiritual consciousness is produced by the love of others as much as self, and the love of God more than self.

It is love that rules our mental world of eternity. And it is truth by which love rules that world.

Celestial consciousness is produced by "mutual love" in society and "conjugial love" for conjugial pairs in heaven.

In the afterlife we congregate and live in spiritual societies. They are quite different from natural societies on earth. In a society on earth everyone loves self first, and loves others only to the extent that they can receive benefit from them. If self-love cannot benefit from particular others, it hates them and wishes to banish or destroy them. Such is the spiritual insanity of self-love. It defies all logic.

Since our personality at birth clings to love of self first, we continue in natural consciousness until we are willing to undergo regeneration by God. Then we begin to be conscious of the activity going on in our spiritual consciousness. This completely changes our thinking and feeling in our daily life, which grows from love of self first, to love of others first and love of God before self.

Love and desire for spiritual truth brings to our awareness and consciousness spiritual ideas that are active in our spiritual anatomy.

Those who come into the afterlife without undergoing regeneration are therefore still functioning in natural consciousness. They then join societies that agree with their love, morality, and perspective. These communities create a mental "hell" for each other that tends to deteriorate in consciousness to the savage extremes of human insanity and bestiality. And they would go even beyond this unimaginable cruelty and butchery to even more extremes, were it not for the fact that God continually is unconsciously present in their mind and guides them away from worse hells that can be imagined.

The more they enter deeply into their insanities and enjoy them, the less they are willing to consider backtracking and leaving hell. They are frequently being offered the opportunity of living in heaven. But they refuse with unimaginable rage and hatred even at the mention of the idea because heavenly loves are so deeply opposed to their selfish loves that the idea sickens and frightens them. This is the real answer to those who are disturbed at the idea of "eternal hells", thinking that it is Divine injustice and cruelty to create a punishment that is endless, that never, never ceases.

Selfish love feels annihilated at the notion of God and of a society based on mutual love where each loves the other more than self. This mental state of mutual love is what produces the activity in our celestial consciousness. The superiority of this type of society is demonstrated by this fact, which was witnessed by Swedenborg thousands of times, that *every individual communicates their own thoughts and feelings to every other individual in that celestial society.*

This beautiful and enriching celestial pattern is the pattern of mutual love.

Selfish loves does not want to share thoughts and feelings with others, and wants to retain to self all its enjoyments and understandings. Selfish love is depressed when seeing others come into good fortune and success. Selfish love feels rage and the desire for revenge when people favor someone else in any activity or area of life. It defies all logic.

56. Interview With Heavenly Couples on the Delights of Marital Relations

Now we return to Swedenborg's report. In this second event Swedenborg is visiting the houses of a heaven in which conjugial couples live as neighbors in a heavenly society.

———————————

Swedenborg writes:
The second experience.

One morning I was woken up by the sweetest singing, heard coming from some height above me. So in the earliest moments of waking, a period which is inward, peaceful and sweet compared with the rest of the day, I could for some while remain in the spirit as if outside the body, and give the most detailed attention to the affection expressed by the singing. Singing in heaven is simply a mental affection which is expressed through the mouth as a modulation of sound, since it is the sound, distinct from the speaker's words, coming from the affection of his love which gives life to speech. In that state I perceived that it was the affection for the delights of conjugial love, which wives in heaven had made into a song. I could tell this was so by the sound of the singing, in which those varied delights were reproduced in wonderful ways.

After this I got up, and looked out into the spiritual world, and saw to the east what looked like golden rain below the sun there. It was morning dew falling so densely that it seemed to my view like golden rain as it caught the rays of the sun. This made me still more fully awake, so I went out in spirit and asked an angel whom I chanced to meet whether he had seen the golden rain falling from the sun.

[2] 'Yes,' he answered, 'I see it every time I meditate about conjugial love,' and then he turned his gaze in that direction. 'That rain,' he said, 'falls on a hall where three husbands live with their wives in the middle of the eastern park. The reason such rain is seen falling* from the sun over that hall is that there wisdom about conjugial love and its delights abides with them, about conjugial love with the husbands and about its delights with their wives. But I perceive that you are meditating about the delights of conjugial love, so I will take you to that hall and introduce you.'

He took me through park-land to some houses built of olive wood with two cedar columns in front of the door. He introduced me to the husbands, and asked if I might talk with their wives in their presence.

They agreed and summoned them. The wives looked piercingly at my eyes, so I asked, 'Why do you do that?'

'We can,' they said, 'see exactly what is your inclination and so affection, and thus what you are thinking about sexual love. We see you are meditating deeply but chastely about it. What,' they asked, 'do you want us to tell you about it?'

'Please be so good,' I answered, 'as to tell me something about the delights of conjugial love.' Their husbands agreed and said, 'Yes, you can reveal something about that if you like; they have chaste ears.'

[3] 'Who was it,' they asked, 'told you to question us about the delights of that love? Why not our husbands?' 'This angel with me,' I replied, 'whispered in my ear that it is wives who receive and feel those delights, since they are born to be loves, and all delights belong to love.'

They replied to this with a smile, 'Be careful, and don't say anything like that, except with ambiguous meaning, because we women have wisdom deeply stored in our hearts, and we do not disclose it to any husband unless he enjoys truly conjugial love. There are many reasons for this, which we keep hidden away.'

'Our wives,' said the husbands, 'know every state of our minds, and nothing escapes their notice. They see, perceive and feel anything that proceeds from our will, but we in turn perceive nothing in our wives. Wives have this privilege, because they are very tender loves and as it were burning with zeal to preserve

friendship and trust in marriage, and thus a happy life for both. They take care to maintain this for their husbands and themselves due to the wisdom inherent in their love, which is so full of prudence that they are unwilling and thus unable to say they love, but only that they are loved.'

'Why,' I asked, 'are they unwilling and thus unable?' They replied that if the slightest hint of this escaped their lips, a chill would grip their husbands, and banish them from their bed, their bedroom and their sight. 'But this,' they said, 'happens to those who do not regard marriage as holy, and therefore do not love their wives with spiritual love. It is different in the case of those who do; in their minds that love is spiritual and from this it becomes natural in the body. We in this hall enjoy natural love arising from spiritual, so we entrust our husbands with our secrets about the delights of conjugial love.'

[4] Then I pressed them strongly to reveal some of these secrets to me too. At once they started looking towards the window facing the south, where we saw a shining white dove, with its wings glistening as if of silver and its head decorated with a crest as if of gold, standing on a branch from which sprang an olive. When the dove tried to stretch its wings, the wives said, 'We will reveal something; when that dove appears, it is a sign that we may.'

'Every man,' they said, 'has five senses, sight, hearing, smell, taste and touch. But we also have a sixth, which allows us to feel all the delights of our husband's conjugial love. We have this feeling in the palms of our hands, when we touch our husbands' chests, arms, hands or cheeks, but particularly their chests. We also feel it when they touch us. All the happiness and charm of the thoughts in their minds, and all the joys and pleasures in their consciousness, and the amusement and cheerfulness in their chests are passed from them to us and take a form, becoming perceptible, capable of being felt and touched. We can tell them apart as accurately and exactly as the ear can tell apart the notes of a song, or the tongue the tastes of delicacies. In short, our husbands' spiritual pleasures put on a kind of natural embodiment in us. Our husbands therefore call us the sense organs of chaste conjugial love, and so of its delights. This sense our sex has comes into and remains in existence, continues and grows the more our husbands love us for wisdom and judgment, and we in turn love them for the same qualities in them. This sense our sex has is called in the heavens the sport of wisdom with its love and of love with its wisdom.'

[5] These remarks filled me with a longing to ask many more questions, for instance, about the various kinds of delights. 'The variety is endless,' they said, 'but we do not wish to say more, and so we cannot, because the dove in our window has flown off with the olive branch in its claws.' I waited for it to come back, but in vain. Meanwhile I asked the husbands, 'Do you not have a similar sense of conjugial love?' 'We have,' they replied, 'a general sense, but not a particular one. We feel a general blessedness, pleasure and charm arising from the particular ones our wives feel. This general feeling we get from them is like the tranquility of peace.'

When they had said this, we saw through the window a swan standing on the branch of a fig-tree; it unfolded its wings and flew away. On seeing this the husbands said, 'This is our sign to keep quiet about conjugial love. Come back again from time to time, and perhaps more will be revealed.' So they turned away, and we left. . ~Swedenborg, Conjugial Love, CL 155bis

---

Swedenborg used the expression "memorable relation" or "experience" when recounting an event that he witnessed in the spiritual world. Hundreds of such ethnographic descriptions can be found throughout Swedenborg's 37 volumes. In this selection he is interviewing the wives of conjugial couples in one of the countless heavens on the kind of delights people in celestial consciousness feel in marital relations. The husbands gave permission for the interview because they sensed that Swedenborg's interest was scientific and not salacious. They were thus agreeing to cooperate with Swedenborg for the sake of his research.

Swedenborg was being assisted by an angel who was also in celestial consciousness. The angel advised Swedenborg to focus on the wives because women feel the love more intensely and clearly than men, an opinion he rationalized by saying that women *"are born to be loves, and all delights belong to love".*

The interview reveals that husbands in lower consciousness feel impotent when they perceive the wife to take the lead in sexual activity. The wives were warning Swedenborg not to reveal to men in natural consciousness that the husband's sexual urge and hence potency is sourced in the wife's desire to keep their husbands feeling masculine and loved. These three wives explained that it made no harm to reveal this secret to their own husbands because they were in spiritual consciousness and were able to accept, and even love, the fact that their wife experiences the enjoyments of marital relations.

Regarding the anatomy of the human mind, I already stated that the created unit of human beings is the pair or a spiritually conjoined conjugial couple. This is the actual unit of "one angel". Our mental anatomy has this property built-in from creation. This is why it is said that in God's scheme of creation everyone is born for others and no one is born for self. The heavenly society of mutual love is possible only with a celestial society made of conjugial pairs. No one who is not a pair can survive in the atmosphere of celestial light and heat.

It was Swedenborg's discovery that love-substance and truth-substance issue from the Spiritual Sun that governs the mental world of humanity. All our individual mental world is in the same spiritual environment. It is only after we lose the physical avatar that we can perceive this. Immediately upon completion of the three-day dying-resuscitation procedure, every individual receives sensory input from the mental world of eternity and can see and interact with others who are already there.

Our individual and collective mental world is said to be "in eternity" because as we very well know, we can think or imagine anything as in a dream where we create mental space, mental time, and mental objects of our choosing and desire. This is what each of us do in the activity of sleeping and dreaming. We are being conscious and creative in constructing dramatic scenes in which we get involved as a character. Actually, very involved many times.

So we are already very familiar with the spiritual world of the afterlife because we are born in it and never can leave it! Never, because we are living immortal human beings.

It is only our conscious awareness that is focused and captured, or encapsulated and restricted, by the materialism of the physical input we receive from the sensory organs of our avatar, which is given to us at the birth of our spiritual body that is located in the mental world of eternity. *So we are born into eternity and immortality.*

We need to remember that we are anatomical constructions in the mental world and our substance is not matter but feeling and thought, that is, love-substance and truth-substance. These are living anatomical substances that are conjoined into one in God's Divine-Human infinite spiritual body. God's feelings and intentions are united in a Divine marriage with God's thinking and omniscience.

Love-substance with its truth-substance stream out from the Spiritual Sun into the mental environment of human beings. Although united in God's mind they are not united in the minds of human beings. They separate from each other and now are absorbed as two things by our mental body. We receive love-substance into our affective system of feelings and intentions, but we receive truth-substance into our cognitive system of thoughts and reasonings.

The entire theme of an individual's life with the avatar is to grow up, to become mentally mature, and to start regeneration, a process of personality change that equips us with traits that are adequate for living a happy life in the afterlife of eternity.

The goal of regeneration is to reunite love-substance and truth-substance. These two are dynamic and powerful elements in our motivational system. When united they are called the spiritual marriage within individual consciousness. They mirror and are a prerequisite to the conjugial marriage of the united and conjoined pair. This is the completion of the human person and is then called an angel. This celestial person can now grow and evolve endlessly to eternity.

In natural consciousness we cannot undergo regeneration because our love and our truth has been modified genetically over the generations. Everything in our personality structure now favors the "me first" attitude and intention.

57. Honeymoon Love

Celestial love is to feel the deepest and greatest satisfaction and delight when one can benefit another through one's talents and disposition. And at the same time, to feel the deepest remorse and gnawing suffering when we contribute to the discomfort or injury of another.

Now consider the mutual love of pairs in romantic love. This is called "conjugial Love" and is the love of all loves that God created. It begins as a celestial love with the pair, before it is corrupted by their "first fight" through disagreement, jealousy, or anger. In the honeymoon phase of romantic love everything is agreeable and of little importance in comparison to the love. It is an eternal love, immortal, forever. There is no thought that some day it might end. There is certainty that it will go on forever.

Conjugial love is like mutual love when applied to the romantic pair in love with each other. *Each loves the other more than self, and each greatly fears anything that threatens to kill that love between them.* Hence it is that the fear to injure their conjugial love is far greater than their self-centered desire to dominate, control, or hurt the other's feelings.

Take for example the notion of "equity" in marriage or for couples who live together. This is a business model that appeals to modern attitudes of gender equality and freedom of the individual. Health professionals and life-coaches recommend and teach this arrangement principle as necessary and advantageous. People see a certain satisfying logic to it. It makes sense when there are disagreements, injustices, and resentments on the part of one or both regarding who does how much of the daily "chores" in running a household or apartment together.

It is fair to say that the equity principle in modern marriages has worked to protect women from the traditional gender bias practices that favored the rights, comforts, and attitudes of the husband over the wife. The principle of equity compelled many men to participate more directly in household chores and sharing the burden of raising children and taking care of aged parents.

Once equity is in place, however, where does the love of the couple go? The wife needs love to be happy and to survive spiritually. So does the husband, though he often isn't aware of this. The fact is that equity has nowhere to go but down. There commence fights of equity in which the two compete against each other and no longer feel like a unified pair. The wife feels this first, then the husband. It is now necessary for a spiritual revolution in their marriage, if they are going to recapture the original celestial love they had for each other.

The ability to achieve a new conjugial consciousness is available to them. This is to practice mutual love with each other.

In my own experience of more than four decades of marriage, I noted several intermediate steps, each lasting a decade or more. There is undoubtedly great variation among couples in how long each step must last for them, whether short or quite long. But the quality in each step may be similar regardless of how long the step must last before going further.

First, there was the politics of equity that silenced our initial conjugial love. Fights were regular, disagreements were daily. The wife grows more and more lonely in the pair, feeling abandoned and disrespected by the husband, and consequently hopeless she is hopeless. She has to give up her basic needs of feeling like a woman and being a woman. The husband grows more and more independent and secretive. Both are going in the opposite direction of unification, pair-hood, and mutual love.

Everything good collapses. Now the husband can rescue the situation, if he would. He has the ability to compel himself to put her in a position prior to himself in all things, great or small. As long as he desperately sticks to this spiritual insight, and compels himself to perform it, the marriage will be saved for conjugial love.

But there are intermediate stages. The husband does not stick all the time to his spiritual insight. He allows himself exceptions during which he falls back to his earlier arrogant treatment of her, disagreeing, yelling, insulting, disrespecting, embarrassing, and hurting his wife. This destroys her confidence in their conjugial love. What the husband is doing is a terrible spiritual crime or sin against his wife, against God, and against his celestial consciousness.

But eventually he learns this evil up and down charade well enough to be able to avoid it altogether. The wife's conjugial love returns through the confidence that she gains in her husband, until it has become a certainty in her mind that his new personality is now against the former behaviors and attitudes.

Some people who read my earlier books on what I used to call "*The Doctrine of the Wife*" (still on the Web if you search that tile). A general and frequent comment by men readers was that my doctrine is too one sided and gives all the advantage to the wife. Hence it is not just or spiritual. The principle rule in practicing the doctrine of the wife is that "the husband should never disagree with his wife" and that this rule is not reciprocal. A wife disagrees with her husband for pair-hood reasons and purposes, while a husband does so for independence and equity.

The husband's disagreements with the wife come from his desire for greater independence and therefore they work against pair-hood; while the wife's disagreements with the husband come from the desire to strengthen pair-hood.

58. Heaven Is A Collective Humanity Of Love

In the afterlife of mental eternity there is a special sphere or zone in the mental world of eternity. It is called heaven in the human mind. When we are willing to enter that zone of consciousness we would be living as a conjugial pair, two souls with total one-mindedness. We would be using the language of communication that is proper for that level of mental functioning. In the mental world it is our mental functioning that constitutes the environment of our spiritual body, also called our mental body.

At the celestial level in our mental anatomy we spontaneously think and speak in a celestial-rational language and system of reasoning. Human beings who are willing to function in that region are called "angels". *All angels love others more than they love themselves.* Living together in community as an "angelic society" they each live in their own magnificent houses, walk the streets, parks, and gardens, enjoy architecture, art, food, and marital relations. They daily perform certain useful functions to people in other levels of consciousness function.

Swedenborg experienced active and conscious presence with those who lived in the heaven of eternity. In order to talk to and interview people in celestial consciousness, Swedenborg's consciousness was temporarily elevated by God into the celestial level of functioning. After his consciousness returned back to a spiritual-natural consciousness, Swedenborg was able to translate his celestial experience into a natural language, which was mostly 17th century Neo Latin, and sometimes his native tongue Swedish.

So we have an objective idea of what we are like as "angels" in heaven. I used the expression "willing to function in that region" because *it is the individual who determines its zone of consciousness*. You yourself are determining your current level of mental functioning, what is called consciousness. Consider the anatomical fact love is the gravity of the mental world. More than the gravity, the substance and the form of our thinking and feeling. The loves we cling to determine the level of our thinking and reasoning.

Every human love has a state or zone of closure, consummation, and completeness that is in the mental world of our personality and self. Each love is a specific mental activity in some anatomical layer of the spiritual body or mind. The activity of love is sourced in human celestial consciousness. Love-substance descends from God's mind into the human layers of mental anatomy. It is absorbed fully at the celestial layers of consciousness. It is then passed downwards to the spiritual and then natural consciousness levels. Each descent gives us an awareness and understanding of God's love-substance that is rationally explainable at that level of thinking and reasoning.

In other words, when we think in spiritual consciousness of being angels in heaven we think of its outward appearance, as for instance the beauty of the homes, the love and respect that all neighbors show for each other, the quality of their lifestyle and uses, and the way they talk and reason. This is a correct way of thinking about heaven in outward appearance. It is essential for children's spiritual health to be given this naturalistic depiction of heaven. Children fully understand this level of description and feel joy and delight when they are told about it. And it is a true and valid depiction of the outward perspective on heaven. We can define it as an intermediate state of knowledge of heaven.

Above this level of thinking, in celestial consciousness, we have an inner view from our love. This is the realization that *heaven is a collective humanity of love*. The mental state of each individual constitutes the center of the collective focus. There is instantaneous telepathic communication between each individual with every other individual in that angelic society. This includes feelings, emotions, sensations, intentions, and thoughts.

It is awesome to try to think about this in detail. This is a description of you and me and everyone else of what we are like in the celestial layer of mental functioning. It tells the unimaginable enhancement of our self as individuals. *The most evolved stage of individuation is finally achieved within the collective conscious of a heavenly community in eternity.*

This thought becomes even more impressive when we realize that the *sharing-of-one-with-all-and-all-with-one* principle extends itself as a sphere to all the other anatomical layers of mental consciousness.

The language and reasoning of in natural consciousness is very familiar to us. The language of spiritual consciousness is inborn or spontaneous when we are active in that anatomical layer of the mental world of eternity. Consider that our mental world is organic and anatomical and is constructed out of love-substance and truth-substance available in the environment of our mental world. This environment is substantive and anatomical.

When we operate in celestial consciousness the thoughts we have are strictly celestial. We are unable to experience natural ideas or spiritual ideas when we are in celestial ideas. And vice versa: we understand nothing about celestial ideas in lower levels of consciousness. Nevertheless, the ideas in the three layers of functioning are linked by the laws of correspondences.

Celestial language and topics are about love and its affections, especially conjugial love and love unto God. The topics angels discuss with each other are about their relationship to God, the relationship between love and truth, their relationship in pair and in collective society, and various specific topics that deal with carrying out one's daily uses to others.

The contrast to celestial topics is the spiritual insanity of what is called "infernal" or evil reasoning. This language and its thinking is spontaneous with those who live in one of the many hells in the mental world of eternity. The rank order of insanities in the hells corresponds to the rank order of truths in the heavens. The highest and deepest truths of heaven are specifically denied and hated by the lowest insanities in hell. This shows that there is communication by correspondence between all zones of the mental world.

Now here is a very practical question: How do I prepare myself so that I will be willing to love others more than I love myself?

Since this is what determines whether or not I live in heaven forever.

I have provided many answers for this question. The full title of this Volume is: "Rational Theistic self-analysis (RTS) For Achieving Wholeness Here and in the Afterlife". To achieve wholeness is to become fully individuated within the collectivity of mutual love. This is the achievement of wholeness. The central focus of the ideas I have covered is that every individual is born for others and no one is born for himself or herself. We need to penetrate the meaning and actuality of this love principle. To be born for others is to love others. When we love others we cannot harm them or treat them with disrespect, first, and second, we are motivated to treat them well, to wish them well, and to do useful things for them. This is to love others.

Part of RTS thinking is to realize and understand that we are born selfish by inheritance and genetics, and that it is impossible for us to willingly love others.

But what is impossible to us is possible to God. It is from God that we receive the motivation to love others. Our task is to willingly accept positive motivation from God and to approve of it. *Eventually, we not only approve of doing good to others, but experience a deep sense of reward and joy when we are able to perform these goods and uses for others.*

This is then the training we need for learning to love others.

First, *we are to understand rationally that our motivation to love others comes solely from God.*
Second, *we need to compel ourselves to avoid harming or disrespecting others.*
Third, *we need to compel ourselves to do good to others, to perform uses for them, to wish them well, and to act with good will towards them.*

Fourth *and finally, we strive to do these things because it is how we can love God. Hence everything we do validates the spiritual reality that we are born for others, and that for their sake we are to love God more than anything.*

You can see that in order to be successful we need to go through these four steps every day dozens of times for years. There are dozens of occasions in the course of each day when we have the opportunity to resist disrespecting or harming someone and to put up an effort to make the person more comfortable or to benefit the person in some way, emotionally or physically. This is a lot of effort, a lot of work every day for years! Is it worth it? Just consider the alternatives!

This is the preparation needed for entering heaven in eternity.

So it is easy and straightforward to understand what we need to do to enter heaven and be happy and fulfilled to eternity.

> *All angels love others more than they love themselves.*

59. Some Ancient Greek Philosophers Speak Again

You may have seen movies or theater plays that are set in the context of famous ancient philosophers like Plato or Socrates or Epicurus. Here now is a selection from Swedenborg in which he describes attending a conference or gathering of people in the afterlife who had lived at that time and in that culture. At this gathering in the spiritual world one of the Ancient Greek teachers caused "newcomers" who had just completed their three-day resuscitation procedure, to be summoned and be present at the gathering so that they may respond to the question, "What is news from earth?"

In the literature on Swedenborg for the past two centuries some critics have pointed to these types of reports by Swedenborg as examples of

Swedenborg's style of writing that attempts to present new ideas of a philosophical and theological nature in the form of allegory and theatrical imagination.

This type of explanation is sourced in natural consciousness that reasons in one dimension, which leads it to deny that there is a spiritual or mental world that is separate and independent of matter, time, and space on earth. Such a notion is viewed as fiction or imaginative allegory. In other words, the mind is not real, God's existence has not yet been proven, and we are all mortal, not immortal. From this "monism" perspective the report below by Swedenborg will be seen as allegorical, and as a result we are not witnessing real people having an actual discussion that Swedenborg objectively observed and reported.

But we see things differently if we are willing to activate the rationality of our thinking to the level of spiritual consciousness. Now we can put a meaningful context to Swedenborg's report. Now we realize that

- dual consciousness is possible
- that Swedenborg was a man of genius, rationality, and integrity
- that God exists and wants us to know about the afterlife
- that human beings are immortal and Plato and Socrates and those others must be somewhere in their own identity
- that given Swedenborg's Divinely given mission he came into contact with everyone that he needed to write about

Now here is the selection:

_____

Swedenborg writes:
I shall add here two accounts of experiences, of which this is the first.

When I was going home from the contest of wisdom (described above in 132), I saw on the way an angel dressed in blue. He came and walked beside me, and said: 'I see that you have come away from the contest of wisdom, and that you took great pleasure in what you heard there. But I perceive that you are not fully in this world, because you are at the same time in the natural world, so you do not know about our Olympic sports. At these the wise men of antiquity meet, and learn from newcomers from your world what changes of state and what vicissitudes wisdom has up to the present undergone and is still undergoing. If you like, I will take you to the place where many of the wise men of antiquity live together with their sons, that is, their disciples'.

So he took me to a place on the border between the north and the east, and when I had a view in that direction from a piece of high ground, I caught sight of a city with two hills at one side, the one nearer the city being the lower of the two. 'This city,' he told me, 'is called Athenaeum, the lower hill is called Parnassium, the higher Heliconeum. They bear these names because in the city and its neighbourhood the wise men of ancient Greece live, men such as Pythagoras, Socrates, Aristippus and Xenophon (Greek philosophers of the 6th, 5th and 4th centuries B.C. with their disciples and recruits.)

I asked about Plato and Aristotle. He told me that they and their followers were in a different region, because they had taught about reasoning, purely intellectual matters, but the others about moral issues relevant to the conduct of life.

[2] He said that scholars from the city of Athenaeum were frequently sent on embassies to the educated Christians of the day, to report what they thought about God, the creation of the universe, the immortality of the soul, the condition of man as compared with that of animals, and other matters which belong to inner wisdom. He told me that the crier had announced a meeting for that day, a sign that their emissaries had met some newcomers from the earth and heard some interesting news.

We saw a lot of people coming out of the city and its neighbourhood, some of them with laurel-wreaths on the heads, some holding palm-fronds in their hands, some with books under their arms, and some with pens tucked under the hair of the left temple. We joined them and went up together, and found on the hill an octagonal palace, which they called the Palladium. When we went in, we found eight hexagonal recesses, in each of which there was a bookcase, as well as a table, at which those who wore laurels sat down. In the Palladium proper we saw seats carved out of stone, on which the remainder seated themselves.

[3] Then a door on the left was opened, and by it two newcomers from the earth were brought in. When they had been welcomed, one of those wearing laurels asked them, 'What news is there from earth?'

'The news,' they said, 'is that in forests men have been found resembling animals, or animals resembling men. It was recognised from their faces and bodies that they had been born men, but that at the age of two or three they had been lost or abandoned in the forests. It was said that these creatures could not voice any of their thoughts, nor learn how to make articulate sounds so as to utter words. Neither did they know what food was fit for them, as animals do, but they put in their mouths what grew in the forest whether clean or dirty, and much more of the same kind. From these facts some of our learned men made many guesses and some drew many deductions about the condition of men as compared with that of animals.'

[4] On hearing this some of the wise men of antiquity asked, 'What were their guesses and deductions from these facts?' The newcomers replied that there was a great deal, but it could be reduced to the following:
(a) Man by his nature and also from birth is more stupid and so more vile than any animal, and if not taught becomes like one.
(b) He can be taught because he has learnt to make articulate sounds, and so to talk; and by this means he has begun to express his thoughts; and by degrees he has done so more and more, until he could frame the laws of living together, many of which, however, have been imprinted on animals from birth.
(c) Animals equally with men are capable of reasoning.
(d) If therefore animals could talk, they would reason as cleverly on all subjects as men. A proof of this is that they think from reason and prudence just as much as men.
(e) The intellect is merely a modification of sunlight with the co-operation of heat by means of the ether, so that it is simply an activity of a more inward nature. This activity can be raised to such a height that it looks like wisdom.
(f) It is therefore useless to believe that man lives after death any more than an animal does, except that perhaps for a few days after death an exhalation of the life of the body may appear as a cloud in the form of a ghost, before being dispersed into nature. This is very much as when a twig picked out of the ashes of a fire may appear to retain the likeness of its shape.
(g) Consequently religion, which teaches that life continues after death, is an invention so that the simple may be kept inwardly obedient by its laws, just as they are kept outwardly obedient by the civil law.

They added that these were the reasonings of those who were only clever, not intelligent. 'What do the intelligent think?' they asked. The reply was that they had not heard, but they were of the opinion that they thought the same.

On hearing this all who were sitting at the tables said: 'What times they live in on earth now! What sad changes has wisdom undergone! It seems to have been turned into foolish cleverness. The sun has set and is beneath the earth, diametrically opposite its noon position. How can anyone fail to know from the evidence of the people abandoned in the forests, that this is what man is like if he receives no instruction? Surely he is what he is taught to be. By birth he is more ignorant than animals. He must then learn to walk and to talk. If he did not learn to walk, would he stand upright on his feet? And if he did not learn to talk, would he be able to utter any of his thoughts? Surely everyone is what he is taught to be, crazy if taught falsities, wise if taught truths? And if he is crazy from being taught falsities, does he not imagine himself to be wiser than the man who is wise from being taught truths? Are there not foolish and deranged people who are no more human beings than those who were found in the forests? Are not those who have lost their memory like them?

[2] 'From both these sets of facts we draw the conclusion that a man is not a man without instruction, and is not an animal either, but he is a form capable of receiving in himself what makes a man human, so that he is not born a man, but becomes one. Man has by birth a form such that he can be an instrument for the reception of life from God, with a view to being a subject into which God can put all good, and by union with Himself make blessed for ever. We perceive from what you say that wisdom at the present time is so far extinct or turned to foolishness, that there is total ignorance about the terms upon which human being live as compared with those on which animals live. As a result, they do not know either anything about how a person lives after death. But those who are able, but unwilling, to know about this, and so deny its reality, as many of you Christians do, can be likened to the people found in the forests. It is not that they have become so stupid through being deprived of instruction, but they have made themselves stupid by relying on the fallacies of the senses, which are the darkness that conceals truths.'

But then someone standing in the middle of the Palladium and holding a palm-frond in his hand said: 'Please unravel this mystery. How could a man having been created a form of God be changed into the form of a devil? I am well aware that the angels of heaven are forms of God, and the angels of hell are forms of the devil, and that these two are completely opposite forms, one of madness, the other of wisdom. Tell me, then, how could man created as a form of God pass from daylight into such a night as to be able to deny the existence of God and everlasting life?'

[2] The teachers replied one after the other, first the Pythagoreans, then the Socratics, and afterwards the rest. But among them there was a certain follower of Plato, who was the last to speak. His opinion, which was adopted, went like this. The people of the age of Saturn, the golden age, knew and acknowledged that they were forms for the reception of life from God, and consequently they had wisdom written on their souls and their hearts, so that they saw truth by the light of truth, and truths enabled them to perceive good by the pleasure of its love. 'But,' he said, 'as in the following periods the human race retreated from the acknowledgment that all the truths of wisdom and thus all the good of love they had was continually flowing in from God, they ceased to be dwelling-places of God, and then too they stopped talking with God and mixing with angels. For the interiors of their minds were diverted from their previous direction, which was being raised upwards by God towards God, and they were turned further and further aside, outwards towards the world, and so directed by God to God by way of the world. Finally they were turned in the opposite direction, which is downwards towards oneself. Because a person who is inwardly turned upside down or away cannot look to God, people separated themselves from God and became forms of hell, and so of the devil.

[3] 'It follows from this that in the earliest ages people acknowledged with heart and soul that all the good of love, and so all the truth of wisdom, came to them from God, and also that this good and truth were God's in them, so that they were purely receivers of life from God; which is why they were called images of God, sons of God and born of God. But in the following ages people no longer acknowledged this with their heart and soul, but were influenced by some incorrect belief, later by historical faith and finally merely professing it with their lips. Acknowledging anything of this kind merely by professing it with the lips is not acknowledging it, but is in fact denying it at heart.

'These facts enable us to see what wisdom is like on earth among present-day Christians. They can still be inspired by God as the result of a written revelation, while not being aware of the difference between man and an animal. Thus many people believe that if a man lives after death, so too must an animal; or because an animal does not live after death, neither can man. Surely our spiritual light, which enlightens our mental vision, is in their case turned to thick darkness; and their natural light, which only enlightens the bodily vision, has become dazzling light to them?'

After this speech all turned to the two newcomers and thanked them for coming and bringing them their report; and they begged them to carry back to their brethren a report of what they had heard. The newcomers replied that they would strengthen their people in their belief in this truth, that in so far as they attribute all the good of charity and all the truth of faith to the Lord and not to themselves, so far are they human beings and so far do they become angels of heaven. ~Swedenborg, Conjugial Love, CL 151-154bis

---

Swedenborg is presenting his own eyewitness account that he witnessed of a gathering of ancient Greek philosophers that took place in the mental world of eternity, or as he called it, "the spiritual world". This sounds like fiction to thinking in natural consciousness, as I mentioned. I find it interesting the way these people in the afterlife engage in a timeless activity of their past on earth. Each time it occurs that they have the experience of attending such a conference, it feels entirely new and fresh. They love figuring out and judging the self-reports in accordance with their own spiritual personality. This cultural personality is familiar to us from learning portrayals of ancient history settings.

I recall that when I entered middle school in the 1950's in Belgium I was given a choice of being registered in the "classic Greek and Latin" curriculum or the "modern science curriculum". I chose the Classic program. I find it interesting to read in Swedenborg's report that the true classics in ancient times knew that human beings were immortal due to their connection to God. They also knew that our ability to think and act involves the activity of God's actual power and not our own. I was not aware of this from my classic education.

I suppose that the spiritual wisdom and knowledge that people display in this gathering was not something they already possessed when they were still active on earth in historical times. Since their passing into the spiritual world they must have attended many gatherings before this one, of "newcomers" who keep showing up every day in the world of spirits when they awaken from the dying-resuscitation procedure. Swedenborg was Divinely led to attend this particular gathering at this time so that he could witness their thinking during

Swedenborg's time, which was two thousand years after their century on earth about whom we read in ancient literature.

About Volume 1.
Dreams and the Spiritual World

If a man knows more than others, he becomes lonely. ~Carl Jung, Memories, Dreams, Reflections, 1962

The Word is the only doctrine which teaches how a man must live in the world in order to be happy to eternity. ~Swedenborg, Heavenly Secrets, AC 8939

For us humans, once alive, always alive. You are now in the natural phase of your eternity. The three-day dying-resuscitation procedure ends that phase and begins the spiritual phase of immortality. ~Leon James

Carl Jung   Emanuel Swedenborg   Leon James

The ideas of Carl Jung (1875-1961) and Emanuel Swedenborg (1688-1772) have brought to psychology a whole new direction that gives people the ability to think about themselves as immortal spiritual beings.

Thanks to these two giants of psychology people today are receiving knowledge about the spiritual reality in which they are born and in which they live forever. *Reality is spiritual.* Spiritual consciousness reveals that everything in the universe was created by God so that it may serve and be useful to the human race.

No thing exists that does not in some way contribute to the goal of human existence and life.

This is a human universe.

Why then does reality seem so cold, so materialistic, so dark and inhuman? I will use the ideas of Jung and Swedenborg to show that this constricted and unhappy view of reality is a false appearance that we perceive and experience when we blind ourselves to the spiritual depth that lies within the human mind of every individual.

Jung looked within his mind and discovered through the *process of experiencing* the larger world that exists *within* the human psyche. He allowed his inner senses to be awakened from their slumber and then he could perceive the unfathomable vastness and darkness of the *collective unconscious*, which is what binds together all human minds, past, present, and future.

My thesis, then, is as follows: In addition to our immediate consciousness, which is of a thoroughly personal nature and which we believe to be the only empirical psyche (even if we tack on the personal unconscious as an appendix), there exists a second psychic system of a collective, universal, and impersonal nature which is identical in all individuals. ~Carl Jung, The Archetypes and the Collective Unconscious, 1936, p. 43

What a wonderful truth is expressed in the Jung quote above. This realization extends the reach of scientific knowledge to the immense mental world within the mind. Freud's materialistic thinking barred him from knowing anything about the most fundamental aspects of the mind and of human psychology. He immediately broke his relationship with Jung when Jung made this declaration about the existence of an independent and objective "second psychic system" in the human mind. This was Jung's greatness.

The whole Self of every human being lies in that vast collective mental universe of eternity that is apart from time, apart from space, and apart from the limits of physical matter. Jung taught that to be psychologically healthy and whole, or *self-realized* and *individuated*, every person must go on the spiritual hunt to track the Self down in that vast and murky psychic universe.

It is a scary experience to make this discovery by which we become exposed to the raw and awesome psychic forces that exist in our collective unconscious mind. Every individual's mind exists as an entity

Readers of Jung have discovered this same mental reality in their own experiencing of the depth that lies within the mind of every person.

By looking inward we too can discover the same things that Jung discovered and wrote about. It is human to want to know our present and our future reality.

> *I have now seen quite a number of people die in the time of a great transition, reaching as it were the end of their pilgrimage in sight of the Gates, where the way bifurcates to the land of Hereafter and to the future of mankind and its spiritual adventure. You had a glimpse of the Mysterium Magnum.* ~Carl Jung, Letters Vol. II, p. 604

> *If ever you have the rare opportunity to speak with the devil, then do not forget to confront him in all seriousness. He is your devil after all.* ~Carl Jung, Liber Novus, p. 261

> *Our eternal destiny is in our power through the choices we make in daily life.* ~Leon James

> *Eternity is mental.* ~Leon James

> Death is a drawing together of two worlds, not an end. We are the bridge. ~Carl Jung, J.E.T., p. 95

Whoever lives and believes in Me, shall never die. ~Jesus, New Testament, John xi 25, 26

Those who die and are buried do not die, but pass from an obscure life into a clear one. For the death of the body is merely the continuation and also the perfection of the life. ~Swedenborg, Heavenly Secrets, AC 1854

It is part of being a human being to want to be immortal. The people of the ancient and pre-modern cultures knew that they were immortal. They understood that death brings new life to the person. But modern civilization was shaped by the scientific approach, which turned more and more towards a materialistic or monist foundational premise. As a result, modern people do not know that they are immortal. And yet they desperately want to be immortal!

Once you allow that idea to enter your mind -- the idea that you are immortal, you will perceive a sense of deep relief from the constant normal anxiety about death or dying. It is being thought that the self is going out of existence. This is the modern individual's life-angst or anxiety. Hence the amazing relief we feel when discovering and understanding our immortality. One of the central tasks in the perspective of rational theistic self-analysis" (RTS) is to help you make that discovery of yourself.

Once the death-fear is gone or much lessened, there comes curiosity. Many questions flood the mind, such as these:

a) What is it like to live in the afterlife?
b) Do we have a body?
c) Can we feel pleasure?
d) Can we be intimate with others?
e) What are the afterlife lifestyles?
f) What is there to do?
g) Can we see God?
h) How are we to prepare ourselves now for that life in eternity?
i) What is the most important task we have here on earth?
j) If there is life after death in eternity then why are we born on earth instead of in eternity?
k) Do we have a soulmate with whom we live in happiness to eternity?
l) Is there marriage in the afterlife?

m)　What is our spirit body like and can we feel and do the same things as in the physical body?
n)　What is love?
o)　What is truth?
p)　How does God relate to each individual personally?
q)　Can we meet the people who already live in the afterlife?
r)　Are there spirits and angels?
s)　Is there a devil?
t)　How do we equip our personality with traits of mutual love that allows us to be angels in eternity?
u)　How do we avoid becoming selfish and stupid, unhappy and non-productive, living below the level of our human potential?
v)　Ho do we achieve self-realization and spiritual enlightenment?

Every one of these questions is answered in the three Volumes of this book. The answers are presented as rational explanations based on the empirical observations and vast research compiled by the two giants of psychology, Jung and Swedenborg. In most cases these are answers that can be found elsewhere echoed in pieces and scattered across the world literature of the past three thousand years. The unparalleled genius and knowledge of Jung and Swedenborg provide the basis for presenting a coherent rational and unified scientific theory of the immortal human mind and of God's very close relationship to the human race and to every individual.

More than anyone in history and science Swedenborg has brought to people a definite and specific knowledge of the dying process, the resuscitation after death into the afterlife world of eternity, and *the detailed ethnographic descriptions of lifestyles in the afterlife*, including the landscapes, the people, psychic cities, and habitations of heaven and hell, which are not places but good and bad mental states in every person's mind.

These two together, Jung and Swedenborg, are giants in the history of psychology who enrich our knowledge and imagination of our present and of our immortal future. This book collects their ideas into short quotations and longer selections of what they wrote about the psychic world, God, death, immortality, resurrection, love, dreams, and other vibrant ideas from depth psychology, analytical psychology, and theistic psychology. The author, Leon James, who is knowledgeable in theistic psychology, shows how the ideas of Jung and Swedenborg complement each other, enriching our understanding of the spiritual topics they discuss and have become so vital to our modern technological generation.

Jung said that to look outside is to be blind, but to look inside is to see. And also, that to analyze one's dreams is to wake up.

This book reviews the meaning and psychodynamics of symbolism in dreams and in the unconscious as found in the work of Jung and Swedenborg. Swedenborg's theistic psychology clarifies the spiritual symbolism that is hidden in *Sacred Scripture* in its more interior layer, and what critical role these spiritual-natural "correspondences" play in our psychological development and growth.

> *Every real solution is only reached by intense suffering. ~Carl Jung, Letters Vol. I, p. 233*

Thousands of people are reading Jung's books and deriving benefits in thinking about themselves and understanding the world. Being a trained analyst and counselor is one possible approach to Jung's ideas and principles. Another approach is to read Jung's pages and try to apply their contents to oneself. This involves various areas of focus of the personality such as understanding the psychodynamic symbolism and power of dreams, understanding God and our relationship to God, and discovering the awesomeness of the collective unconscious and how our individual ego is connected to it or is immersed in it.

This is what I have done in Volume 1, reading Jung's collected works available on the Internet and various contemporary commentaries and current blogs on the Web that are concerned with Jung's ideas today. Studying Swedenborg has been a longtime intellectual passion of mine, so it makes sense that when I started studying Jung I interconnected the ideas of Jung and Swedenborg and came to see how they enriched and clarified each other.

I realized that the two authors together provide a deeper understanding of each alone. That is what motivated me to write this book and share that insight.

Jung's writings, lectures, letters, and interviews are all available on the Web. Never before have so many people gotten involved in his ideas. In this book I focus on a highly significant statement Jung made about himself, which was that God was the center of focus and interest all his life. This is a little known fact, especially because of the way Jung talked about God in his published writings. Still today, some "Jungians" or readers of Jung see Jung's involvement with God as an interest in archetypes and comparative religions. They do not acknowledge that Jung had a personal relationship with God on a significant basis.

In Volume 1 of this book I present evidence that clearly shows Jung's central relationship to God that spanned from his childhood days to the last months of his life in this world. I also focus on Jung's great spiritual discovery that he called "the collective unconscious". This may be the most imprtant and most exciting discovery in psychology in the 20th century. Through Jung's work scientific dualism was introduced in modern science. Perhaps not everyone is fully aware of the fact that the collective unconscious does not exist in the physical world. It exists in the psychic world, which is independent of the physical world and exists apart from space and apart from time. This is known in science as "dualism".

Science and technology have indeed conquered the world, but whether the psyche has gained anything is another matter. ~Carl Jung, CW 13, Para 163

Freud and the rest of the prominent scientists of the 20th century rejected and ridiculed the idea of two worlds. To Freud the psychic "world" was not a real world lIke the natural world is a real world. Freud was a materialist, a monist, an opponent of dualism. Psyche, soul, ego, pdychodynamic forces, self, ego, consciousness – these for Freud were not real objects since they were psychological or mental, and those are not real. To realize this is quite shocking about Freud since this view renders all of Freudian psychology merely a mechanical metaphor, not psychological reality. I present some views on Freud that Jung shared in an interview and in some of his articles. Jung said that Freud had no genuine understanding of dream analysis because his rigid materialism and passionate atheism put up a block to the reality of the psyche and psychic world.

Jung's discovery of the psychic world as independent reality was only the second time in the history of psychology that the perspective of scientific dualism was presented. The first time was about one hundred years before Jung's birth when Swedenborg publsihed his Writings on the ethnography of the psychic world.

Soul and body are not two things. They are one. ~Carl Jung, Zarathustra Seminar, p. 355

Every person consists of three components which follow in order in him: soul, mind, and body. The inmost one is his soul. The intermediate one is his mind. And the outmost one is his body. Everything that flows into a person from the Lord flows first into his inmost component, which is the soul, and descends from there into his intermediate component, which is the mind, and through this into his outmost component, which is the body.

A marriage of good and truth flows in from the Lord in a person in the same way. It flows into his soul directly, and continues from there into the subsequent faculties, and through these to the outmost constituents. And thus conjointly they bring about conjugial love. It is apparent from a consideration of this influx that a married couple is an image of the marriage between good and truth in their inmost qualities and thus in their subsequent ones. ~Swedenborg, Conjugial Love, CL 101

About Volume 3
The RTS Interview

Rational Theistic Self-Analysis (RTS)
Dialog On
Consciousness, Immortality, Personality, Marriage,
God, and Afterlife Lifestyles
Based on the Psychology of Jung and Swedenborg

Our individual consciousness appears to us as an awareness that is omnipresent and alone within our private world of self.

And yet, all consciousness is collective.

If we raise our consciousness to the spiritual level we immediately experience a new consciousness, higher and sharper than the former. We become aware of all sorts of new ideas, explanations, and feelings that stream into our awareness. Thus, a new and higher life begins for the individual.

The process by which we raise our consciousness to the spiritual level is called *regeneration*. This means that we are willing to engage in daily spiritual battles against the many loves that we've acquired that are selfish, harmful, and anti-social. Some of these loves we have from birth by inheritance, and the others we have acquired ourselves from our experiences and lifestyle.

These inherited and acquired selfish loves became integtrated into our personality structure through our attachment to them, the pleasure and enjoyment they give us every day. Thus, they become a part of our normal practice and habit in daily living. We come to accept our selfishness. We allow it to become our very self. We justify it and make it allowable, understandable, and normal. We echo common sayings such as *"Nobody is perfect", "All human beings are flawd", "God overlooks it", "I make up for it by being generous and useful"*, etc.

This kind of justification will take care of now, here on earth. But what about the afterlife? What kind of afterlife can we have in eternity after death? And should we try right now to provide for that future life?

RTS presents spiritual ideas that clarify how our loves *now* are shaping our afterlife in eternity. All people experience their afterlife as either a happy heaven in eternity or a mental hell. Hence it makes good sense to know how to avoid ending up living in our mental hell in eternity.

Then we also need to know how to prepare our personality for the afterlife so that we may live in heaven where only mutual love exists. Selfish loves cannot eixst in a heavenly sphere. Since we live with inherited and acquired selfish loves, how do we stop that and start living with mutual love? *It takes training ourselves to think with effective ideas that are spiritual.*

RTS stands for rational theistic self-analysis. All spiritual ideas are *rational* and we can all understand them through our inborn common sense. *Self-analysis* is necessary in order to raise our consciousness from natural to spiritual. *Theistic* means that we acknowledge that God is everywhere in our mind helping us to think rationally and to be motivated to stop being selfish and to start being altruistic.

RTS is therefore a way of self-discovery and enhancement of consciousness.

RTS is also a practical mental approach to maintaining a daily relationship with God. To love God means to talk or converse with God on everything that is going on. This is what God wants and longs for. Imagine a roommate you have for a whole year sharing the same small apartment but never having looked at each other or talked to each other. This would indeed be strange and abnormal behavior.

God is present in our mind all the time and doing all the things that keep our thoughts and emotions connected and healthy, second by second, since our birth. No other human being can ever be so close and intimate to each of us, as God is. And yet, many of us do not talk or converse with God all day long. The practice of RTS changes that abnormal spiritual mental state and attitude.

We all know that we can be selfish in some situations, perhaps in most situations in our daily lives. In this world it is hard to find people who are kind, loving, strong, passionate, compassionate, generous, brave, decent, helpful, honest, just, intelligent, informed, and patriotic. But it is fairly easy to find people who are selfish, rude, domineering, aggressive, cruel, self-involved, uninformed, disinterested in things of intelligence and rationality, and disdaining wisdom, spirituality, and God.

Our personality is actually a mental batlle ground for these two types of loves. If we pay attention to our experiencing we can actually sense this tug of war between wanting to satisfy some selfish love and wanting to be a good person, loving others more than self, and loving God more than anything. Loving self and loving others both give us delight, enjoyment, pleasure, and satisfaction, but of a different sort. Satisfying a *selfish love* and feeling its delight, is an experience in our natural consciousness. We all know what it feels like.

But satisfying a *mutual love* is an experience in our spiritual consciousness. This gives us a deeper and higher experience, feeling and delight. We value and appreciate the spiritual far more than the natural. That is how we were created.

RTS is composed of spiritual ideas and thinking that are rational and unified. They originate from the highest region of human experience called celestial consciousness. When we are in the celestial mental state, our consciousness is collective in the widest sense. Anything we want to know or is possible to know, is instantly available to our awareness. We do not need to learn something new or do research.

Human beings are created by God to be immortal and to live forever in celestial consciousness.

To achieve this inborn potential we must first develop our natural consciousness. This is completed in early adulthood. It is well adapted to conditions of life on this earth. During adulthood and old age, God gives us the opportunity to undergo the regeneration process. This involves noticing our selfish thinking and attitudes, and then resisting them. Since we cannot fight successfully against our own loves, we must work together with God.

RTS provides a consistent and common sense explanation of the process of regeneration. God provides us with external and physical experiences that arouse some particular selfish love. We experience the intensity of the "pull" in a temptation situation that God provides and supervises. Now it's up to us to fight as-of self for the happiness of our eternal life.

If we give in to the temptation, we are bonded even closer to self-love and its delights. But if we resist the temptation, God causes that bond to loosen. Regeneratdion takes several years to complete since there are so many selfish loves in our personality, and each love must be resisted mulyiple times in various conditions.

RTS stands for rational theistic self-analysis. RTS is a rational method of thinking about the regeneration of our personality and about practicing that mode of thinking in daily life. *The purpose of regeneration is to fundamentally modify our inherited personality structure from selfish love to mutual love.*

When we become willing to undergo regeneration we first consciously put ourselves under obedience to God by acknowledging to ourselves that God is the only one who can remove our selfish loves.

Once we choose to begin such a relationship with God, God will then start to arrange daily situations for us in which we are spiritually tempted to give in to some selfish love, despite our prior resolution to undergo regeneration, which requires that we resist and not give in.

By resisting the temptation we allow God to remove that selfish love from our personality structure. This takes many trials because the individual is not emotionally ready to give up selfish loves. Giving in to these loves brings the individual many different kinds of pleasures and delights.

Regeneration proceeds for years because it takes a long time and many trials for most people to be willing to give up these pleasures and delights.

Though RTS people find out new spiritual facts about their relationship to God and about the immortality of their personality and consciousness.

RTS provides a totally new psychology of the self. The old "psychology of the self" is renamed the new "*theistic psychology of the as-of self*", in recognition that by ourselves we have no power to change or even to act, and that God alone has this power. God's power cannot be given away to the individual so that it may become the individual's power. God's power must therefore be acting within the individual. Therefore God must be directly involved in all our mental activity.

This completely changes our view of ourselves from natural to spiritual.

RTS is then a new way of thinking of ourselves that is spiritual and theistic. Thinking in this new way raises our consciousness from natural to spiritual.

We learn to think in our natural consciousness as we grow up and slowly become mature adults. This way of thinking is called materialistic because it uses only ideas and logic that belong to the physical world. In this natural-rational reasoning process we deny that there are two worlds, one in time-space, the other in eternity apart from time and space. We also deny that there is a separate and independent world of the afterlife, other than here on earth. In natural consciousness we are not capable of thinking and understanding a single spiritual idea or explanation.

But when we raise our consciousness to the spiritual level we think only with spiritual ideas and reasoning. This spiritual-rational thinking does not involve any ideas that belong to the material world. The RTS knowledge base contains only spiritual ideas.

Spiritual-rational thinking requires that we be in a mental state called mutual love. In natural thinking we are in a mental state called self-love or ego-love. The instant we begin to love others more than self we experience an opening of our spiritual consciousness and begin to perceive and understand the amazing new vistas it offers.

About This Book (Volume 2)

Why do we need self-analysis? In this Volume I discuss the fundamental inner need that every individual experiences to achieve elevation of consciousness. Doing this brings the achievement of wholeness in human potential.

Our inborn potentials contain the packets of our deepest loves and happiness. Operating in a higher consciousness allows those inborn packets to open and become active in our personality. We can now see more, think more rationally, and do what we could not do before. We become an 'enhanced' version of ourselves. This brings the joy of fulfilment and a life filled with vitality and self-confidence.

Every individual is born with a unique and endless collection of potentials that are gradually released more and more as we grow in mind and consciousness. Without the steady release of new potentials the individual feels mentally starved. Mental growth must be continuous, as it is with other living things like plants and our body cells. *Vitality and satisfaction in life depend on experiencing the release of our inborn and unique potentials.* We discover new aspects and interests within us, which are affections that were previously hidden from our consciousness.

Many of us believe that this is an automatic process like the growth of the physical body and the maturity of the mind. And yet is clear from the state of our society that positive growth has been interrupted and has changed course into a negative direction or "de-volution" in consciousness. People reach adulthood and flounder in unhappiness and frustration, unable to find the right path for achieving their many inborn potentials, which releases vitality, spiritual intelligence, and life satisfaction. Most of us suffer from a recurrent daily dose of negative emotions. We experience anger, resentment, anxiety, uncertainty, depression, and a dreary collection of neuroses and limitations.

How many adults can say that they are operating at full potential and feel vitality and excitement at the fulfilment of their dreams and plans? There is something lacking in the lives of most of us. Yet hope remains a constant human experience. Most of us do not wish to accpet a life that is less than perfect and exciting with endless possibilities. We want to gain control over our mental growth process so that we may direct it towards that wholeness and self-realization that should be and could be the destiny of everyone. This book takes up that challenge and presents a sure way out of our half-satisfied lives.

The title of this Volume anticipates and encapsulates the method everyone can use to attain this spiritual victory. It puts us on a sure path towards healing our spiritual and psychological condition and restoring happiness, vitality, and fulfilment. The perspective of *rational theistic self-analysis* (RTS) reconnects us to a relationship with God and a spirituality that is based on common sense and our innate ability to understand spiritual truths rationally. This is the meaning of "Reality Is Spiritual".

Few of us know the distinction between religion and a personal relationship with God. We have been created to enjoy and function at two distinct levels of consciousness: natural and spiritual. Natural consciousness gives us the ability to survive but not to thrive. It provides us with intelligence, but not with wisdom. Our view of the world in natural consciousness remains limited and fairly dark. We can make a living, raise a family, assume leadership roles, and contribute our share to the steady advances in civilization and technology. But we remain ignorant of what comnes next and we fall prey to all sorts of unsatisfactory philosophies and theories about where we are going that is beyond this present living and achieving.

There is a way out of this dilemma that God provides to each of us. Spiritual understanding of ourselves and of life gives us that knowledge of our destiny as human beings. Every person is born for a life of eternity and endless growth and development of one's unique innate potentials. Life after death in eternity is social, interactive, exciting, and filled with objects of beauty and function unknown in this world. This is what we have to look forward to!

But most of us are raised in an educational system and culture that is exclusively materialistic in thinking and is driven by a materialistic science that causes us to be estranged from our true spiritual reality. We can overcome this one sided past of oursevles by knowing the facts of our spiritual reality at the center of which is God.

The practice of rational theistic self-analysis (RTS) prepares us for that exciting life after death. Everyone can learn to gain control over their inner mental life where consciousness and experiencing reside. It is there that our true life as human beings begins and proceeds. All we need is to move our natural thinking and intelligence to the level of spiritual consciousness. It is a level everyone already has but is unconscious of.

Spiritual rationality opens up that inner way and makes us conscsious of the exciting events of life that take place there. It is our mental eternity. We are born into it and can never leave it.

This Volume presents the uncomplicated spiritual knowledge that takes us to that exalted life. It is not difficult to understand our spiritual reality. I have found that children between 7 and 10 easily grasp all the basics upon first presentation of these ideas. They seem to find it obvious and self-evident. It is only later that we forget this spiritual-rational knowledge and become unconscious of it until death when we awaken in our spiritual mind. But unless we have prepared ourselves to enter that spiritual consciousness prior to death it will elude us after death. As a result our lot in eternity is indeed dire. People have called it "hell", and it is.

This is why it is critical that we prepare ourselves for the afterlife of eternity by acquiring the knwowledge that gives us the ability to think in spiritual-rational consciousness. All you need to understand, enjoy, and benefit from this book is an open mind that seeks the spiritual rationality of God and our loving relationship to God. *This is not a book about religion.* It is about learning the spiritual facts of our personal, individual, and actual relationship to God regardless of religion, culture, or beliefs.

> *Everything in the physical world is caused by something in the spiritual world. ~Emanuel Swedenborg*

Reader CommentAbout this Book:

> *A TOUR DE FORCE ADDRESSING THE SPIRITUAL NEEDS OF MODERN MANKIND*
>
> *A unique marriage of the Analytical Psychology of Jung and the theology of Swedenborg. I recommend it to everyone with existential questions. Especially those who are inclined to spiritual thinking. Those who have the*

intimation that this so often wretched life carries greater meaning and connection deep within. This is also a practical guide to daily spiritual living. How to become more considerate and caring in all relationships. Moreover, and more importantly to start a living relationship with God, or the Divine Human as Swedenborg prefers. Reading this text was life changing to me.
~Abe Venter, Counseling Psychologist South Africa, October 2016

Reality is Spiritual

Volume 2

The RTS Personality

Rational Theistic Self-Analysis (RTS)
For Achieving Wholeness
Here and in the Afterlife
Based on the Spiritual Psychology
of Jung and Swedenborg

About The Author

Dr. Leon James has been Professor of Psychology at the University Hawaii since 1971. He has also held academic positions at McGill University, Laval University, University of Wisconsin, and University of Illinois. Since 1960 he has conducted research, published articles and books, and taught courses in several scientific specialty subjects that include the following:

social-personality theory and measurement; statistics and research design; psycholinguistics and ethnosemantics; ethnomethodology and intersubjectivity; discourse analysis; language learning and teaching; library and information science; driving psychology; road rage; sidewalk rage; air rage; the spiritual psychology of Emanuel Swedenborg; theistic psychology; cyberpsychology; marriage and couplehood.

Dr. James has been an Instructor and Professor of Psychology for over 50 years and has published research throughout this time. Currently, he is on the Editorial Board of the *Journal of Psychology and Clinical Psychiatry*, *Acta Psychopathologica Journal, Symbiosis: SOJ Psychology, Social Behavior Research and Practice, International Journal of Communication and Linguistic Studies*, and others. He consults with safety organizations and institutions worldwide on driving psychology. He is considered an expert on "road rage", "air rage" and "sidewalk rage", and has given well over one thousand newspaper interviews and media appearances. In 1997 he was among the first to give expert testimony to the Transportation Sub-Committee of the U.S. Congress on the then emerging topic of road rage and aggressive driving. Since then road rage and aggressive driving have continued to increase, killing thousands of victims every year and injuring millions of people yearly. His book with his wife Dr. Diane Nahl titled *Road Rage and Aggressive Driving* (2000) provides behavioral methods to help drivers gain control over their traffic emotions. These methods have been taught to thousands of people throughout the United States who are preparing to obtain a driver's license.

In fifty years of scientific research and writing Leon James introduced more than two thousand *neologisms* or novel expressions that refer to new scientific ideas that he discovered or invented. Some of these expressions have been picked up by others and are in use today. The oldest and most successful of his neologisms is the expression "*semantic satiation*" which was the topic of his Masters Thesis and Ph.D. Dissertation at McGill University in 1962. Semantic satiation refers to the change or loss of meaning of a word when it is repeated beyond a certain frequency (see Wikipedia article). He demonstrated how this neuro-semantic phenomenon applies to various situations, including vocabulary learning, doing simple arithmetic, enjoyment of popular songs, stuttering on the phone, bilingualism, remembering TV commercials, and focusing on visual displays. In the past few years semantic satiation has been researched in dozens of articles in psychology, instruction, business, art, music, and aesthetics. It has now become a popular topic of chat discussions and a name for blogs, chat rooms, bands, albums, and videos. Semantic satiation is also entering the common vocabulary of people in their everyday use.

Another of his neologisms that entered into popular use is the expression "*road rage nursery*" to refer to the back seat of a car. This was meant to alert parents that the way they verbalize and behave behind the wheel in traffic will function as a model for the children in the back seat when they grow up and start driving on their own. Another expression he coined that became popular in the language-teaching field is "*communicative competence*". This idea was meant to make a distinction between mere linguistic competence and the actual ability to use the language for communication. Since then this distinction and term has become of standard use in the field of language teaching and testing.

However most of his neologisms remained unaddressed by others. Some of these are: "*cross-modality transfer effect*", "*ethnosemantic hexagram series*" (viz.: trigram, hexagram, ennead, double hexagram, electric couple), "*existential neologisms*", "*mental anatomy*", "*the mental world of eternity*", "*vertical community*", and "*self-witnessing*". The full list of his neologisms with explanations is available on the Web at:
http://theisticpsychology.org/books/neologisms/neochartp1.htm

For the past thirty years Dr. James focused his research especially on the *Writings of Swedenborg*, looking for ways to transform Swedenborg's spiritual reports and ideas into the language and theory of modern scientific psychology. He coined the expression "theistic psychology" in 1990. Dr. James acknowledges that Emanuel Swedenborg (1688-1772) is the actual founder of theistic psychology, even though Swedenborg himself did not use this expression.

This book is the latest instance of that continuing task of bringing Swedenborg's ideas to the science of theistic psychology and to the practice of rational theistic self-analysis for raising one's consciousness from natural to spiritual.

Analysis is not only a "diagnosis" but rather an understanding and a moral support in the honest experimental attempt one calls "life." ~Carl Jung, Letters Vol I, p. 47

Denying God leads to love of oneself, and this is a ticket to hell. Visual proof for this is provided by the Swedenborg Reports. ~Leon James

Truth is visible to awareness while its love is hidden within it. ~Leon James

*All my doubts are so many sins against God.
~Leon James*

*If truth is the chair, then love is its wood.
If love is the flower, then truth is its stalk.
If truth is water, love is its steam.
If love is heat, truth is its light.
~Leon James*

*Insight is foresight.
~Leon James*

Consciousness is the awareness of experiencing. Therefore such as is the quality of awareness such is the consciousness. Experiencing is what happens. There is no other venue for anything to happen. ~Leon James

The immortality of the person is nothing else than the flow of experiencing that cannot cease. ~Leon James

To love others more than self, and to love God more than anything, is the experiencing of spiritual consciousness. . ~Leon James

A husband loves what he understands. A wife understands what he loves. ~Leon James

In order to understand himself, a spiritual husband relies on his wife. ~Leon James

Anatomically viewed, a husband and a wife together make up one complete human being. The conjoined pair is the complete person. She is his heart and he is her lungs. ~Leon James

Consciousness is omnipresent. God is omnipresent.
Consciousness is human. God is Human.
God creates human beings to be reception organs for consciousness.
An individual's consciousness is unique, human, immortal, and omnipresent.
We receive God's inflowing consciousness at three levels of perfection in our mind: celestial-rational, spiritual-rational, and natural-rational.
~Leon James

To be in the highest heaven in eternity is the experiencing of celestial-rational consciousness. Here we love others more than self for the sake of good that is of God.
To be in the middle heaven in eternity is the experiencing of spiritual-rational consciousness. Here we love others as much as self for the sake of truth that is of God.
To be in the lower heaven in eternity is the experiencing of spiritual-natural consciousness. Here we love others as much as self for the sake of conscience that is from God.
~Leon James

There are three things in a man that a woman wants more than all other things—friendship, cooperation, and wisdom.

A wife wants friendship from her husband because she needs to feel accepted, stimulated, and free. These are the feelings that come from being the best of friends. This includes intimacy and sexuality as an eternal couple.

A wife wants cooperation from her husband because her life is miserable and hard when he resists her in this or that, following his own mind instead of hers.

A wife wants wisdom in her husband so that she could admire him and feel safe and protected from false perspectives and dangerous involvements, which otherwise she might fall prey to. ~Leon James

Leon James started studying *Swedenborg's Writings* in 1981. Full text and free access to most of his theistic psychology books and articles is available at the Theistic Psychology Web Site: http://theisticpsychology.org/index.htm that is managed by Dr. Ian Thompson, physicist, nuclear researcher, and author of the recent *Starting Science from God: Rational Scientific Theories from Theism* (available at Amazon.com and elsewhere).

Every smallest moment of a person's life entails a chain of consequences into eternity. ~Swedenborg

Everyone is created to live to eternity, for he is so created that he may be conjoined with God, and conjunction with God is eternal life. ~Swedenborg

Spiritual power is to desire the well-being of another, and to desire to give to another as far as possible what is within you. ~Swedenborg

God, Immortality and Theistic Psychology Series
by Dr. Leon James

© 2016 Leon James and Diane Nahl

http://www.theisticpsychology.org

BOOKS

Jung and Swedenborg on God and Life After Death (2015) (Print and Digital)

Reality is Spiritual. Volume 1. Dreams and the Spiritual World: Integrating the Psychology of Jung and Swedenborg (2016) (Print and Digital)

Reality is Spiritual Volume 2 Rational Theistic self-analysis (RTS) For Achieving Wholeness Here and in the Afterlife (2016) (current volume)

Experiencing Regeneration: Equipping Our Personality For Living In The Afterlife (2015) (Print and Digital)

The Conjoined Pair: Natural and Spiritual Marriage (2012) (Print and Digital)

A Man of the Field: Forming the New Church Mind in Today's World (3 Volumes) (2014) (Print and Kindle)

WEB DOCUMENTS

The Correspondential Sense of Sacred Scriptures: Proving that there is a Unified Theistic Psychology Hidden within the World's Historical Sacred Writings (2009)
On the web: http://www.theisticpsychology.org/books/ssss.htm

Best Friends in Love and Together Forever: The Natural and Spiritual Dimension of Marriage (2008)
On the web: http://theisticpsychology.org/books/best-friends-in-love.htm

Principles of Theistic Psychology: The Scientific Knowledge of God Extracted from the Correspondential Sense of Sacred Scripture (18 Volumes) (2004-2008)
On the web: http://theisticpsychology.org/books/theistic/index.htm

Moses, Paul, and Swedenborg: Three Steps in Rational Spirituality (1999)
http://theisticpsychology.org/books/rationality/moses.html

Swedenborg Encyclopedia of Theistic Psychology: The Ideas of Emanuel Swedenborg (1668-1772) Expressed In Modern Scientific Psychology (1995-2010) (multiple Volumes)
http://theisticpsychology.org/gloss.html

END OF VOLUME 2

www.ingramcontent.com/pod-product-compliance
Lightning Source LLC
Chambersburg PA
CBHW060236290526
45789CB00001B/72